Natural Language Processing with Java and LingPipe Cookbook

Over 60 effective recipes to develop your Natural Language Processing (NLP) skills quickly and effectively

Breck Baldwin

Krishna Dayanidhi

BIRMINGHAM - MUMBAI

Natural Language Processing with Java and LingPipe Cookbook

Copyright © 2014 Packt Publishing

All rights reserved. No part of this book may be reproduced, stored in a retrieval system, or transmitted in any form or by any means, without the prior written permission of the publisher, except in the case of brief quotations embedded in critical articles or reviews.

Every effort has been made in the preparation of this book to ensure the accuracy of the information presented. However, the information contained in this book is sold without warranty, either express or implied. Neither the authors, nor Packt Publishing, and its dealers and distributors will be held liable for any damages caused or alleged to be caused directly or indirectly by this book.

Packt Publishing has endeavored to provide trademark information about all of the companies and products mentioned in this book by the appropriate use of capitals. However, Packt Publishing cannot guarantee the accuracy of this information.

First published: November 2014

Production reference: 1241114

Published by Packt Publishing Ltd.
Livery Place
35 Livery Street
Birmingham B3 2PB, UK.

ISBN 978-1-78328-467-2

www.packtpub.com

Credits

Authors
Breck Baldwin
Krishna Dayanidhi

Reviewers
Aria Haghighi
Kshitij Judah
Karthik Raghunathan
Altaf Rahman

Commissioning Editor
Kunal Parikh

Acquisition Editor
Sam Wood

Content Development Editor
Ruchita Bhansali

Technical Editors
Mrunal M. Chavan
Shiny Poojary
Sebastian Rodrigues

Copy Editors
Janbal Dharmaraj
Karuna Narayanan
Merilyn Pereira

Project Coordinator
Kranti Berde

Proofreaders
Bridget Braund
Maria Gould
Ameesha Green
Lucy Rowland

Indexers
Monica Ajmera Mehta
Tejal Soni

Production Coordinator
Melwyn D'sa

Cover Work
Melwyn D'sa

About the Authors

Breck Baldwin is the Founder and President of Alias-i/LingPipe. The company focuses on system building for customers, education for developers, and occasional forays into pure research. He has been building large-scale NLP systems since 1996. He enjoys telemark skiing and wrote *DIY RC Airplanes from Scratch: The Brooklyn Aerodrome Bible for Hacking the Skies, McGraw-Hill/TAB Electronics*.

> This book is dedicated to Peter Jackson, who hired me as a consultant for Westlaw, before I founded the company, and gave me the confidence to start it. He served on my advisory board until his untimely death, and I miss him terribly.
>
> Fellow Aristotelian, Bob Carpenter, is the architect and developer behind the LingPipe API. It was his idea to make LingPipe open source, which opened many doors and led to this book.
>
> Mitzi Morris has worked with us over the years and has been instrumental in our challenging NIH work, the author of tutorials, packages, and pitching in where it was needed.
>
> Jeff Reynar was my office mate in graduate school when we hatched the idea of entering the MUC-6 competition, which was the prime mover for creation of the company; he now serves our advisory board.
>
> Our volunteer reviewers deserve much credit; Doug Donahue and Rob Stupay were a big help. Packt Publishing reviewers made the book so much better; I thank Karthik Raghunathan, Altaf Rahman, and Kshitij Judah for their attention to detail and excellent questions and suggestions.
>
> Our editors were the ever patient; Ruchita Bhansali who kept the chapters moving and provided excellent commentary, and Shiny Poojary, our thorough technical editor, who suffered so that you don't have to. Much thanks to both of you.
>
> I could not have done this without my co-author, Krishna, who worked full-time and held up his side of the writing.
>
> Many thanks to my wife, Karen, for her support throughout the book-writing process.

Krishna Dayanidhi has spent most of his professional career focusing on Natural Language Processing technologies. He has built diverse systems, from a natural dialog interface for cars to Question Answering systems at (different) Fortune 500 companies. He also confesses to building those automated speech systems for very large telecommunication companies. He's an avid runner and a decent cook.

> I'd like to thank Bob Carpenter for answering many questions and for all his previous writings, including the tutorials and Javadocs that have informed and shaped this book. Thank you, Bob! I'd also like to thank my co-author, Breck, for convincing me to co-author this book and for tolerating all my quirks throughout the writing process.
>
> I'd like to thank the reviewers, Karthik Raghunathan, Altaf Rahman, and Kshitij Judah, for providing essential feedback, which in some cases changed the entire recipe. Many thanks to Ruchita, our editor at Packt Publishing, for guiding, cajoling, and essentially making sure that this book actually came to be. Finally, thanks to Latha for her support, encouragement, and tolerance.

About the Reviewers

Karthik Raghunathan is a scientist at Microsoft, Silicon Valley, working on Speech and Natural Language Processing. Since first being introduced to the field in 2006, he has worked on diverse problems such as spoken dialog systems, machine translation, text normalization, coreference resolution, and speech-based information retrieval, leading to publications in esteemed conferences such as SIGIR, EMNLP, and AAAI. He has also had the privilege to be mentored by and work with some of the best minds in Linguistics and Natural Language Processing, such as Prof. Christopher Manning, Prof. Daniel Jurafsky, and Dr. Ron Kaplan.

Karthik currently works at the Bing Speech and Language Sciences group at Microsoft, where he builds speech-enabled conversational understanding systems for various Microsoft products such as the Xbox gaming console and the Windows Phone mobile operating system. He employs various techniques from speech processing, Natural Language Processing, machine learning, and data mining to improve systems that perform automatic speech recognition and natural language understanding. The products he has recently worked on at Microsoft include the new improved Kinect sensor for Xbox One and the Cortana digital assistant in Windows Phone 8.1. In his previous roles at Microsoft, Karthik worked on shallow dependency parsing and semantic understanding of web queries in the Bing Search team and on statistical spellchecking and grammar checking in the Microsoft Office team.

Prior to joining Microsoft, Karthik graduated with an MS degree in Computer Science (specializing in Artificial Intelligence), with a distinction in Research in Natural Language Processing from Stanford University. While the focus of his graduate research thesis was coreference resolution (the coreference tool from his thesis is available as part of the Stanford CoreNLP Java package), he also worked on the problems of statistical machine translation (leading Stanford's efforts for the GALE 3 Chinese-English MT bakeoff), slang normalization in text messages (codeveloping the Stanford SMS Translator), and situated spoken dialog systems in robots (helped in developing speech packages, now available as part of the open source Robot Operating System (ROS)).

Karthik's undergraduate work at the National Institute of Technology, Calicut, focused on building NLP systems for Indian languages. He worked on restricted domain-spoken dialog systems for Tamil, Telugu, and Hindi in collaboration with IIIT, Hyderabad. He also interned with Microsoft Research India on a project that dealt with scaling statistical machine translation for resource-scarce languages.

Karthik Raghunathan maintains a homepage at `nlp.stanford.edu/~rkarthik/` and can be reached at `kr@cs.stanford.edu`.

Altaf Rahman is currently a research scientist at Yahoo Labs in California, USA. He works on search queries, understanding problems such as query tagging, query interpretation ranking, vertical search triggering, module ranking, and others. He earned his PhD degree from The University of Texas at Dallas on Natural Language Processing. His dissertation was on the conference resolution problem. Dr. Rahman has publications in major NLP conferences with over 200 citations. He has also worked on other NLP problems: Named Entity Recognition, Part of Speech Tagging, Statistical Parsers, Semantic Classifier, and so on. Earlier, he worked as a research intern in IBM Thomas J. Watson Research Center, Université Paris Diderot, and Google.

www.PacktPub.com

Support files, eBooks, discount offers, and more

For support files and downloads related to your book, please visit `www.PacktPub.com`.

Did you know that Packt offers eBook versions of every book published, with PDF and ePub files available? You can upgrade to the eBook version at `www.PacktPub.com` and as a print book customer, you are entitled to a discount on the eBook copy. Get in touch with us at `service@packtpub.com` for more details.

At `www.PacktPub.com`, you can also read a collection of free technical articles, sign up for a range of free newsletters and receive exclusive discounts and offers on Packt books and eBooks.

`https://www2.packtpub.com/books/subscription/packtlib`

Do you need instant solutions to your IT questions? PacktLib is Packt's online digital book library. Here, you can search, access, and read Packt's entire library of books.

Why subscribe?

- Fully searchable across every book published by Packt
- Copy and paste, print, and bookmark content
- On demand and accessible via a web browser

Free access for Packt account holders

If you have an account with Packt at `www.PacktPub.com`, you can use this to access PacktLib today and view 9 entirely free books. Simply use your login credentials for immediate access.

Table of Contents

Preface	**1**
Chapter 1: Simple Classifiers	**7**
Introduction	8
Deserializing and running a classifier	11
Getting confidence estimates from a classifier	14
Getting data from the Twitter API	19
Applying a classifier to a .csv file	22
Evaluation of classifiers – the confusion matrix	24
Training your own language model classifier	29
How to train and evaluate with cross validation	32
Viewing error categories – false positives	37
Understanding precision and recall	39
How to serialize a LingPipe object – classifier example	40
Eliminate near duplicates with the Jaccard distance	42
How to classify sentiment – simple version	45
Chapter 2: Finding and Working with Words	**51**
Introduction	51
Introduction to tokenizer factories – finding words in a character stream	52
Combining tokenizers – lowercase tokenizer	56
Combining tokenizers – stop word tokenizers	58
Using Lucene/Solr tokenizers	60
Using Lucene/Solr tokenizers with LingPipe	62
Evaluating tokenizers with unit tests	66
Modifying tokenizer factories	68
Finding words for languages without white spaces	70

Chapter 3: Advanced Classifiers — 75
- Introduction — 75
- A simple classifier — 76
- Language model classifier with tokens — 78
- Naïve Bayes — 79
- Feature extractors — 85
- Logistic regression — 87
- Multithreaded cross validation — 93
- Tuning parameters in logistic regression — 97
- Customizing feature extraction — 103
- Combining feature extractors — 105
- Classifier-building life cycle — 106
- Linguistic tuning — 114
- Thresholding classifiers — 119
- Train a little, learn a little – active learning — 126
- Annotation — 136

Chapter 4: Tagging Words and Tokens — 141
- Introduction — 141
- Interesting phrase detection — 142
- Foreground- or background-driven interesting phrase detection — 145
- Hidden Markov Models (HMM) – part-of-speech — 149
- N-best word tagging — 151
- Confidence-based tagging — 153
- Training word tagging — 154
- Word-tagging evaluation — 160
- Conditional random fields (CRF) for word/token tagging — 163
- Modifying CRFs — 167

Chapter 5: Finding Spans in Text – Chunking — 173
- Introduction — 174
- Sentence detection — 174
- Evaluation of sentence detection — 178
- Tuning sentence detection — 182
- Marking embedded chunks in a string – sentence chunk example — 184
- Paragraph detection — 186
- Simple noun phrases and verb phrases — 189
- Regular expression-based chunking for NER — 191
- Dictionary-based chunking for NER — 193
- Translating between word tagging and chunks – BIO codec — 195

HMM-based NER	198
Mixing the NER sources	205
CRFs for chunking	208
NER using CRFs with better features	214

Chapter 6: String Comparison and Clustering — 221

Introduction	221
Distance and proximity – simple edit distance	222
Weighted edit distance	224
The Jaccard distance	227
The Tf-Idf distance	230
Using edit distance and language models for spelling correction	234
The case restoring corrector	239
Automatic phrase completion	240
Single-link and complete-link clustering using edit distance	243
Latent Dirichlet allocation (LDA) for multitopic clustering	248

Chapter 7: Finding Coreference Between Concepts/People — 257

Introduction	257
Named entity coreference with a document	258
Adding pronouns to coreference	261
Cross-document coreference	266
The John Smith problem	281

Index — 291

Preface

Welcome to the book you will want to have by your side when you cross the door of a new consulting gig or take on a new Natural Language Processing (NLP) problem. This book starts as a private repository of LingPipe recipes that Baldwin continually referred to when facing repeated but twitchy NLP problems with system building. We are an open source company but the code never merited sharing. Now they are shared.

Honestly, the LingPipe API is an intimidating and opaque edifice to code against like any rich and complex Java API. Add in the "black arts" quality needed to get NLP systems working and we have the perfect conditions to satisfy the need for a recipe book that minimizes theory and maximizes the practicality of getting the job done with best practices sprinkled in from 20 years in the business.

This book is about getting the job done; damn the theory! Take this book and build the next generation of NLP systems and send us a note about what you did.

LingPipe is the best tool on the planet to build NLP systems with; this book is the way to use it.

What this book covers

Chapter 1, *Simple Classifiers*, explains that a huge percentage of NLP problems are actually classification problems. This chapter covers very simple but powerful classifiers based on character sequences and then brings in evaluation techniques such as cross-validation and metrics such as precision, recall, and the always-BS-resisting confusion matrix. You get to train yourself on your own and download data from Twitter. The chapter ends with a simple sentiment example.

Chapter 2, *Finding and Working with Words*, is exactly as boring as it sounds but there are some high points. The last recipe will show you how to tokenize Chinese/Japanese/Vietnamese languages, which doesn't have whitespaces, to help define words. We will show you how to wrap Lucene tokenizers, which cover all kinds of fun languages such as Arabic. Almost everything later in the book relies on tokenization.

Chapter 3, *Advanced Classifiers*, introduces the star of modern NLP systems—logistic regression classifiers. 20 years of hard-won experience lurks in this chapter. We will address the life cycle around building classifiers and how to create training data, cheat when creating training data with active learning, and how to tune and make the classifiers work faster.

Chapter 4, *Tagging Words and Tokens*, explains that language is about words. This chapter focuses on ways of applying categories to tokens, which in turn drives many of the high-end uses of LingPipe such as entity detection (people/places/orgs in text), part-of-speech tagging, and more. It starts with tag clouds, which have been described as "mullet of the Internet" and ends with a foundational recipe for conditional random fields (CRF), which can provide state-of-the-art performance for entity-detection tasks. In between, we will address confidence-tagged words, which is likely to be a very important dimension of more sophisticated systems.

Chapter 5, *Finding Spans in Text – Chunking*, shows that text is not words alone. It is collections of words, usually in spans. This chapter will advance from word tagging to span tagging, which brings in capabilities such as finding sentences, named entities, and basal NPs and VPs. The full power of CRFs are addressed with discussions on feature extraction and tuning. Dictionary approaches are discussed as they are ways of combining chunkings.

Chapter 6, *String Comparison and Clustering*, focuses on comparing text with each other, independent of a trained classifier. The technologies range from the hugely practical spellchecking to the hopeful but often frustrating Latent Dirichelet Allocation (LDA) clustering approach. Less presumptive technologies such as single-link and complete-link clustering have driven major commercial successes for us. Don't ignore this chapter.

Chapter 7, *Finding Coreference Between Concepts/People*, lays the future but unfortunately, you won't get the ultimate recipe, just our best efforts so far. This is one of the bleeding edges of industrial and academic NLP efforts that has tremendous potential. Potential is why we include our efforts to help grease the way to see this technology in use.

What you need for this book

You need some NLP problems and a solid foundation in Java, a computer, and a developer-savvy approach.

Who this book is for

If you have NLP problems or you want to educate yourself in comment NLP issues, this book is for you. With some creativity, you can train yourself into being a solid NLP developer, a beast so rare that they are seen about as often as unicorns, with the result of more interesting job prospects in hot technology areas such as Silicon Valley or New York City.

Conventions

In this book, you will find a number of styles of text that distinguish between different kinds of information. Here are some examples of these styles and an explanation of their meaning.

Java is a pretty awful language to put into a recipe book with a 66-character limit on lines for code. The overriding convention is that the code is ugly and we apologize.

Code words in text, database table names, folder names, filenames, file extensions, pathnames, dummy URLs, user input, and Twitter handles are shown as follows: "Once the string is read in from the console, then `classifier.classify(input)` is called, which returns `Classification`."

A block of code is set as follows:

```
public static List<String[]> filterJaccard(List<String[]> texts,
TokenizerFactory tokFactory, double cutoff) {
  JaccardDistance jaccardD = new JaccardDistance(tokFactory);
```

When we wish to draw your attention to a particular part of a code block, the relevant lines or items are set in bold:

```
public static void consoleInputBestCategory(
BaseClassifier<CharSequence> classifier) throws IOException {
  BufferedReader reader = new BufferedReader(
    new InputStreamReader(System.in));
  while (true) {
    System.out.println("\nType a string to be classified. " + "
      Empty string to quit.");
    String data = reader.readLine();
    if (data.equals("")) {
      return;
    }
    Classification classification = classifier.classify(data);
    System.out.println("Best Category: " +
      classification.bestCategory());
  }
}
```

Any command-line input or output is written as follows:

```
tar -xvzf lingpipeCookbook.tgz
```

New terms and **important words** are shown in bold. Words that you see on the screen, in menus or dialog boxes for example, appear in the text like this: "Click on **Create a new application**."

> Warnings or important notes appear in a box like this.

> Tips and tricks appear like this.

Reader feedback

Feedback from our readers is always welcome. Let us know what you think about this book—what you liked or may have disliked. Reader feedback is important for us to develop titles that you really get the most out of.

To send us general feedback, simply send an e-mail to `feedback@packtpub.com`, and mention the book title via the subject of your message.

If there is a topic that you have expertise in and you are interested in either writing or contributing to a book, see our author guide on `www.packtpub.com/authors`.

Send hate/love/neutral e-mails to `cookbook@lingpipe.com`. We do care, we won't do your homework for you or prototype your startup for free, but do talk to us.

Customer support

Now that you are the proud owner of a Packt book, we have a number of things to help you to get the most from your purchase.

We do offer consulting services and even have a pro-bono (free) program as well as a start up support program. NLP is hard, this book is most of what we know but perhaps we can help more.

Downloading the example code

You can download the example code files for all Packt books you have purchased from your account at `http://www.packtpub.com`. If you purchased this book elsewhere, you can visit `http://www.packtpub.com/support` and register to have the files e-mailed directly to you.

All the source for the book is available at `http://alias-i.com/book.html`.

Errata

Although we have taken every care to ensure the accuracy of our content, mistakes do happen. If you find a mistake in one of our books—maybe a mistake in the text or the code—we would be grateful if you would report this to us. By doing so, you can save other readers from frustration and help us improve subsequent versions of this book. If you find any errata, please report them by visiting `http://www.packtpub.com/submit-errata`, selecting your book, clicking on the **errata submission form** link, and entering the details of your errata. Once your errata are verified, your submission will be accepted and the errata will be uploaded on our website, or added to any list of existing errata, under the Errata section of that title. Any existing errata can be viewed by selecting your title from `http://www.packtpub.com/support`.

Piracy

Piracy of copyright material on the Internet is an ongoing problem across all media. At Packt, we take the protection of our copyright and licenses very seriously. If you come across any illegal copies of our works, in any form, on the Internet, please provide us with the location address or website name immediately so that we can pursue a remedy.

Please contact us at `copyright@packtpub.com` with a link to the suspected pirated material.

We appreciate your help in protecting our authors, and our ability to bring you valuable content.

Questions

You can contact us at `questions@packtpub.com` if you are having a problem with any aspect of the book, and we will do our best to address it.

Hit `http://lingpipe.com` and go to our forum for the best place to get questions answered and see if you have a solution already.

Simple Classifiers

In this chapter, we will cover the following recipes:

- Deserializing and running a classifier
- Getting confidence estimates from a classifier
- Getting data from the Twitter API
- Applying a classifier to a .csv file
- Evaluation of classifiers – the confusion matrix
- Training your own language model classifier
- How to train and evaluate with cross validation
- Viewing error categories – false positives
- Understanding precision and recall
- How to serialize a LingPipe object – classifier example
- Eliminate near duplicates with the Jaccard distance
- How to classify sentiment – simple version

Introduction

This chapter introduces the LingPipe toolkit in the context of its competition and then dives straight into text classifiers. Text classifiers assign a category to text, for example, they assign the language to a sentence or tell us if a tweet is positive, negative, or neutral in sentiment. This chapter covers how to use, evaluate, and create text classifiers based on language models. These are the simplest machine learning-based classifiers in the LingPipe API. What makes them simple is that they operate over characters only—later, classifiers will have notions of words/tokens and even more. However, don't be fooled, character-language models are ideal for language identification, and they were the basis of some of the world's earliest commercial sentiment systems.

This chapter also covers crucial evaluation infrastructure—it turns out that almost everything we do turns out to be a classifier at some level of interpretation. So, do not skimp on the power of cross validation, definitions of precision/recall, and F-measure.

The best part is that you will learn how to programmatically access Twitter data to train up and evaluate your own classifiers. There is a boring bit concerning the mechanics of reading and writing LingPipe objects from/to disk, but other than that, this is a fun chapter. The goal of this chapter is to get you up and running quickly with the basic care and feeding of machine-learning techniques in the domain of **natural language processing** (**NLP**).

LingPipe is a Java toolkit for NLP-oriented applications. This book will show you how to solve common NLP problems with LingPipe in a problem/solution format that allows developers to quickly deploy solutions to common tasks.

LingPipe and its installation

LingPipe 1.0 was released in 2003 as a dual-licensed open source NLP Java library. At the time of writing this book, we are coming up on 2000 hits on Google Scholar and have thousands of commercial installs, ranging from universities to government agencies to Fortune 500 companies.

Current licensing is either AGPL (`http://www.gnu.org/licenses/agpl-3.0.html`) or our commercial license that offers more traditional features such as indemnification and non-sharing of code as well as support.

Projects similar to LingPipe

Nearly all NLP projects have awful acronyms so we will lay bare our own. **LingPipe** is the short form for **linguistic pipeline**, which was the name of the `cvs` directory in which Bob Carpenter put the initial code.

LingPipe has lots of competition in the NLP space. The following are some of the more popular ones with a focus on Java:

- **NLTK**: This is the dominant Python library for NLP processing.
- **OpenNLP**: This is an Apache project built by a bunch of smart folks.
- **JavaNLP**: This is a rebranding of Stanford NLP tools, again built by a bunch of smart folks.
- **ClearTK**: This is a University of Boulder toolkit that wraps lots of popular machine learning frameworks.
- **DkPro**: Technische Universität Darmstadt from Germany produced this UIMA-based project that wraps many common components in a useful manner. UIMA is a common framework for NLP.
- **GATE**: GATE is really more of a framework than competition. In fact, LingPipe components are part of their standard distribution. It has a nice graphical "hook the components up" capability.
- **Learning Based Java** (**LBJ**): LBJ is a special-purpose programming language based on Java, and it is geared toward machine learning and NLP. It was developed at the Cognitive Computation Group of the University of Illinois at Urbana Champaign.
- **Mallet**: This name is the short form of **MAchine Learning for LanguagE Toolkit**. Apparently, reasonable acronym generation is short in supply these days. Smart folks built this too.

Here are some pure machine learning frameworks that have broader appeal but are not necessarily tailored for NLP tasks:

- **Vowpal Wabbit**: This is very focused on scalability around Logistic Regression, Latent Dirichelet Allocation, and so on. Smart folks drive this.
- **Factorie**: It is from UMass, Amherst and an alternative offering to Mallet. Initially it focused primarily on graphic models, but now it also supports NLP tasks.
- **Support Vector Machine** (**SVM**): SVM light and `libsvm` are very popular SVM implementations. There is no SVM implementation in LingPipe, because logistic regression does this as well.

So, why use LingPipe?

It is very reasonable to ask why choose LingPipe with such outstanding free competition mentioned earlier. There are a few reasons:

- **Documentation**: The class-level documentation in LingPipe is very thorough. If the work is based on academic work, that work is cited. Algorithms are laid out, the underlying math is explained, and explanations are precise. What the documentation lacks is a "how to get things done" perspective; however, this is covered in this book.

- **Enterprise/server optimized**: LingPipe is designed from the ground up for server applications, not for command-line usage (though we will be using the command line extensively throughout the book).

- **Coded in the Java dialect**: LingPipe is a native Java API that is designed according to standard Java class design principles (Joshua Bloch's *Effective Java*, by Addison-Wesley), such as consistency checks on construction, immutability, type safety, backward-compatible serializability, and thread safety.

- **Error handling**: Considerable attention is paid to error handling through exceptions and configurable message streams for long-running processes.

- **Support**: LingPipe has paid employees whose job is to answer your questions and make sure that LingPipe is doing its job. The rare bug gets fixed in under 24 hours typically. They respond to questions very quickly and are very willing to help people.

- **Consulting**: You can hire experts in LingPipe to build systems for you. Generally, they teach developers how to build NLP systems as a byproduct.

- **Consistency**: The LingPipe API was designed by one person, Bob Carpenter, with an obsession of consistency. While it is not perfect, you will find a regularity and eye to design that can be missing in academic efforts. Graduate students come and go, and the resulting contributions to university toolkits can be quite varied.

- **Open source**: There are many commercial providers, but their software is a black box. The open source nature of LingPipe provides transparency and confidence that the code is doing what we ask it to do. When the documentation fails, it is a huge relief to have access to code to understand it better.

Downloading the book code and data

You will need to download the source code for this cookbook, with supporting models and data from `http://alias-i.com/book.html`. Untar and uncompress it using the following command:

```
tar -xvzf lingpipeCookbook.tgz
```

Downloading the example code

You can download the example code files for all Packt books you have purchased from your account at `http://www.packtpub.com`. If you purchased this book elsewhere, you can visit `http://www.packtpub.com/support` and register to have the files e-mailed directly to you.

Alternatively, your operating system might provide other ways of extracting the archive. All recipes assume that you are running the commands in the resulting cookbook directory.

Downloading LingPipe

Downloading LingPipe is not strictly necessary, but you will likely want to be able to look at the source and have a local copy of the Javadoc.

The download and installation instructions for LingPipe can be found at `http://alias-i.com/lingpipe/web/install.html`.

The examples from this chapter use command-line invocation, but it is assumed that the reader has sufficient development skills to map the examples to their preferred IDE/ant or other environment.

Deserializing and running a classifier

This recipe does two things: introduces a very simple and effective language ID classifier and demonstrates how to deserialize a LingPipe class. If you find yourself here from a later chapter, trying to understand deserialization, I encourage you to run the example program anyway. It will take 5 minutes, and you might learn something useful.

Our language ID classifier is based on character language models. Each language model gives you the probability of the text, given that it is generated in that language. The model that is most familiar with the text is the first best fit. This one has already been built, but later in the chapter, you will learn to make your own.

How to do it...

Perform the following steps to deserialize and run a classifier:

1. Go to the `cookbook` directory for the book and run the command for OSX, Unix, and Linux:

   ```
   java -cp lingpipe-cookbook.1.0.jar:lib/lingpipe-4.1.0.jar com.lingpipe.cookbook.chapter1.RunClassifierFromDisk
   ```

   For Windows invocation (quote the classpath and use ; instead of :):

   ```
   java -cp "lingpipe-cookbook.1.0.jar;lib\lingpipe-4.1.0.jar" com.lingpipe.cookbook.chapter1.RunClassifierFromDisk
   ```

   We will use the Unix style command line in this book.

Simple Classifiers

2. The program reports the model being loaded and a default, and prompts for a sentence to classify:

   `Loading: models/3LangId.LMClassifier`

   `Type a string to be classified. Empty string to quit.`

   `The rain in Spain falls mainly on the plain.`

   `english`

   `Type a string to be classified. Empty string to quit.`

   `la lluvia en España cae principalmente en el llano.`

   `spanish`

   `Type a string to be classified. Empty string to quit.`

   スペインの雨は主に平野に落ちる。

   `japanese`

3. The classifier is trained on English, Spanish, and Japanese. We have entered an example of each—to get some Japanese, go to `http://ja.wikipedia.org/wiki/`. These are the only languages it knows about, but it will guess on any text. So, let's try some Arabic:

   `Type a string to be classified. Empty string to quit.`

   المطر في اسبانيا يقع أساسا على سهل.

   `japanese`

4. It thinks it is Japanese because this language has more characters than English or Spanish. This in turn leads that model to expect more unknown characters. All the Arabic characters are unknown.

5. If you are working with a Windows terminal, you might encounter difficulty entering UTF-8 characters.

How it works...

The code in the jar is `cookbook/src/com/lingpipe/cookbook/chapter1/RunClassifierFromDisk.java`. What is happening is that a pre-built model for language identification is deserialized and made available. It has been trained on English, Japanese, and Spanish. The training data came from Wikipedia pages for each language. You can see the data in `data/3LangId.csv`. The focus of this recipe is to show you how to deserialize the classifier and run it—training is handled in the *Training your own language model classifier* recipe in this chapter. The entire code for the `RunClassifier FromDisk.java` class starts with the package; then it imports the start of the `RunClassifierFromDisk` class and the start of `main()`:

```
package com.lingpipe.cookbook.chapter1;
import java.io.File;
```

```
import java.io.IOException;

import com.aliasi.classify.BaseClassifier;
import com.aliasi.util.AbstractExternalizable;
import com.lingpipe.cookbook.Util;
public class RunClassifierFromDisk {
  public static void main(String[] args) throws
  IOException, ClassNotFoundException {
```

The preceding code is a very standard Java code, and we present it without explanation. Next is a feature in most recipes that supplies a default value for a file if the command line does not contain one. This allows you to use your own data if you have it, otherwise it will run from files in the distribution. In this case, a default classifier is supplied if there is no argument on the command line:

```
String classifierPath = args.length > 0 ? args[0]
  : "models/3LangId.LMClassifier";
System.out.println("Loading: " + classifierPath);
```

Next, we will see how to deserialize a classifier or another LingPipe object from disk:

```
File serializedClassifier = new File(classifierPath);
@SuppressWarnings("unchecked")
BaseClassifier<String> classifier
  = (BaseClassifier<String>)
  AbstractExternalizable.readObject(serializedClassifier);
```

The preceding code snippet is the first LingPipe-specific code, where the classifier is built using the static `AbstractExternalizable.readObject` method.

This class is employed throughout LingPipe to carry out a compilation of classes for two reasons. First, it allows the compiled objects to have final variables set, which supports LingPipe's extensive use of immutables. Second, it avoids the messiness of exposing the I/O methods required for externalization and deserialization, most notably, the no-argument constructor. This class is used as the superclass of a private internal class that does the actual compilation. This private internal class implements the required `no-arg` constructor and stores the object required for `readResolve()`.

The reason we use `Externalizable` instead of `Serializable` is to avoid breaking backward compatibility when changing any method signatures or member variables. `Externalizable` extends `Serializable` and allows control of how the object is read or written. For more information on this, refer to the excellent chapter on serialization in Josh Bloch's book, *Effective Java, 2nd Edition*.

Simple Classifiers

`BaseClassifier<E>` is the foundational classifier interface, with `E` being the type of object being classified in LingPipe. Look at the Javadoc to see the range of classifiers that implements the interface—there are 10 of them. Deserializing to `BaseClassifier<E>` hides a good bit of complexity, which we will explore later in the *How to serialize a LingPipe object – classifier example* recipe in this chapter.

The last line calls a utility method, which we will use frequently in this book:

```
Util.consoleInputBestCategory(classifier);
```

This method handles interactions with the command line. The code is in `src/com/lingpipe/cookbook/Util.java`:

```java
public static void consoleInputBestCategory(
BaseClassifier<CharSequence> classifier) throws IOException {
  BufferedReader reader = new BufferedReader(
    new InputStreamReader(System.in));
  while (true) {
    System.out.println("\nType a string to be classified. "
      + " Empty string to quit.");
    String data = reader.readLine();
    if (data.equals("")) {
      return;
    }
    Classification classification = classifier.classify(data);
    System.out.println("Best Category: " +
      classification.bestCategory());
  }
}
```

Once the string is read in from the console, then `classifier.classify(input)` is called, which returns `Classification`. This, in turn, provides a `String` label that is printed out. That's it! You have run a classifier.

Getting confidence estimates from a classifier

Classifiers tend to be a lot more useful if they give more information about how confident they are of the classification—this is usually a score or a probability. We often threshold classifiers to help fit the performance requirements of an installation. For example, if it was vital that the classifier never makes a mistake, then we could require that the classification be very confident before committing to a decision.

LingPipe classifiers exist on a hierarchy based on the kinds of estimates they provide. The backbone is a series of interfaces—don't freak out; it is actually pretty simple. You don't need to understand it now, but we do need to write it down somewhere for future reference:

- `BaseClassifier<E>`: This is just your basic classifier of objects of type `E`. It has a `classify()` method that returns a classification, which in turn has a `bestCategory()` method and a `toString()` method that is of some informative use.
- `RankedClassifier<E> extends BaseClassifier<E>`: The `classify()` method returns `RankedClassification`, which extends `Classification` and adds methods for `category(int rank)` that says what the 1st to *n*th classifications are. There is also a `size()` method that indicates how many classifications there are.
- `ScoredClassifier<E> extends RankedClassifier<E>`: The returned `ScoredClassification` adds a `score(int rank)` method.
- `ConditionalClassifier<E> extends RankedClassifier<E>`: `ConditionalClassification` produced by this has the property that the sum of scores for all categories must sum to 1 as accessed via the `conditionalProbability(int rank)` method and `conditionalProbability(String category)`. There's more; you can read the Javadoc for this. This classification will be the work horse of the book when things get fancy, and we want to know the confidence that the tweet is English versus the tweet is Japanese versus the tweet is Spanish. These estimates will have to sum to 1.
- `JointClassifier<E> extends ConditionalClassifier<E>`: This provides `JointClassification` of the input and category in the space of all the possible inputs, and all such estimates sum to 1. This is a sparse space, so values are log based to avoid underflow errors. We don't see a lot of use of this estimate directly in production.

It is obvious that there has been a great deal of thought put into the classification stack presented. This is because huge numbers of industrial NLP problems are handled by a classification system in the end.

It turns out that our simplest classifier—in some arbitrary sense of simple—produces the richest estimates, which are joint classifications. Let's dive in.

Simple Classifiers

Getting ready

In the previous recipe, we blithely deserialized to `BaseClassifier<String>` that hid all the details of what was going on. The reality is a bit more complex than suggested by the hazy abstract class. Note that the file on disk that was loaded is named `3LangId.LMClassifier`. By convention, we name serialized models with the type of object it will deserialize to, which, in this case, is `LMClassifier`, and it extends `BaseClassifier`. The most specific typing for the classifier is:

```
LMClassifier<CompiledNGramBoundaryLM,
      MultivariateDistribution> classifier
  = (LMClassifier <CompiledNGramBoundaryLM,
    MultivariateDistribution>) AbstractExternalizable.readObject(new
File(args[0]));
```

The cast to `LMClassifier<CompiledNGramBoundaryLM, MultivariateDistribution>` specifies the type of distribution to be `MultivariateDistribution`. The Javadoc for `com.aliasi.stats.MultivariateDistribution` is quite explicit and helpful in describing what this is.

> `MultivariateDistribution` implements a discrete distribution over a finite set of outcomes, numbered consecutively from zero.

The Javadoc goes into a lot of detail about `MultivariateDistribution`, but it basically means that we can have an n-way assignment of probabilities that sum to 1.

The next class in the cast is for `CompiledNGramBoundaryLM`, which is the "memory" of the `LMClassifier`. In fact, each language gets its own. This means that English will have a separate language model from Spanish and so on. There are eight different kinds of language models that could have been used as this part of the classifier—consult the Javadoc for the `LanguageModel` interface. Each **language model** (**LM**) has the following properties:

- The LM will provide a probability that it generated the text provided. It is robust against data that it has not seen before, in the sense that it won't crash or give a zero probability. Arabic just comes across as a sequence of unknown characters for our example.

- The sum of all the possible character sequence probabilities of any length is 1 for boundary LMs. Process LMs sum the probability to 1 over all sequences of the same length. Look at the Javadoc for how this bit of math is done.

- Each language model has no knowledge of data outside of its category.

- The classifier keeps track of the marginal probability of the category and factors this into the results for the category. Marginal probability is saying that we tend to see two-thirds English, one-sixth Spanish, and one-sixth Japanese in Disney tweets. This information is combined with the LM estimates.
- The LM is a compiled version of `LanguageModel.Dynamic` that we will cover in the later recipes that discuss training.

`LMClassifier` that is constructed wraps these components into a classifier.

Luckily, the interface saves the day with a more aesthetic deserialization:

```
JointClassifier<String> classifier = (JointClassifier<String>)
AbstractExternalizable.readObject(new File(classifierPath));
```

The interface hides the guts of the implementation nicely and this is what we are going with in the example program.

How to do it...

This recipe is the first time we start peeling away from what classifiers can do, but first, let's play with it a bit:

1. Get your magic shell genie to conjure a command prompt with a Java interpreter and type:

   ```
   java -cp lingpipe-cookbook.1.0.jar:lib/lingpipe-4.1.0.jar: com.
   lingpipe.cookbook.chapter1.RunClassifierJoint
   ```

2. We will enter the same data as we did earlier:

   ```
   Type a string to be classified. Empty string to quit.
   The rain in Spain falls mainly on the plain.
   Rank Categ Score     P(Category|Input)    log2 P(Category,Input)
   0=english -3.60092 0.9999999999           -165.64233893156052
   1=spanish -4.50479 3.04549412621E-13      -207.2207276413206
   2=japanese -14.369 7.6855682344E-150      -660.989401136873
   ```

As described, `JointClassification` carries through all the classification metrics in the hierarchy rooted at `Classification`. Each level of classification shown as follows adds to the classifiers preceding it:

- `Classification` provides the first best category as the rank 0 category.
- `RankedClassification` adds an ordering of all the possible categories with a lower rank corresponding to greater likelihood of the category. The `rank` column reflects this ordering.

Simple Classifiers

- ▶ `ScoredClassification` adds a numeric score to the ranked output. Note that scores might or might not compare well against other strings being classified depending on the type of classifier. This is the column labeled `Score`. To understand the basis of this score, consult the relevant Javadoc.

- ▶ `ConditionalClassification` further refines the score by making it a category probability conditioned on the input. The probabilities of all categories will sum up to 1. This is the column labeled `P(Category|Input)`, which is the traditional way to write *probability of the category given the input*.

- ▶ `JointClassification` adds the $\log_2$ (log base 2) probability of the input and the category—this is the joint probability. The probabilities of all categories and inputs will sum up to 1, which is a very large space indeed with very low probabilities assigned to any pair of category and string. This is why $\log_2$ values are used to prevent numerical underflow. This is the column labeled `log 2 P(Category, Input)`, which is translated as *the $\log_2$ probability of the category and input*.

Look at the Javadoc for the `com.aliasi.classify` package for more information on the metrics and classifiers that implement them.

How it works...

The code is in `src/com/lingpipe/cookbook/chapter1/RunClassifierJoint.java`, and it deserializes to a `JointClassifier<CharSequence>`:

```
public static void main(String[] args) throws IOException,
  ClassNotFoundException {
  String classifierPath  = args.length > 0 ? args[0] :
    "models/3LangId.LMClassifier";
  @SuppressWarnings("unchecked")
    JointClassifier<CharSequence> classifier
    = (JointClassifier<CharSequence>)
    AbstractExternalizable.readObject(new File(classifierPath));
  Util.consoleInputPrintClassification(classifier);
}
```

It makes a call to `Util.consoleInputPrintClassification(classifier)`, which minimally differs from `Util.consoleInputBestCategory(classifier)`, in that it uses the `toString()` method of classification to print. The code is as follows:

```
public static void consoleInputPrintClassification(BaseClassifier<Cha
rSequence>
classifier) throws IOException {
  BufferedReader reader = new BufferedReader(new
    InputStreamReader(System.in));
  while (true) {
```

```java
    System.out.println("\nType a string to be classified." + Empty 
string to quit.");
    String data = reader.readLine();
    if (data.equals("")) {
      return;
    }
    Classification classification = classifier.classify(data);
    System.out.println(classification);
  }
}
```

We got a richer output than we expected, because the type is `Classification`, but the `toString()` method will be applied to the runtime type `JointClassification`.

See also

- There is detailed information in *Chapter 6, Character Language Models* of *Text Analysis with LingPipe 4*, by *Bob Carpenter* and *Breck Baldwin*, *LingPipe Publishing* (http://alias-i.com/lingpipe-book/lingpipe-book-0.5.pdf) on language models.

Getting data from the Twitter API

We use the popular `twitter4j` package to invoke the Twitter Search API, and search for tweets and save them to disk. The Twitter API requires authentication as of Version 1.1, and we will need to get authentication tokens and save them in the `twitter4j.properties` file before we get started.

Getting ready

If you don't have a Twitter account, go to `twitter.com/signup` and create an account. You will also need to go to `dev.twitter.com` and sign in to enable yourself for the developer account. Once you have a Twitter login, we'll be on our way to creating the Twitter OAuth credentials. Be prepared for this process to be different from what we are presenting. In any case, we will supply example results in the `data` directory. Let's now create the Twitter OAuth credentials:

1. Log in to `dev.twitter.com`.
2. Find the little pull-down menu next to your icon on the top bar.
3. Choose **My Applications**.
4. Click on **Create a new application**.
5. Fill in the form and click on **Create a Twitter application**.

Simple Classifiers

6. The next page contains the OAuth settings.
7. Click on the **Create my access token** link.
8. You will need to copy **Consumer key** and **Consumer secret**.
9. You will also need to copy **Access token** and **Access token secret**.
10. These values should go into the `twitter4j.properties` file in the appropriate locations. The properties are as follows:

    ```
    debug=false
    oauth.consumerKey=ehUOExampleEwQLQpPQ
    oauth.consumerSecret=aTHUGTBgExampleaW3yLvwdJYlhWY74
    oauth.accessToken=1934528880-fiMQBJCBExamplegK6otBG3XXazLv
    oauth.accessTokenSecret=y0XExampleGEHdhCQGcn46F8Vx2E
    ```

How to do it...

Now, we're ready to access Twitter and get some search data using the following steps:

1. Go to the directory of this chapter and run the following command:

    ```
    java -cp lingpipe-cookbook.1.0.jar:lib/twitter4j-core-
    4.0.1.jar:lib/opencsv-2.4.jar:lib/lingpipe-4.1.0.jar com.lingpipe.
    cookbook.chapter1.TwitterSearch
    ```

2. The code displays the output file (in this case, a default value). Supplying a path as an argument will write to this file. Then, type in your query at the prompt:

    ```
    Writing output to data/twitterSearch.csv
    Enter Twitter Query:disney
    ```

3. The code then queries Twitter and reports every 100 tweets found (output truncated):

    ```
    Tweets Accumulated: 100
    Tweets Accumulated: 200
    ...
    Tweets Accumulated: 1500
    writing to disk 1500 tweets at data/twitterSearch.csv
    ```

This program uses the search query, searches Twitter for the term, and writes the output (limited to 1500 tweets) to the `.csv` file name that you specified on the command line or uses a default.

Chapter 1

How it works...

The code uses the `twitter4j` library to instantiate `TwitterFactory` and searches Twitter using the user-entered query. The start of `main()` at `src/com/lingpipe/cookbook/chapter1/TwitterSearch.java` is:

```
String outFilePath = args.length > 0 ? args[0] : "data/twitterSearch.csv";
File outFile = new File(outFilePath);
System.out.println("Writing output to " + outFile);
BufferedReader reader = new BufferedReader(new InputStreamReader(System.in));
System.out.print("Enter Twitter Query:");
String queryString = reader.readLine();
```

The preceding code gets the outfile, supplying a default if none is provided, and takes the query from the command line.

The following code sets up the query according to the vision of the twitter4j developers. For more information on this process, read their Javadoc. However, it should be fairly straightforward. In order to make our result set more unique, you'll notice that when we create the query string, we will filter out retweets using the `-filter:retweets` option. This is only somewhat effective; see the *Eliminate near duplicates with the Jaccard distance* recipe later in this chapter for a more complete solution:

```
Twitter twitter = new TwitterFactory().getInstance();
Query query = new Query(queryString + " -filter:retweets");
query.setLang("en");//English
query.setCount(TWEETS_PER_PAGE);
query.setResultType(Query.RECENT);
```

We will get the following result:

```
List<String[]> csvRows = new ArrayList<String[]>();
while(csvRows.size() < MAX_TWEETS) {
  QueryResult result = twitter.search(query);
  List<Status> resultTweets = result.getTweets();
  for (Status tweetStatus : resultTweets) {
    String row[] = new String[Util.ROW_LENGTH];
    row[Util.TEXT_OFFSET] = tweetStatus.getText();
    csvRows.add(row);
  }
  System.out.println("Tweets Accumulated: " + csvRows.size());
```

```
    if ((query = result.nextQuery()) == null) {
      break;
    }
  }
}
```

The preceding snippet is a pretty standard code slinging, albeit without the usual hardening for external facing code—try/catch, timeouts, and retries. One potentially confusing bit is the use of `query` to handle paging through the search results—it returns `null` when no more pages are available. The current Twitter API allows a maximum of 100 results per page, so in order to get 1500 results, we need to rerun the search until there are no more results, or until we get 1500 tweets. The next step involves a bit of reporting and writing:

```
System.out.println("writing to disk " + csvRows.size()
  + " tweets at " + outFilePath);
Util.writeCsvAddHeader(csvRows, outFile);
```

The list of tweets is then written to a `.csv` file using the `Util.writeCsvAddHeader` method:

```
public static void writeCsvAddHeader(List<String[]> data, File file)
throws IOException {
  CSVWriter csvWriter = new CSVWriter
    (new OutputStreamWriter(new
    FileOutputStream(file),Strings.UTF8));
  csvWriter.writeNext(ANNOTATION_HEADER_ROW);
  csvWriter.writeAll(data);
  csvWriter.close();
}
```

We will be using this `.csv` file to run the language ID test in the next section.

See also

For more details on using the Twitter API and twitter4j, please go to their documentation pages:

- http://twitter4j.org/javadoc/
- https://dev.twitter.com/docs

Applying a classifier to a .csv file

Now, we can test our language ID classifier on the data we downloaded from Twitter. This recipe will show you how to run the classifier on the `.csv` file and will set the stage for the evaluation step in the next recipe.

How to do it...

Applying a classifier to the `.csv` file is straightforward! Just perform the following steps:

1. Get a command prompt and run:

   ```
   java -cp lingpipe-cookbook.1.0.jar:lib/lingpipe-4.1.0.jar:lib/
   twitter4j-core-4.0.1.jar:lib/opencsv-2.4.jar com.lingpipe.
   cookbook.chapter1.ReadClassifierRunOnCsv
   ```

2. This will use the default CSV file from the `data/disney.csv` distribution, run over each line of the CSV file, and apply a language ID classifier from `models/3LangId.LMClassifier` to it:

   InputText: When all else fails #Disney

   Best Classified Language: english

   InputText: ES INSUPERABLE DISNEY !! QUIERO VOLVER:(

   Best Classified Language: Spanish

3. You can also specify the input as the first argument and the classifier as the second one.

How it works...

We will deserialize a classifier from the externalized model that was described in the previous recipes. Then, we will iterate through each line of the `.csv` file and call the classify method of the classifier. The code in `main()` is:

```
String inputPath = args.length > 0 ? args[0] : "data/disney.csv";
String classifierPath = args.length > 1 ? args[1] :
  "models/3LangId.LMClassifier";
@SuppressWarnings("unchecked") BaseClassifier<CharSequence> classifier
= (BaseClassifier<CharSequence>) AbstractExternalizable.readObject(new
File(classifierPath));
List<String[]> lines = Util.readCsvRemoveHeader(new File(inputPath));
for(String [] line: lines) {
  String text = line[Util.TEXT_OFFSET];
  Classification classified = classifier.classify(text);
  System.out.println("InputText: " + text);
  System.out.println("Best Classified Language: " + classified.
bestCategory());
}
```

Simple Classifiers

The preceding code builds on the previous recipes with nothing particularly new. `Util.readCsvRemoveHeader`, shown as follows, just skips the first line of the `.csv` file before reading from disk and returning the rows that have non-null values and non-empty strings in the `TEXT_OFFSET` position:

```
public static List<String[]> readCsvRemoveHeader(File file) throws
IOException {
  FileInputStream fileIn = new FileInputStream(file);
  InputStreamReader inputStreamReader = new
    InputStreamReader(fileIn,Strings.UTF8);
  CSVReader csvReader = new CSVReader(inputStreamReader);
  csvReader.readNext();  //skip headers
  List<String[]> rows = new ArrayList<String[]>();
  String[] row;
  while ((row = csvReader.readNext()) != null) {
    if (row[TEXT_OFFSET] == null || row[TEXT_OFFSET].equals("")) {
      continue;
    }
    rows.add(row);
  }
  csvReader.close();
  return rows;
}
```

Evaluation of classifiers – the confusion matrix

Evaluation is incredibly important in building solid NLP systems. It allows developers and management to map a business need to system performance, which, in turn, helps communicate system improvement to vested parties. "Well, uh, the system seems to be doing better" does not hold the gravitas of "Recall has improved 20 percent, and the specificity is holding well with 50 percent more training data".

This recipe provides the steps for the creation of truth or *gold standard* data and tells us how to use this data to evaluate the performance of our precompiled classifier. It is as simple as it is powerful.

Getting ready

You might have noticed the headers from the output of the CSV writer and the suspiciously labeled column, `TRUTH`. Now, we get to use it. Load up the tweets we provided earlier or convert your data into the format used in our `.csv` format. An easy way to get novel data is to run a query against Twitter with a multilingual friendly query such as `Disney`, which is our default supplied data.

Open the CSV file and annotate the language you think the tweet is in for at least 10 examples each of *e* for English and *n* for non-English. There is a `data/disney_e_n.csv` file in the distribution; you can use this if you don't want to deal with annotating data. If you are not sure about a tweet, feel free to ignore it. Unannotated data is ignored. Have a look at the following screenshot:

	A	B	C	
1	SCORE	GUESS	TRUTH	TRUTH
2			e	When all else fails #Disney
3			n	昨日の幸せな気持ちのまま今日はLANDにいっちゃうよ♡はあ、幸せ♡笑
4			e	Best part of having a neice now is having an excuse to relive all the old Disney movies
5			e	I can't wait for Disney though
6			e	request now "let's get tricky" by @bellathorne and @ROSHON on @radiodisney!!! just
7			n	100均のDisneyが可愛いよぉ~(/ _ ;)♥帰る前に買っていこう。そしてプリンセスって、
8			e	I fully love the Disney Channel I do not care
9			n	@greenath_ t'as de la chance d'aller a Disney putain j'y ai jamais été moi.
10			e	AHH! What a talent! Love ya girl! @ShoshanaBean in Disney-Style Spell Block Tango!
11			n	Prefiro gastar uma baba de dinheiro pra ir pra cancun doq pra Disney por exemplo
12			n	@meeelp mas que venha um filhinho mais fofo que o próprio pai, com covinha e amar
13			e	"@rpdavlin: I want to go to a college in California so I can go to Disney Land whenever
14			e	Cant sleep so im watching.. Beverley Hills Chihuahua.. Yep thats right, I'm watching a
15			n	なんか、Twitterアップデートしたらさ…(^◇^;)
16			e	Miley isn't Hannah anymore, Demi isn't Sonny anymore, Selena isn't Alex anymore. Di
17			n	ES INSUPERABLE DISNEY !! QUIERO VOLVER:(
18			n	Creo q fue lo peor q pude hacer mirar los videos de disney
19			n	Malisimos los nuevos dibujitos de disney, nickelodeon, cartoon, etc, no me gustannn
20			n	@Hukaaaa_disney ネオマウスという役で出てきてました（笑）聞いた瞬間マジフィニ
21			e	@FernandaAbarca_ how did you become an artist for Dream Works. I wanna do that fo
22				Disney channel should have played "Mom's got a date with a vampire"
23				Some imagination, huh? #fantasmic #studios # glowwiththeshow #disney #disneynerd

Screenshot of the spreadsheet with human annotations for English 'e' and non-English 'n'. It is known as truth data or gold standard data because it represents the phenomenon correctly.

Often, this data is called **gold standard data**, because it represents the truth. The "gold" in "gold standard" is quite literal. Back it up and store it with longevity in mind—it is most likely that it is the single-most valuable collection of bytes on your hard drive, because it is expensive to produce in any quantity and the cleanest articulation of what is being done. Implementations come and go; evaluation data lives on forever. The John Smith corpus from the *The John Smith problem* recipe, in *Chapter 7*, *Finding Coreference Between Concepts/People*, is the canonical evaluation corpus for that particular problem and lives on as the point of comparison for a line of research that started in 1997. The original implementation is long forgotten.

Simple Classifiers

How to do it...

Perform the following steps to evaluate the classifiers:

1. Enter the following in the command prompt; this will run the default classifier on the texts in the default gold standard data. Then, it will compare the classifier's best category against what was annotated in the TRUTH column:

   ```
   java -cp lingpipe-cookbook.1.0.jar:lib/opencsv-2.4.jar:lib/
   lingpipe-4.1.0.jar com.lingpipe.cookbook.chapter1.
   RunConfusionMatrix
   ```

2. This class will then produce the confusion matrix:

   ```
   reference\response
         \e,n,
         e 11,0,
         n 1,9,
   ```

The confusion matrix is aptly named since it confuses almost everyone initially, but it is, without a doubt, the best representation of classifier output, because it is very difficult to hide bad classifier performance with it. In other words, it is an excellent BS detector. It is the unambiguous view of what the classifier got right, what it got wrong, and what it thought was the right answer.

The sum of each row represents the items that are known by truth/reference/gold standard to belong to the category. For English (e) there were 11 tweets. Each column represents what the system thought was in the same labeled category. For English (e), the system thought 11 tweets were English and none were non-English (n). For the non-English category (n), there are 10 cases in truth, of which the classifier thought 1 was English (incorrectly) and 9 were non-English (correctly). Perfect system performance will have zeros in all the cells that are not located diagonally, from the top-left corner to the bottom-right corner.

The real reason it is called a confusion matrix is that it is relatively easy to see categories that the classifier is confusing. For example, British English and American English would likely be highly confusable. Also, confusion matrices scale to multiple categories quite nicely, as will be seen later. Visit the Javadoc for a more detailed explanation of the confusion matrix—it is well worth mastering.

How it works...

Building on the code from the previous recipes in this chapter, we will focus on what is novel in the evaluation setup. The entirety of the code is in the distribution at `src/com/lingpipe/cookbook/chapter1/RunConfusionMatrix.java`. The start of `main()` is shown in the following code snippet. The code starts by reading from the arguments that look for non-default CSV data and serialized classifiers. Defaults, which this recipe uses, are shown here:

```
String inputPath = args.length > 0 ? args[0] :
  "data/disney_e_n.csv";
String classifierPath = args.length > 1 ? args[1] :
  "models/1LangId.LMClassifier";
```

Next, the language model and the `.csv` data will be loaded. The method differs slightly from the `Util.CsvRemoveHeader` explanation, in that it only accepts rows that have a value in the TRUTH column—see `src/com/lingpipe/cookbook/Util.java` if this is not clear:

```
@SuppressWarnings("unchecked")
BaseClassifier<CharSequence> classifier
  = (BaseClassifier<CharSequence>) AbstractExternalizable.
readObject(new File(classifierPath));

List<String[]> rows = Util.readAnnotatedCsvRemoveHeader(new
  File(inputPath));
```

Next, the categories will be found:

```
String[] categories = Util.getCategories(rows);
```

The method will accumulate all the category labels from the TRUTH column. The code is simple and is shown here:

```
public static String[] getCategories(List<String[]> data) {
  Set<String> categories = new HashSet<String>();
  for (String[] csvData : data) {
    if (!csvData[ANNOTATION_OFFSET].equals("")) {
      categories.add(csvData[ANNOTATION_OFFSET]);
    }
  }
  return categories.toArray(new String[0]);
}
```

The code will be useful when we run arbitrary data, where the labels are not known at compile time.

Simple Classifiers

Then, we will set up `BaseClassfierEvaluator`. This requires the classifier to be evaluated. The categories and a `boolean` value that controls whether inputs are stored in the classifier for construction will also be set up:

```
boolean storeInputs = false;
BaseClassifierEvaluator<CharSequence> evaluator = new
   BaseClassifierEvaluator<CharSequence>(classifier, categories,
   storeInputs);
```

Note that the classifier can be null and specified at a later time; the categories must exactly match those produced by the annotation and the classifier. We will not bother configuring the evaluator to store the inputs, because we are not going to use this capability in this recipe. See the *Viewing error categories – false positives* recipe for an example in which the inputs are stored and accessed.

Next, we will do the actual evaluation. The loop will iterate over each row of the information in the `.csv` file, build a `Classified<CharSequence>`, and pass it off to the evaluator's `handle()` method:

```
for (String[] row : rows) {
   String truth = row[Util.ANNOTATION_OFFSET];
   String text = row[Util.TEXT_OFFSET];
   Classification classification = new Classification(truth);
   Classified<CharSequence> classified
      = new Classified<CharSequence>(text,classification);
   evaluator.handle(classified);
}
```

The fourth line will create a classification object with the value from the truth annotation—*e* or *n* in this case. This is the same type as the one `BaseClassifier<E>` returns for the `bestCategory()` method. There is no special type for truth annotations. The next line adds in the text that the classification applies to and we get a `Classified<CharSequence>` object.

The last line of the loop will apply the handle method to the created classified object. The evaluator assumes that data supplied to its handle method is a truth annotation, which is handled by extracting the data being classified, applying the classifier to this data, getting the resulting `firstBest()` classification, and finally noting whether the classification matches that of what was just constructed with the truth. This happens for each row of the `.csv` file.

Outside the loop, we will print out the confusion matrix with `Util.createConfusionMatrix()`:

```
System.out.println(Util.confusionMatrixToString(evaluator.
confusionMatrix()));
```

Examining this code is left to the reader. That's it; we have evaluated our classifier and printed out the confusion matrix.

There's more...

The evaluator has a complete `toString()` method that is a bit of a fire hose for information on just how well your classifier did. Those aspects of the output will be covered in later recipes. The Javadoc is quite extensive and well worth reading.

Training your own language model classifier

The world of NLP really opens up when classifiers are customized. This recipe provides details on how to customize a classifier by collecting examples for the classifier to learn from—this is called training data. It is also called gold standard data, truth, or ground truth. We have some from the previous recipe that we will use.

Getting ready

We will create a customized language ID classifier for English and other languages. Creation of training data involves getting access to text data and then annotating it for the categories of the classifier—in this case, annotation is the language. Training data can come from a range of sources. Some possibilities include:

- Gold standard data such as the one created in the preceding evaluation recipe.
- Data that is somehow already annotated for the categories you care about. For example, Wikipedia has language-specific versions, which make easy pickings to train up a language ID classifier. This is how we created the `3LangId.LMClassifier` model.
- Be creative—where is the data that helps guide a classifier in the right direction?

Language ID doesn't require much data to work well, so 20 tweets per language will start to reliably distinguish strongly different languages. The amount of training data will be driven by evaluation—more data generally improves performance.

The example assumes that around 10 tweets of English and 10 non-English tweets have been annotated by people and put in `data/disney_e_n.csv`.

How to do it...

In order to train your own language model classifier, perform the following steps:

1. Fire up a terminal and type the following:

   ```
   java -cp lingpipe-cookbook.1.0.jar:lib/opencsv-2.4.jar:lib/lingpipe-4.1.0.jar com.lingpipe.cookbook.chapter1.TrainAndRunLMClassifier
   ```

Simple Classifiers

2. Then, type some English in the command prompt, perhaps, a Kurt Vonnegut quotation, to see the resulting `JointClassification`. See the *Getting confidence estimates from a classifier* recipe for the explanation of the following output:

   ```
   Type a string to be classified. Empty string to quit.
   So it goes.
   Rank Categ Score         P(Category|Input)      log2 P(Category,Input)
   0=e -4.24592987919  0.9999933712053       -55.19708842949149
   1=n -5.56922173547  6.62884502334E-6      -72.39988256112824
   ```

3. Type in some non-English, such as the Spanish title of Borge's *The Garden of the Forking Paths*:

   ```
   Type a string to be classified. Empty string to quit.
   El Jardín de senderos que se bifurcan
   Rank Categ Score         P(Category|Input)      log2 P(Category,Input)
   0=n -5.6612148689  0.999989087229795    -226.44859475801326
   1=e -6.0733050528  1.091277041753E-5    -242.93220211249715
   ```

How it works...

The program is in `src/com/lingpipe/cookbook/chapter1/TrainAndRunLMClassifier.java`; the contents of the `main()` method start with:

```
String dataPath = args.length > 0 ? args[0] :
  "data/disney_e_n.csv";
List<String[]> annotatedData =
  Util.readAnnotatedCsvRemoveHeader(new File(dataPath));
String[] categories = Util.getCategories(annotatedData);
```

The preceding code gets the contents of the `.csv` file and then extracts the list of categories that were annotated; these categories will be all the non-empty strings in the annotation column.

The following `DynamicLMClassifier` is created using a static method that requires the array of categories and `int`, which is the order of the language models. With an order of 3, the language model will be trained on all 1 to 3 character sequences of the text training data. So "I luv Disney" will produce training instances of "I", " ", " l", "l", " lu", "u", "uv", "luv", and so on. The `createNGramBoundary` method appends a special token to the beginning and end of each text sequence; this token can help if the beginnings or ends are informative for classification. Most text data is sensitive to beginnings/ends, so we will choose this model:

```
int maxCharNGram = 3;
DynamicLMClassifier<NGramBoundaryLM> classifier =
  DynamicLMClassifier.createNGramBoundary(categories,maxCharNGram);
```

The following code iterates over the rows of training data and creates `Classified<CharSequence>` in the same way as shown in the *Evaluation of classifiers – the confusion matrix* recipe for evaluation. However, instead of passing the `Classified` object to an evaluation handler, it is used to train the classifier.

```
for (String[] row: annotatedData) {
  String truth = row[Util.ANNOTATION_OFFSET];
  String text = row[Util.TEXT_OFFSET];
  Classification classification
     = new Classification(truth);
  Classified<CharSequence> classified =
     new Classified<CharSequence>(text,classification);
  classifier.handle(classified);
}
```

No further steps are necessary, and the classifier is ready for use by the console:

```
Util.consoleInputPrintClassification(classifier);
```

There's more...

Training and using the classifier can be interspersed for classifiers based on `DynamicLM`. This is generally not the case with other classifiers such as `LogisticRegression`, because they use all the data to compile a model that can carry out classifications.

There is another method for training the classifier that gives you more control over how the training goes. The following is the code snippet for this:

```
Classification classification = new Classification(truth);
Classified<CharSequence> classified = new
   Classified<CharSequence>(text,classification);
classifier.handle(classified);
```

Alternatively, we can have the same effect with:

```
int count = 1;
classifier.train(truth,text,count);
```

The `train()` method allows an extra degree of control for training, because it allows for the count to be explicitly set. As we explore LingPipe classifiers, we will often see an alternate way of training that allows for some additional control beyond what the `handle()` method provides.

Character-language model-based classifiers work very well for tasks where character sequences are distinctive. Language identification is an ideal candidate for this, but it can also be used for tasks such as sentiment, topic assignment, and question answering.

Simple Classifiers

See also

The Javadoc for LingPipe's classifiers are quite extensive on the underlying math that drives the technology.

How to train and evaluate with cross validation

The earlier recipes have shown how to evaluate classifiers with truth data and how to train with truth data but how about doing both? This great idea is called cross validation, and it works as follows:

1. Split the data into *n* distinct sets or folds—the standard *n* is 10.
2. For *i* from 1 to *n*:
   - Train on the *n - 1* folds defined by the exclusion of fold *i*
   - Evaluate on fold *i*
3. Report the evaluation results across all folds *i*.

This is how most machine-learning systems are tuned for performance. The work flow is as follows:

1. See what the cross validation performance is.
2. Look at the error as determined by an evaluation metric.
3. Look at the actual errors—yes, the data—for insights into how the system can be improved.
4. Make some changes
5. Evaluate it again.

Cross validation is an excellent way to compare different approaches to a problem, try different classifiers, motivate normalization approaches, explore feature enhancements, and so on. Generally, a system configuration that shows increased performance on cross validation will also show increased performance on new data. What cross validation does not do, particularly with active learning strategies discussed later, is reliably predict performance on new data. Always apply the classifier to new data before releasing production systems as a final sanity check. You have been warned.

Cross validation also imposes a negative bias compared to a classifier trained on all possible training data, because each fold is a slightly weaker classifier, in that it only has 90 percent of the data on 10 folds.

Rinse, lather, and repeat is the mantra of building state-of-the-art NLP systems.

Getting ready

Note how different this approach is from other classic computer-engineering approaches that focus on developing against a functional specification driven by unit tests. This process is more about refining and adjusting the code to work better as determined by the evaluation metrics.

How to do it...

To run the code, perform the following steps:

1. Get to a command prompt and type:

   ```
   java -cp lingpipe-cookbook.1.0.jar:lib/opencsv-2.4.jar:lib/lingpipe-4.1.0.jar com.lingpipe.cookbook.chapter1.RunXValidate
   ```

2. The result will be:

   ```
   Training data is: data/disney_e_n.csv
   Training on fold 0
   Testing on fold 0
   Training on fold 1
   Testing on fold 1
   Training on fold 2
   Testing on fold 2
   Training on fold 3
   Testing on fold 3
   reference\response
        \e,n,
        e 10,1,
        n 6,4,
   ```

   The preceding output will make more sense in the following section.

How it works...

This recipe introduces an `XValidatingObjectCorpus` object that manages cross validation. It is used heavily in training classifiers. Everything else should be familiar from the previous recipes. The `main()` method starts with:

```
String inputPath = args.length > 0 ? args[0] : "data/disney_e_n.csv";
System.out.println("Training data is: " + inputPath);
List<String[]> truthData = Util.readAnnotatedCsvRemoveHeader(new File(inputPath));
```

Simple Classifiers

The preceding code gets us the data from the default or a user-entered file. The next two lines introduce `XValidatingObjectCorpus`—the star of this recipe:

```
int numFolds = 4;
XValidatingObjectCorpus<Classified<CharSequence>> corpus = Util.
loadXValCorpus(truthData, numFolds);
```

The `numFolds` variable controls how the data that is just loaded will be partitioned—it will be in four partitions in this case. Now, we will look at the `Util.loadXValCorpus(truthData, numfolds)` subroutine:

```
public static XValidatingObjectCorpus<Classified<CharSequence>>
loadXValCorpus(List<String[]> rows, int numFolds) throws IOException {
  XValidatingObjectCorpus<Classified<CharSequence>> corpus
= new XValidatingObjectCorpus<Classified<CharSequence>>(numFolds);
  for (String[] row : rows) {
    Classification classification = new
      Classification(row[ANNOTATION_OFFSET]);
    Classified<CharSequence> classified = new
      Classified<CharSequence>(row[TEXT_OFFSET],classification);
    corpus.handle(classified);
  }
  return corpus;
}
```

`XValidatingObjectCorpus<E>` constructed will contain all the truth data in the form of `Objects E`. In this case, we are filling the corpus with the same object used to train and evaluate in the previous recipes in this chapter—`Classified<CharSequence>`. This will be handy, because we will be using the objects to both train and test our classifier. The `numFolds` parameter specifies how many partitions of the data to make. It can be changed later.

The following `for` loop should be familiar, in that, it should iterate over all the annotated data and creates the `Classified<CharSequence>` object before applying the `corpus.handle()` method, which adds it to the corpus. Finally, we will return the corpus. It is worth taking a look at the Javadoc for `XValidatingObjectCorpus<E>` if you have any questions.

Returning to the body of `main()`, we will permute the corpus to mix the data, get the categories, and set up `BaseClassifierEvaluator<CharSequence>` with a null value where we supplied a classifier in a previous recipe:

```
corpus.permuteCorpus(new Random(123413));
String[] categories = Util.getCategories(truthData);
boolean storeInputs = false;
BaseClassifierEvaluator<CharSequence> evaluator
= new BaseClassifierEvaluator<CharSequence>(null, categories,
storeInputs);
```

Now, we are ready to do the cross validation:

```
int maxCharNGram = 3;
for (int i = 0; i < numFolds; ++i) {
  corpus.setFold(i);
  DynamicLMClassifier<NGramBoundaryLM> classifier =
    DynamicLMClassifier.createNGramBoundary(categories,
    maxCharNGram);
  System.out.println("Training on fold " + i);
  corpus.visitTrain(classifier);
  evaluator.setClassifier(classifier);
  System.out.println("Testing on fold " + i);
  corpus.visitTest(evaluator);
}
```

On each iteration of the `for` loop, we will set which fold is being used, which, in turn, will select the training and testing partition. Then, we will construct `DynamicLMClassifier` and train it by supplying the classifier to `corpus.visitTrain(classifier)`. Next, we will set the evaluator's classifier to the one we just trained. The evaluator is passed to the `corpus.visitTest(evaluator)` method where the contained classifier is applied to the test data that it was not trained on. With four folds, 25 percent of the data will be test data at any given iteration, and 75 percent of the data will be training data. Data will be in the test partition exactly once and three times in the training. The training and test partitions will never contain the same data unless there are duplicates in the data.

Once the loop has finished all iterations, we will print a confusion matrix discussed in the *Evaluation of classifiers – the confusion matrix* recipe:

```
System.out.println(
  Util.confusionMatrixToString(evaluator.confusionMatrix()));
```

There's more...

This recipe introduces quite a few moving parts, namely, cross validation and a corpus object that supports it. The `ObjectHandler<E>` interface is also used a lot; this can be confusing to developers not familiar with the pattern. It is used to train and test the classifier. It can also be used to print the contents of the corpus. Change the contents of the `for` loop to `visitTrain` with `Util.corpusPrinter`:

```
System.out.println("Training on fold " + i);
corpus.visitTrain(Util.corpusPrinter());
corpus.visitTrain(classifier);
evaluator.setClassifier(classifier);
System.out.println("Testing on fold " + i);
corpus.visitTest(Util.corpusPrinter());
```

Simple Classifiers

Now, you will get an output that looks like:

```
Training on fold 0
Malis?mos los nuevos dibujitos de disney, nickelodeon, cartoon,
etc, no me gustannn:n
@meeelp mas que venha um filhinho mais fofo que o pr?prio pai, com
covinha e amando a Disney kkkkkkkkkkkkkkkk:n
@HedyHAMIDI au quartier pas a Disney moi:n
I fully love the Disney Channel I do not care ?:e
```

The text is followed by : and the category. Printing the training/test folds is a good sanity check for whether the corpus is properly populated. It is also a nice glimpse into how the `ObjectHandler<E>` interface works—here, the source is from `com/lingpipe/cookbook/Util.java`:

```java
public static ObjectHandler<Classified<CharSequence>> corpusPrinter () 
{
  return new ObjectHandler<Classified<CharSequence>>() {
    @Override
    public void handle(Classified<CharSequence> e) {
      System.out.println(e.toString());
    }
  };
}
```

There is not much to the returned class. There is a single `handle()` method that just prints the `toString()` method of `Classified<CharSequence>`. In the context of this recipe, the classifier instead invokes `train()` on the text and classification, and the evaluator takes the text, runs it past the classifier, and compares the result to the truth.

Another good experiment to run is to report performance on each fold instead of all folds. For small datasets, you will see very large variations in performance. Another worthwhile experiment is to permute the corpus 10 times and see the variations in performance that come from different partitioning of the data.

Another issue is how data is selected for evaluation. To text process applications, it is important to not leak information between test data and training data. Cross validation over 10 days of data will be much more realistic if each day is a fold rather than a 10-percent slice of all 10 days. The reason is that a day's data will likely be correlated, and this correlation will produce information about that day in training and testing, if days are allowed to be in both train and test. When evaluating the final performance, always select data from after the training data epoch if possible, to better emulate production environments where the future is not known.

Viewing error categories – false positives

We can achieve the best possible classifier performance by examining the errors and making changes to the system. There is a very bad habit among developers and machine-learning folks to not look at errors, particularly as systems mature. Just to be clear, at the end of a project, the developers responsible for tuning the classifier should be very familiar with the domain being classified, if not expert in it, because they have looked at so much data while tuning the system. If the developer cannot do a reasonable job of emulating the classifiers that you are tuning, then you are not looking at enough data.

This recipe performs the most basic form of looking at what the system got wrong in the form of false positives, which are examples from training data that the classifier assigned to a category, but the correct category was something else.

How to do it...

Perform the following steps in order to view error categories using false positives:

1. This recipe extends the previous *How to train and evaluate with cross validation* recipe by accessing more of what the evaluation class provides. Get a command prompt and type:

    ```
    java -cp lingpipe-cookbook.1.0.jar:lib/opencsv-2.4.jar:lib/lingpipe-4.1.0.jar com.lingpipe.cookbook.chapter1.ReportFalsePositivesOverXValidation
    ```

2. This will result in:

    ```
    Training data is: data/disney_e_n.csv
    reference\response
             \e,n,
           e 10,1,
           n 6,4,
    False Positives for e
    Malisímos los nuevos dibujitos de disney, nickelodeon, cartoon, etc, no me gustannn : n
    @meeelp mas que venha um filhinho mais fofo que o próprio pai, com covinha e amando a Disney kkkkkkkkkkkkkkkk : n
    @HedyHAMIDI au quartier pas a Disney moi : n
    @greenath_ t'as de la chance d'aller a Disney putain j'y ai jamais été moi. : n
    ```

Simple Classifiers

```
Prefiro gastar uma baba de dinheiro pra ir pra cancun doq pra
Disney por exemplo : n

ES INSUPERABLE DISNEY !! QUIERO VOLVER:( : n

False Positives for n

request now "let's get tricky" by @bellathorne and @ROSHON on @
radiodisney!!! just call 1-877-870-5678 or at http://t.co/
cbne5yRKhQ!! <3 : e
```

3. The output starts with a confusion matrix. Then, we will see the actual six instances of false positives for p from the lower left-hand side cell of the confusion matrix labeled with the category that the classifier guessed. Then, we will see false positives for n, which is a single example. The true category is appended with :, which is helpful for classifiers that have more than two categories.

How it works...

This recipe is based on the previous one, but it has its own source in `com/lingpipe/cookbook/chapter1/ReportFalsePositivesOverXValidation.java`. There are two differences. First, `storeInputs` is set to `true` for the evaluator:

```
boolean storeInputs = true;
BaseClassifierEvaluator<CharSequence> evaluator = new BaseClassifierEv
aluator<CharSequence>(null, categories, storeInputs);
```

Second, a `Util` method is added to print false positives:

```
for (String category : categories) {
  Util.printFalsePositives(category, evaluator, corpus);
}
```

The preceding code works by identifying a category of focus—e or English tweets—and extracting all the false positives from the classifier evaluator. For this category, false positives are tweets that are non-English in truth, but the classifier thought they were English. The referenced `Util` method is as follows:

```
public static <E> void printFalsePositives(String category,
BaseClassifierEvaluator<E> evaluator, Corpus<ObjectHandler<Classified
<E>>> corpus) throws IOException {
  final Map<E,Classification> truthMap = new
    HashMap<E,Classification>();
  corpus.visitCorpus(new ObjectHandler<Classified<E>>() {
    @Override
    public void handle(Classified<E> data) {
      truthMap.put(data.getObject(),data.getClassification());
    }
  });
```

The preceding code takes the corpus that contains all the truth data and populates `Map<E,Classification>` to allow for lookup of the truth annotation, given the input. If the same input exists in two categories, then this method will not be robust but will record the last example seen:

```
List<Classified<E>> falsePositives = evaluator.
falsePositives(category);
System.out.println("False Positives for " + category);
for (Classified<E> classified : falsePositives) {
  E data = classified.getObject();
  Classification truthClassification = truthMap.get(data);
  System.out.println(data + " : " +
    truthClassification.bestCategory());
  }
}
```

The code gets the false positives from the evaluator and then iterates over all them with a lookup into `truthMap` built in the preceding code and prints out the relevant information. There are also methods to get false negatives, true positives, and true negatives in `evaluator`.

The ability to identify mistakes is crucial to improving performance. The advice seems obvious, but it is very common for developers to not look at mistakes. They will look at system output and make a rough estimate of whether the system is good enough; this does not result in top-performing classifiers.

The next recipe works through more evaluation metrics and their definition.

Understanding precision and recall

The false positive from the preceding recipe is one of the four possible error categories. All the categories and their interpretations are as follows:

- For a given category X:
    - **True positive**: The classifier guessed X, and the true category is X
    - **False positive**: The classifier guessed X, but the true category is a category that is different from X
    - **True negative**: The classifier guessed a category that is different from X, and the true category is different from X
    - **False negative**: The classifier guessed a category different from X, but the true category is X

Simple Classifiers

With these definitions in hand, we can define the additional common evaluation metrics as follows:

- Precision for a category X is true positive / (false positive + true positive)
    - The degenerate case is to make one very confident guess for 100 percent precision. This minimizes the false positives but will have a horrible recall.
- Recall or sensitivity for a category X is true positive / (false negative + true positive)
    - The degenerate case is to guess all the data as belonging to category X for 100 percent recall. This minimizes false negatives but will have horrible precision.
- Specificity for a category X is true negative / (true negative + false positive)
    - The degenerate case is to guess that all data is not in category X.

The degenerate cases are provided to make clear what the metric is focused on. There are metrics such as f-measure that balance precision and recall, but even then, there is no inclusion of true negatives, which can be highly informative. See the Javadoc at `com.aliasi.classify.PrecisionRecallEvaluation` for more details on evaluation.

- In our experience, most business needs map to one of the three scenarios:
- **High precision / high recall**: The language ID needs to have both good coverage and good accuracy; otherwise, lots of stuff will go wrong. Fortunately, for distinct languages where a mistake will be costly (such as Japanese versus English or English versus Spanish), the LM classifiers perform quite well.
- **High precision / usable recall**: Most business use cases have this shape. For example, a search engine that automatically changes a query if it is misspelled better not make lots of mistakes. This means it looks pretty bad to change "Breck Baldwin" to "Brad Baldwin", but no one really notices if "Bradd Baldwin" is not corrected.
- **High recall / usable precision**: Intelligence analysis looking for a particular needle in a haystack will tolerate a lot of false positives in support of finding the intended target. This was an early lesson from our DARPA days.

How to serialize a LingPipe object – classifier example

In a deployment situation, trained classifiers, other Java objects with complex configuration, or training are best accessed by deserializing them from a disk. The first recipe did exactly this by reading in `LMClassifier` from the disk with `AbstractExternalizable`. This recipe shows how to get the language ID classifier written out to the disk for later use.

Serializing `DynamicLMClassifier` and reading it back in results in a different class, which is an instance of `LMClassifier` that performs the same as the one just trained except that it can no longer accept training instances because counts have been converted to log probabilities and the backoff smoothing arcs are stored in suffix trees. The resulting classifier is much faster.

In general, most of the LingPipe classifiers, language models, and **hidden Marcov models** (**HMM**) implement both the `Serializable` and `Compilable` interfaces.

Getting ready

We will work with the same data as we did in the *Viewing error categories – false positives* recipe.

How to do it...

Perform the following steps to serialize a LingPipe object:

1. Go to the command prompt and convey:

   ```
   java -cp lingpipe-cookbook.1.0.jar:lib/opencsv-2.4.jar:lib/
   lingpipe-4.1.0.jar com.lingpipe.cookbook.chapter1.
   TrainAndWriteClassifierToDisk
   ```

2. The program will respond with the default file values for input/output:

   ```
   Training on data/disney_e_n.csv
   ```
   ```
   Wrote model to models/my_disney_e_n.LMClassifier
   ```

3. Test if the model works by invoking the *Deserializing and running a classifier* recipe while specifying the classifier file to be read in:

   ```
   java -cp lingpipe-cookbook.1.0.jar:lib/lingpipe-4.1.0.jar com.
   lingpipe.cookbook.chapter1.LoadClassifierRunOnCommandLine models/
   my_disney_e_n.LMClassifier
   ```

4. The usual interaction follows:

   ```
   Type a string to be classified. Empty string to quit.
   ```
   ```
   The rain in Spain
   ```
   ```
   Best Category: e
   ```

How it works...

The contents of `main()` from `src/com/lingpipe/cookbook/chapter1/TrainAndWriteClassifierToDisk.java` start with the materials covered in the previous recipes of the chapter to read the `.csv` files, set up a classifier, and train it. Please refer back to it if any code is unclear.

Simple Classifiers

The new bit for this recipe happens when we invoke the `AbtractExternalizable.compileTo()` method on `DynamicLMClassifier`, which compiles the model and writes it to a file. This method is used like the `writeExternal` method from Java's `Externalizable` interface:

```
AbstractExternalizable.compileTo(classifier,outFile);
```

This is all you need to know folks to write a classifier to a disk.

There's more...

There is an alternate way to serialize that is amenable to more variations of data sources for serializations that are not based on the `File` class. An alternate way to write a classifier is:

```
FileOutputStream fos = new FileOutputStream(outFile);
ObjectOutputStream oos = new ObjectOutputStream(fos);
classifier.compileTo(oos);
oos.close();
fos.close();
```

Additionally, `DynamicLM` can be compiled without involving the disk with a static `AbstractExternalizable.compile()` method. It will be used in the following fashion:

```
@SuppressWarnings("unchecked")
LMClassifier<LanguageModel, MultivariateDistribution> compiledLM
 = (LMClassifier<LanguageModel, MultivariateDistribution>)
    AbstractExternalizable.compile(classifier);
```

The compiled version is a lot faster but does not allow further training instances.

Eliminate near duplicates with the Jaccard distance

It often happens that the data has duplicates or near duplicates that should be filtered. Twitter data has lots of duplicates that can be quite frustrating to work with even with the `-filter:retweets` option available for the search API. A quick way to see this is to sort the text in the spreadsheet, and tweets with common prefixes will be neighbors:

485	A Disney deveria fazer uma princesa sem cabelos, para que cada menina no mundo que luta contra o câncer
486	A Disney Halloween Playlist http://t.co/deCWqIw47u via @Weidknecht
487	A Disney Halloween Playlist http://t.co/UXhK7DRQUo via @Weidknecht
488	A Disney le falta crear una princesa que sin su principe azul tambien viva feliz.
489	A Disney le falta crear una princesa que también sin príncipe viva feliz ;)
490	A Disney le falta crear una princesa que también sin príncipe viva feliz.
491	A Disney le falta crear una princesa que también sin príncipe viva feliz.
492	A Disney le falta crear una princesa que también sin príncipe viva feliz.
493	A Disney le falta crear una princesa que también sin príncipe viva feliz.
494	A Disney le falta crear una princesa que también sin príncipe viva feliz. -.- #AsiDeSimple
495	A disney movie never fails to make me happy. ♥
496	A Disney Pixar le falta crear una princesa que también sin príncipe viva feliz.

Duplicate tweets that share a prefix

This sort only reveals shared prefixes; there are many more that don't share a prefix. This recipe will allow you to find other sources of overlap and threshold, the point at which duplicates are removed.

How to do it...

Perform the following steps to eliminate near duplicates with the Jaccard distance:

1. Type in the command prompt:

   ```
   java -cp lingpipe-cookbook.1.0.jar:lib/opencsv-2.4.jar:lib/
   lingpipe-4.1.0.jar com.lingpipe.cookbook.chapter1.
   DeduplicateCsvData
   ```

2. You will be overwhelmed with a torrent of text:

   ```
   Tweets too close, proximity 1.00
       @britneyspears do you ever miss the Disney days? and iilysm
   please follow me. kiss from Turkey #AskBritneyJean ??
       @britneyspears do you ever miss the Disney days? and iilysm
   please follow me. kiss from Turkey #AskBritneyJean ???
   Tweets too close, proximity 0.50
       Sooo, I want to have a Disney Princess movie night....
       I just want to be a Disney Princess
   ```

3. Two example outputs are shown—the first is a near-exact duplicate with only a difference in a final `?`. It has a proximity of `1.0`; the next example has proximity of `0.50`, and the tweets are different but have a good deal of word overlap. Note that the second case does not share a prefix.

How it works...

This recipe jumps a bit ahead of the sequence, using a tokenizer to drive the deduplication process. It is here because the following recipe, for sentiment, really needs deduplicated data to work well. *Chapter 2, Finding and Working with Words*, covers tokenization in detail.

The source for `main()` is:

```
String inputPath = args.length > 0 ? args[0] : "data/disney.csv";
String outputPath = args.length > 1 ? args[1] : "data/disneyDeduped.
csv";
List<String[]> data = Util.readCsvRemoveHeader(new File(inputPath));
System.out.println(data.size());
```

There is nothing new in the preceding code snippet, but the following code snippet has `TokenizerFactory`:

```
TokenizerFactory tokenizerFactory = new RegExTokenizerFactory("\\w+");
```

Briefly, the tokenizer breaks the text into text sequences defined by matching the regular expression \w+ (the first \ escapes the second one in the preceding code—it is a Java thing). It matches contiguous word characters. The string "Hi, you here??" produces tokens "Hi", "you", and "here". The punctuation is ignored.

Next up, `Util.filterJaccard` is called with a cutoff of .5, which roughly eliminates tweets that overlap with half their words. Then, the filter data is written to disk:

```
double cutoff = .5;
List<String[]> dedupedData = Util.filterJaccard(data,
tokenizerFactory, cutoff);
System.out.println(dedupedData.size());
Util.writeCsvAddHeader(dedupedData, new File(outputPath));
}
```

The `Util.filterJaccard()` method's source is as follows:

```
public static List<String[]> filterJaccard(List<String[]> texts,
TokenizerFactory tokFactory, double cutoff) {
  JaccardDistance jaccardD = new JaccardDistance(tokFactory);
```

In the preceding snippet, a `JaccardDistance` class is constructed with a tokenizer factory. The Jaccard distance divides the intersection of tokens from the two strings over the union of tokens from both strings. Look at the Javadoc for more information.

The nested `for` loops in the following example explore each row with every other row until a higher threshold proximity is found or until all data has been looked at. Do not use this for large datasets because it is the $O(n^2)$ algorithm. If no row is above proximity, then the row is added to `filteredTexts`:

```
List<String[]> filteredTexts = new ArrayList<String[]>();
for (int i = 0; i < texts.size(); ++i) {
  String targetText = texts.get(i)[TEXT_OFFSET];
  boolean addText = true;
  for (int j = i + 1; j < texts.size(); ++j ) {
```

```
      String comparisionText = texts.get(j)[TEXT_OFFSET];
      double proximity = 
        jaccardD.proximity(targetText,comparisionText);
      if (proximity >= cutoff) {
        addText = false;
        System.out.printf(" Tweets too close, proximity %.2f\n",
  proximity);
        System.out.println("\t" + targetText);
        System.out.println("\t" + comparisionText);
        break;
      }
    }
    if (addText) {
      filteredTexts.add(texts.get(i));
    }
  }
  return filteredTexts;
}
```

There are much better ways to efficiently filter the texts at a cost of extra complexity—a simple reverse-word lookup index to compute an initial covering set will be vastly more efficient—search for a shingling text lookup for O(n) to O(n log(n)) approaches.

Setting the threshold can be a bit tricky, but looking a bunch of data should make the appropriate cutoff fairly clear for your needs.

How to classify sentiment – simple version

Sentiment has become the classic business-oriented classification task—what executive can resist an ability to know on a constant basis what positive and negative things are being said about their business? Sentiment classifiers offer this capability by taking text data and classifying it into positive and negative categories. This recipe addresses the process of creating a simple sentiment classifier, but more generally, it addresses how to create classifiers for novel categories. It is also a 3-way classifier, unlike the 2-way classifiers we have been working with.

Our first sentiment system was built for BuzzMetrics in 2004 using language model classifiers. We tend to use logistic regression classifiers now, because they tend to perform better. *Chapter 3*, *Advanced Classifiers*, covers logistic regression classifiers.

Simple Classifiers

How to do it...

The previous recipes focused on language ID—how do we shift the classifier over to the very different task of sentiment? This will be much simpler than one might think—all that needs to change is the training data, believe it or not. The steps are as follows:

1. Use the Twitter search recipe to download tweets about a topic that has positive/negative tweets about it. A search on `disney` is our example, but feel free to branch out. This recipe will work with the supplied CSV file, `data/disneySentiment_annot.csv`.

2. Load the created `data/disneySentiment_annot.csv` file into your spreadsheet of choice. There are already some annotations done.

3. As in the *Evaluation of classifiers – the confusion matrix* recipe, annotate the `true class` column for one of the three categories:

    - The `p` annotation stands for positive. The example is "Oh well, I love Disney movies. #hateonit".
    - The `n` annotation stands for negative. The example is "Disney really messed me up yo, this is not the way things are suppose to be".
    - The `o` annotation stands for other. The example is "Update on Downtown Disney. http://t.co/SE39z73vnw".
    - Leave blank tweets that are not in English, irrelevant, both positive and negative, or you are unsure about.

4. Keep annotating until the smallest category has at least 10 examples.

5. Save the annotations.

6. Run the previous recipe for cross validation, providing the annotated file's name:

    ```
    java -cp lingpipe-cookbook.1.0.jar:lib/lingpipe-4.1.0.jar:lib/opencsv-2.4.jar com.lingpipe.cookbook.chapter1.RunXValidate data/disneyDedupedSentiment.csv
    ```

7. The system will then run a four-fold cross validation and print a confusion matrix. Look at the *How to train and evaluate with cross validation* recipe if you need further explanation:

    ```
    Training on fold 0
    Testing on fold 0
    Training on fold 1
    Testing on fold 1
    Training on fold 2
    Testing on fold 2
    Training on fold 3
    ```

```
Testing on fold 3
reference\response
    \p,n,o,
    p 14,0,10,
    n 6,0,4,
    o 7,1,37,
```

That's it! Classifiers are entirely dependent on training data for what they classify. More sophisticated techniques will bring richer features into the mix than character ngrams, but ultimately, the labels imposed by training data are the knowledge being imparted to the classifier. Depending on your view, the underlying technology is magical or astoundingly simple minded.

How it works...

Most developers are surprised that the only difference between language ID and sentiment is the labeling applied to the data for training. The language model classifier is applying an individual language model for each category and also noting the marginal distribution of the categories in the estimates.

There's more...

Classifiers are pretty dumb but very useful if they are not expected to work outside their capabilities. Language ID works great as a classification problem because the observed events are tightly tied to the classification being done—the words and characters of a language. Sentiment is more difficult because the observed events, in this case, are exactly the same as the language ID and are less strongly associated with the end classification. For example, the phrase "I love" is a good predictor of the sentence being English but not as clear a predictor that the sentiment is positive, negative, or other. If the tweet is "I love Disney", then we have a positive statement. If the tweet is "I love Disney, not", then it is negative. Addressing the complexities of sentiment and other more complex phenomenon tends to be resolved in the following ways:

- Create more training data. Even relatively dumb techniques such as language model classifiers can perform very well given enough data. Humanity is just not that creative in ways to gripe about, or praise, something. The *Train a little, learn a little – active learning* recipe of *Chapter 3, Advanced Classifiers*, presents a clever way to do this.

- Use fancier classifiers that in turn use fancier features (observations) about the data to get the job done. Look at the logistic regression recipes for more information. For the negation case, a feature that looked for a negative phrase in the tweet might help. This could get arbitrarily sophisticated.

Simple Classifiers

Note that a more appropriate way to take on the sentiment problem can be to create a binary classifier for *positive* and *not positive* and a binary classifier for *negative* and *not negative*. The classifiers will have separate training data and will allow for a tweet to be both positive and negative.

Common problems as a classification problem

Classifiers form the foundations of many industrial NLP problems. This recipe goes through the process of encoding some common problems into a classification-based solution. We will pull from real-world examples that we have built whenever possible. You can think of them as mini recipes.

Topic detection

Problem: Take footnotes from financial documents (10Qs and 10Ks) and determine whether an **eXtensible Business Reporting Language** (**XBRL**) category is applied like "forward looking financial statements". Turns out that foot notes are where all the action happens. For example, is the footnote referring to retired debt? Performance needed to be greater than 90 percent precision with acceptable recall.

Solution: This problem closely mirrors how we approached language ID and sentiment. The actual solution involves a sentence recognizer that detects the footnotes—see *Chapter 5, Finding Spans in Text – Chunking*—and then creates training data for each of the XBRL categories. We used the confusion matrix output to help refine the XBRL categories that the system was struggling to distinguish. Merging categories was a possibility, and we did merge them. This system is based on language model classifiers. If done now, we would use logistic regression.

Question answering

Problem: Identify FAQs in a large dataset of text-based customer support data and develop the answers and ability to automatically deliver answers with 90 percent precision.

Solution: Perform clustering analysis over logs to find FAQs—see *Chapter 6, String Comparison and Clustering*. This will result in a very large set of FAQs that are really **Infrequently Asked Questions** (**IAQs**); this means that the prevalence of an IAQ can be as low as 1/20000. Positive data is fairly easy to find for a classifier, but negative data is too expensive to create on any kind of balanced distribution—for every positive case, one will expect 19999 negative case. The solution is to assume that any random sample of a large size will contain very few positives and to just use this as negative data. A refinement is to run a trained classifier over the negatives to find high-scoring cases and annotate them to pull out the positives that might be found.

Degree of sentiment

Problem: Classify a sentiment on a scale of 1 to 10 based on the degree of negativeness to positiveness.

Solution: Even though our classifiers provide a score that can be mapped on a 1-to-10 scale, this is not what the background computation is doing. To correctly map to a degree scale, one will have to annotate the distinction in training data—this tweet is a 1, this tweet is a 3, and so on. We will then train a 10-way classifier, and the first best category should, in theory, be the degree. We write *in theory* because despite regular customer requests for this, we have never found a customer that was willing to support the required annotation.

Non-exclusive category classification

Problem: The desired classifications are not mutually exclusive. A tweet can say both positive and negative things, for example, "Loved Mickey, hated Pluto". Our classifiers assume that categories are mutually exclusive.

Solution: We regularly use multiple binary classifiers in place of one *n*-way or multinomial classifiers. The classifiers will be trained for positive/non-positive and negative/non-negative. A tweet can then be annotated `n` and `p`.

Person/company/location detection

Problem: Detect mentions of people in text data.

Solution: Believe it or not, this breaks down into a word classification problem. See *Chapter 6, String Comparison and Clustering*.

It is generally fruitful to look at any novel problem as a classification problem, even if classifiers don't get used as the underlying technology. It can help clarify what the underlying technology actually needs to do.

2
Finding and Working with Words

In this chapter, we cover the following recipes:

- Introduction to tokenizer factories – finding words in a character stream
- Combining tokenizers – lowercase tokenizer
- Combining tokenizers – stop word tokenizers
- Using Lucene/Solr tokenizers
- Using Lucene/Solr tokenizers with LingPipe
- Evaluating tokenizers with unit tests
- Modifying tokenizer factories
- Finding words for languages without white spaces

Introduction

An important part of building NLP systems is to work with the appropriate unit for processing. This chapter addresses the abstraction layer associated with the word level of processing. This is called tokenization, which amounts to grouping adjacent characters into meaningful chunks in support of classification, entity finding, and the rest of NLP.

LingPipe provides a broad range of tokenizer needs, which are not covered in this book. Look at the Javadoc for tokenizers that do stemming, Soundex (tokens based on what English words sound like), and more.

Finding and Working with Words

Introduction to tokenizer factories – finding words in a character stream

LingPipe tokenizers are built on a common pattern of a base tokenizer that can be used on its own, or can be as the source for subsequent filtering tokenizers. Filtering tokenizers manipulate the tokens/white spaces provided by the base tokenizer. This recipe covers our most commonly used tokenizer, `IndoEuropeanTokenizerFactory`, which is good for languages that use the Indo-European style of punctuation and word separators—examples include English, Spanish, and French. As always, the Javadoc has useful information.

> `IndoEuropeanTokenizerFactory` creates tokenizers with built-in support for alpha-numerics, numbers, and other common constructs in Indo-European languages.
>
> The tokenization rules are roughly based on those used in MUC-6 but are necessarily more fine grained, because the MUC tokenizers are based on lexical and semantic information, such as whether a string is an abbreviation.

MUC-6 refers to the Message Understanding Conference that originated the idea of government-sponsored competitions between contractors in 1995. The informal term was *Bake off*, in reference to the Pillsbury Bake-Off that started in 1949, and one of the authors was a participant as postdoc in MUC-6. MUC drove much of the innovation in the evaluation of NLP systems.

LingPipe tokenizers are built using the LingPipe `TokenizerFactory` interface, which provides a way of invoking different types of tokenizers using the same interface. This is very useful in creating filtered tokenizers, which are constructed as a chain of tokenizers and modify their output in some way. A `TokenizerFactory` instance might be created either as a basic tokenizer, which takes simple parameters in its construction, or as a filtered tokenizer, which takes other tokenizer factory objects as parameters. In either case, an instance of `TokenizerFactory` has a single `tokenize()` method, which takes input as a character array, a start index, and the number of characters to process and outputs a `Tokenizer` object. The `Tokenizer` object represents the state of tokenizing a particular slice of string and provides a stream of tokens. While `TokenizerFactory` is thread safe and/or serializable, tokenizer instances are typically neither thread safe nor serializable. The `Tokenizer` object provides methods to iterate over the tokens in the string and to provide token positions of the tokens in the underlying text.

Getting ready

Download the JAR file and source for the book if you have not already done so.

How to do it...

It is all pretty simple. The following are the steps to get started with tokenization:

1. Go to the `cookbook` directory and invoke the following class:

   ```
   java -cp "lingpipe-cookbook.1.0.jar:lib/lingpipe-4.1.0.jar" com.lingpipe.cookbook.chapter2.RunBaseTokenizerFactory
   ```

   This will lead us to a command prompt, which asks us to type in some text:

   ```
   type a sentence to see tokens and white spaces
   ```

2. If we type a sentence such as: `It's no use growing older if you only learn new ways of misbehaving yourself`, we will get the following output:

   ```
   It's no use growing older if you only learn new ways of
   misbehaving yourself.
   Token:'It'
   WhiteSpace:''
   Token:'''
   WhiteSpace:''
   Token:'s'
   WhiteSpace:' '
   Token:'no'
   WhiteSpace:' '
   Token:'use'
   WhiteSpace:' '
   Token:'growing'
   WhiteSpace:' '
   Token:'older'
   WhiteSpace:' '
   Token:'if'
   WhiteSpace:' '
   Token:'you'
   WhiteSpace:' '
   Token:'only'
   WhiteSpace:' '
   Token:'learn'
   WhiteSpace:' '
   Token:'new'
   WhiteSpace:' '
   Token:'ways'
   WhiteSpace:' '
   ```

Finding and Working with Words

```
Token:'of'
WhiteSpace:' '
Token:'misbehaving'
WhiteSpace:' '
Token:'yourself'
WhiteSpace:''
Token:'.'
WhiteSpace:' '
```

3. Examine the output and note what the tokens and white spaces are. The text is from the short story, *The Stampeding of Lady Bastable*, by Saki.

How it works...

The code is so simple that it can be included in its entirety as follows:

```
package com.lingpipe.cookbook.chapter2;

import java.io.BufferedReader;
import java.io.IOException;
import java.io.InputStreamReader;

import com.aliasi.tokenizer.IndoEuropeanTokenizerFactory;
import com.aliasi.tokenizer.Tokenizer;
import com.aliasi.tokenizer.TokenizerFactory;

public class RunBaseTokenizerFactory {

  public static void main(String[] args) throws IOException {
    TokenizerFactory tokFactory =
      IndoEuropeanTokenizerFactory.INSTANCE;
    BufferedReader reader = new BufferedReader(
      new InputStreamReader(System.in));

    while (true) {
      System.out.println("type a sentence to " + "see
        the tokens and white spaces");
      String input = reader.readLine();
      Tokenizer tokenizer = tokFactory.tokenizer
        (input.toCharArray(), 0, input.length());
      String token = null;
      while ((token = tokenizer.nextToken()) != null) {
        System.out.println("Token:'" + token + "'");
        System.out.println("WhiteSpace:'" +
          tokenizer.nextWhitespace() + "'");

    }
```

```
      }
    }
  }
```

This recipe starts with the creation of `TokenizerFactory tokFactory` in the first statement of the `main()` method. Note that a singleton `IndoEuropeanTokenizerFactory.INSTANCE` is used. The factory will produce tokenizers for a given string, which is evident in the line, `Tokenizer tokenizer = tokFactory.tokenizer(input.toCharArray(), 0, input.length())`. The entered string is converted to a character array with `input.toCharArray()` as the first argument to the `tokenizer` method and the start and finish offsets provided into the created character array.

The resulting `tokenizer` provides tokens for the provided slice of character array, and the white spaces and tokens are printed out in the `while` loop. Calling the `tokenizer.nextToken()` method does a few things:

- The method returns the next token or null if there is no next token. The null then ends the loop; otherwise, the loop continues.
- The method also increments the corresponding white space. There is always a white space with a token, but it might be the empty string.

`IndoEuropeanTokenizerFactory` assumes a fairly standard abstraction over characters that break down as follows:

- Characters from the beginning of the `char` array to the first token are ignored and not reported as white space
- Characters from the end of the last token to the end of the `char` array are reported as the next white space
- White spaces can be the empty string because of two adjoining tokens—note the apostrophe in the output and corresponding white spaces

This means that it is not possible to reconstruct the original string necessarily if the input does not start with a token. Fortunately, tokenizers are easily modified for customized needs. We will see this later in the chapter.

There's more...

Tokenization can be arbitrarily complex. The LingPipe tokenizers are intended to cover most common uses, but you might need to create your own tokenizer to have fine-grained control, for example, Victoria's Secret with "Victoria's" as the token. Consult the source for `IndoEuropeanTokenizerFactory` if such customization is needed, to see how arbitrary tokenization is done here.

Finding and Working with Words

Combining tokenizers – lowercase tokenizer

We mentioned in the previous recipe that LingPipe tokenizers can be basic or filtered. Basic tokenizers, such as the Indo-European tokenizer, don't need much in terms of parameterization, none at all as a matter of fact. However, filtered tokenizers need a tokenizer as a parameter. What we're doing with filtered tokenizers is invoking multiple tokenizers where a base tokenizer is usually modified by a filter to produce a different tokenizer.

LingPipe provides several basic tokenizers, such as `IndoEuropeanTokenizerFactory` or `CharacterTokenizerFactory`. A complete list can be found in the Javadoc for LingPipe. In this section, we'll show you how to combine an Indo-European tokenizer with a lowercase tokenizer. This is a fairly common process that many search engines implement for Indo-European languages.

Getting ready

You will need to download the JAR file for the book and have Java and Eclipse set up so that you can run the example.

How to do it...

This works just the same way as the previous recipe. Perform the following steps:

1. Invoke the `RunLowerCaseTokenizerFactory` class from the command line:

    ```
    java -cp "lingpipe-cookbook.1.0.jar:lib/lingpipe-4.1.0.jar" com.lingpipe.cookbook.chapter2.RunLowerCaseTokenizerFactory
    ```

2. Then, in the command prompt, let's use the following example:

    ```
    type a sentence below to see the tokens and white spaces are:
    This is an UPPERCASE word and these are numbers 1 2 3 4.5.
    Token:'this'
    WhiteSpace:' '
    Token:'is'
    WhiteSpace:' '
    Token:'an'
    WhiteSpace:' '
    Token:'uppercase'
    WhiteSpace:' '
    Token:'word'
    WhiteSpace:' '
    Token:'and'
    WhiteSpace:' '
    ```

```
Token:'these'
WhiteSpace:' '
Token:'are'
WhiteSpace:' '
Token:'numbers'
WhiteSpace:' '
Token:'1'
WhiteSpace:' '
Token:'2'
WhiteSpace:' '
Token:'3'
WhiteSpace:' '
Token:'4.5'
WhiteSpace:''
Token:'.'
WhiteSpace:''
```

How it works...

You can see in the preceding output that all the tokens are converted to lowercase, including the word UPPERCASE, which was typed in uppercase. As this example uses an Indo-European tokenizer as its base tokenizer, you can see that the number 4.5 is retained as 4.5 instead of being broken up into 4 and 5.

The way we put tokenizers together is very simple:

```java
public static void main(String[] args) throws IOException {

  TokenizerFactory tokFactory =
    IndoEuropeanTokenizerFactory.INSTANCE;
  tokFactory = new LowerCaseTokenizerFactory(tokFactory);
  tokFactory = new WhitespaceNormTokenizerFactory(tokFactory);

  BufferedReader reader = new BufferedReader(new
    InputStreamReader(System.in));

  while (true) {
    System.out.println("type a sentence below to see
      the tokens and white spaces are:");
    String input = reader.readLine();
    Tokenizer tokenizer =
      tokFactory.tokenizer(input.toCharArray(), 0,
      input.length());
    String token = null;
```

```
    while ((token = tokenizer.nextToken()) != null) {
      System.out.println("Token:'" + token + "'");
      System.out.println("WhiteSpace:'" +
        tokenizer.nextWhitespace() + "'");
    }
   }
}
```

Here, we created a tokenizer that returns case and white space normalized tokens produced using an Indo-European tokenizer. The tokenizer created from the tokenizer factory is a filtered tokenizer that starts with the Indo-European base tokenizer, which is then modified by `LowerCaseTokenizer` to produce the lowercase tokenizer. This is then once again modified by `WhiteSpaceNormTokenizerFactory` to produce a lowercase, white space-normalized Indo-European tokenizer.

Case normalization is applied where the case of words doesn't matter much; for example, search engines often store case-normalized words in their indexes. Now, we will use case-normalized tokens in the upcoming examples on classifiers.

See also

- For more details on how filtered tokenizers are built, see the Javadoc for the abstract class, `ModifiedTokenizerFactory`.

Combining tokenizers – stop word tokenizers

Similarly to the way in which we put together a lowercase and white space normalized tokenizer, we can use a filtered tokenizer to create a tokenizer that filters out stop words. Once again, using search engines as our example, we can remove commonly occurring words from our input set so as to normalize the text. The stop words that are typically removed convey very little information by themselves, although they might convey information in context.

The input is tokenized using whatever base tokenizer is set up, and then, the resulting tokens are filtered out by the stop tokenizer to produce a token stream that is free of the stop words specified when the stop tokenizer is initialized.

Getting ready

You will need to download the JAR file for the book and have Java and Eclipse set up so that you can run the example.

How to do it...

As we did earlier, we will go through the steps of interacting with the tokenizer:

1. Invoke the `RunStopTokenizerFactory` class from the command line:

   ```
   java -cp "lingpipe-cookbook.1.0.jar:lib/lingpipe-4.1.0.jar" com.lingpipe.cookbook.chapter2.RunStopTokenizerFactory
   ```

2. Then, in the prompt, let's use the following example:

   ```
   type a sentence below to see the tokens and white spaces:
   the quick brown fox is jumping
   Token:'quick'
   WhiteSpace:' '
   Token:'brown'
   WhiteSpace:' '
   Token:'fox'
   WhiteSpace:' '
   Token:'jumping'
   WhiteSpace:''
   ```

3. Note that we lose adjacency information. In the input, we have `fox is jumping`, but the tokens came out as `fox` followed by `jumping`, because `is` was filtered. This can be a problem for token-based processes that need accurate adjacency information. In the *Foreground- or background-driven interesting phrase detection* recipe of *Chapter 4, Tagging Words and Tokens*, we will show a length-based filtering tokenizer that preserves adjacency.

How it works...

The stop words used in this `StopTokenizerFactory` filter are just a very short list of words, `is`, `of`, `the`, and `to`. Obviously, this list can be much longer if required. As you saw in the preceding output, the words `the` and `is` have been removed from the tokenized output. This is done with a very simple step: we instantiate `StopTokenizerFactory` in `src/com/lingpipe/cookbook/chapter2/RunStopTokenizerFactory.java`. The relevant code is:

```
TokenizerFactory tokFactory =
   IndoEuropeanTokenizerFactory.INSTANCE;
tokFactory = new LowerCaseTokenizerFactory(tokFactory);
Set<String> stopWords = new HashSet<String>();
stopWords.add("the");
stopWords.add("of");
stopWords.add("to");
```

Finding and Working with Words

```
stopWords.add("is");

tokFactory = new StopTokenizerFactory(tokFactory, stopWords);
```

As we're using `LowerCaseTokenizerFactory` as one of the filters in the tokenizer factory, we can get away with the stop words that contain only lowercase words. If we want to preserve the case of the input tokens and continue to remove the stop words, we will need to add uppercase or mixed-case versions as well.

See also

- The complete list of filtered tokenizers provided by LingPipe can be found on the Javadoc page at `http://alias-i.com/lingpipe/docs/api/com/aliasi/tokenizer/ModifyTokenTokenizerFactory.html`

Using Lucene/Solr tokenizers

The very popular search engine, Lucene, includes many analysis modules, which provide general purpose tokenizers as well as language-specific tokenizers from Arabic to Thai. As of Lucene 4, most of these different analyzers can be found in separate JAR files. We will cover Lucene tokenizers, because they can be used as LingPipe tokenizers, as you will see in the next recipe.

Much like the LingPipe tokenizers, Lucene tokenizers also can be split into basic tokenizers and filtered tokenizers. Basic tokenizers take a reader as input, and filtered tokenizers take other tokenizers as input. We will look at an example of using a standard Lucene analyzer along with a lowercase-filtered tokenizer. A Lucene analyzer essentially maps a field to a token stream. So, if you have an existing Lucene index, you can use the analyzer with the field name instead of the raw tokenizer, as we will show in the later part of this chapter.

Getting ready

You will need to download the JAR file for the book and have Java and Eclipse set up so that you can run the example. Some of the Lucene analyzers used in the examples are part of the `lib` directory. However, if you'd like to experiment with other language analyzers, download them from the Apache Lucene website at `https://lucene.apache.org`.

How to do it...

Remember that we are not using a LingPipe tokenizer in this recipe but introducing the Lucene tokenizer classes:

1. Invoke the `RunLuceneTokenizer` class from the command line:

   ```
   java -cp lingpipe-cookbook.1.0.jar:lib/lucene-analyzers-common-
   4.6.0.jar:lib/lucene-core-4.6.0.jar com.lingpipe.cookbook.
   chapter2.RunLuceneTokenize
   ```

2. Then, in the prompt, let's use the following example:

   ```
   the quick BROWN fox jumped
   type a sentence below to see the tokens and white spaces:
   The rain in Spain.
   Token:'the' Start: 0 End:3
   Token:'rain' Start: 4 End:8
   Token:'in' Start: 9 End:11
   Token:'spain' Start: 12 End:17
   ```

How it works...

Let's review the following code to see how the Lucene tokenizers differ in invocation from the previous examples—the relevant part of the code from `src/com/lingpipe/cookbook/chapter2/RunLuceneTokenizer.java` is:

```
BufferedReader reader = new BufferedReader(new
  InputStreamReader(System.in));

while (true) {
```

The preceding snippet sets up `BufferedReader` from the command line and starts a perpetual `while()` loop. Next, the prompt is provided, the `input` is read, and it is used to construct a `Reader` object:

```
System.out.println("type a sentence below to
  see the tokens and white spaces:");
String input = reader.readLine();
Reader stringReader = new StringReader(input);
```

All the input is now wrapped up, and it is time to construct the actual tokenizer:

```
TokenStream tokenStream = new StandardTokenizer(Version.
LUCENE_46,stringReader);

tokenStream = new LowerCaseFilter(Version.LUCENE_46,tokenStream);
```

Finding and Working with Words

The input text is used to construct `StandardTokenizer` with Lucene's versioning system supplied—this produces an instance of `TokenStream`. Then, we used `LowerCaseFilter` to create the final filtered `tokenStream` with the base `tokenStream` as an argument.

In Lucene, we need to attach the attributes we're interested in from the token stream; this is done by the `addAttribute` method:

```
CharTermAttribute terms =
  tokenStream.addAttribute(CharTermAttribute.class);
OffsetAttribute offset =
  tokenStream.addAttribute(OffsetAttribute.class);
tokenStream.reset();
```

Note that in Lucene 4, once the tokenizer has been instantiated, the `reset()` method must be called before using the tokenizer:

```
while (tokenStream.incrementToken()) {
  String token = terms.toString();
  int start = offset.startOffset();
  int end = offset.endOffset();
  System.out.println("Token:'" + token + "'"
    + " Start: " + start + " End:" + end);
}
```

The `tokenStream` is wrapped up with the following:

```
tokenStream.end();
tokenStream.close();
```

See also

An excellent introduction to Lucene is in *Text Processing with Java*, Mitzi Morris, *Colloquial Media Corporation*, where the guts of what we explained earlier are made clearer than what we can provide in a recipe.

Using Lucene/Solr tokenizers with LingPipe

We can use these Lucene tokenizers with LingPipe; this is useful because Lucene has such a rich set of them. We are going to show how to wrap a Lucene `TokenStream` into a LingPipe `TokenizerFactory` by extending the `Tokenizer` abstract class.

How to do it...

We will shake things up a bit and have a recipe that is not interactive. Perform the following steps:

1. Invoke the `LuceneAnalyzerTokenizerFactory` class from the command line:

   ```
   java -cp lingpipe-cookbook.1.0.jar:lib/lucene-analyzers-common-
   4.6.0.jar:lib/lucene-core-4.6.0.jar:lib/lingpipe-4.1.0.jar com.
   lingpipe.cookbook.chapter2.LuceneAnalyzerTokenizerFactory
   ```

2. The `main()` method in the class specifies the input:

   ```
   String text = "Hi how are you? " + "Are the numbers
     1 2 3 4.5 all integers?";
   Analyzer analyzer = new StandardAnalyzer(Version.LUCENE_46);
   TokenizerFactory tokFactory = new
     LuceneAnalyzerTokenizerFactory
   (analyzer, "DEFAULT");
   Tokenizer tokenizer =
     tokFactory.tokenizer(text.toCharArray(), 0,
     text.length());

   String token = null;
   while ((token = tokenizer.nextToken()) != null) {
     String ws = tokenizer.nextWhitespace();
     System.out.println("Token:'" + token + "'");
     System.out.println("WhiteSpace:'" + ws + "'");
   }
   ```

3. The preceding snippet creates a Lucene `StandardAnalyzer` and uses it to construct a LingPipe `TokenizerFactory`. The output is as follows—the `StandardAnalyzer` filters stop words, so the token `are` is filtered:

   ```
   Token:'hi'
   WhiteSpace:'default'
   Token:'how'
   WhiteSpace:'default'
   Token:'you'
   WhiteSpace:'default'
   Token:'numbers'
   WhiteSpace:'default'
   ```

4. The white spaces report as `default` because the implementation does not accurately provide white spaces but goes with a default. We will discuss this limitation in the *How it works...* section.

Finding and Working with Words

How it works...

Let's take a look at the `LuceneAnalyzerTokenizerFactory` class. This class implements the LingPipe `TokenizerFactory` interface by wrapping a Lucene analyzer. We will start with the class definition from `src/com/lingpipe/cookbook/chapter2/LuceneAnalyzerTokenizerFactory.java`:

```
public class LuceneAnalyzerTokenizerFactory
  implements TokenizerFactory, Serializable {

  private static final long serialVersionUID =
    8376017491713196935L;
  private Analyzer analyzer;
  private String field;
  public LuceneAnalyzerTokenizerFactory
    (Analyzer analyzer, String field) {
    super();
    this.analyzer = analyzer;
    this.field = field;
  }
```

The constructor stores the analyzer and the name of the field as private variables. As this class implements the `TokenizerFactory` interface, we need to implement the `tokenizer()` method:

```
public Tokenizer tokenizer(char[] charSeq , int start, int length) {
  Reader reader = new CharArrayReader(charSeq,start,length);
  TokenStream tokenStream = analyzer.tokenStream(field,reader);
  return new LuceneTokenStreamTokenizer(tokenStream);
}
```

The `tokenizer()` method creates a new character-array reader and passes it to the Lucene analyzer to convert it to a `TokenStream`. An instance of `LuceneTokenStreamTokenizer` is created based on the token stream. `LuceneTokenStreamTokenizer` is a nested static class that extends LingPipe's `Tokenizer` class:

```
static class LuceneTokenStreamTokenizer extends Tokenizer {
  private TokenStream tokenStream;
  private CharTermAttribute termAttribute;
  private OffsetAttribute offsetAttribute;

  private int lastTokenStartPosition = -1;
  private int lastTokenEndPosition = -1;

  public LuceneTokenStreamTokenizer(TokenStream ts) {
    tokenStream = ts;
    termAttribute = tokenStream.addAttribute(
```

```
      CharTermAttribute.class);
    offsetAttribute =
      tokenStream.addAttribute(OffsetAttribute.class);
}
```

The constructor stores `TokenStream` and attaches the term and the offset attributes. In the previous recipe, we saw that the term and the offset attributes contain the token string, and the token start and end offsets into the input text. The token offsets are also initialized to -1 before any tokens are found:

```
@Override
public String nextToken() {
  try {
    if (tokenStream.incrementToken()){
      lastTokenStartPosition =
        offsetAttribute.startOffset();
      lastTokenEndPosition =
        offsetAttribute.endOffset();
      return termAttribute.toString();
    } else {
      endAndClose();
      return null;
    }
  } catch (IOException e) {
    endAndClose();
    return null;
  }
}
```

We will implement the `nextToken()` method and use the `incrementToken()` method of the token stream to retrieve any tokens from the token stream. We will set the token start and end offsets using `OffsetAttribute`. If the token stream is finished or the `incrementToken()` method throws an I/O exception, we will end and close the `TokenStream`.

The `nextWhitespace()` method has some limitations, because `offsetAttribute` is focused on the current token where LingPipe tokenizers quantize the input into the next token and next offset. A general solution here will be quite challenging, because there might not be any well-defined white spaces between tokens—think character ngrams. So, the `default` string is supplied just to make it clear. The method is:

```
@Override
public String nextWhitespace() {
  return "default";
}
```

The code also covers how to serialize the tokenizer, but we will not cover this in the recipe.

Finding and Working with Words

Evaluating tokenizers with unit tests

We will not evaluate Indo-European tokenizers like the other components of LingPipe with measures such as precision and recall. Instead, we will develop them with unit tests, because our tokenizers are heuristically constructed and expected to perform perfectly on example data—if a tokenizer fails to tokenize a known case, then it is a bug, not a reduction in performance. Why is this? There are a few reasons:

- Many tokenizers are very "mechanistic" and are amenable to the rigidity of the unit test framework. For example, the `RegExTokenizerFactory` is obviously a candidate to unit test rather than an evaluation harness.

- The heuristic rules that drive most tokenizers are very general, and there is no issue of over-fitting training data at the expense of a deployed system. If you have a known bad case, you can just go and fix the tokenizer and add a unit test.

- Tokens and white spaces are assumed to be semantically neutral, which means that tokens don't change depending on context. This is not totally true with our Indo-European tokenizer, because it treats . differently if it is part of a decimal or at the end of a sentence, for example, `3.14 is pi.`:

    ```
    Token:'3.14'
    WhiteSpace:' '
    Token:'is'
    WhiteSpace:' '
    Token:'pi'
    WhiteSpace:''
    Token:'.'
    WhiteSpace:''.
    ```

It might be appropriate to use an evaluation metric for statistics-based tokenizers; this is discussed in the *Finding words for languages without white spaces* recipe in this chapter. See the *Evaluation of sentence detection* recipe in *Chapter 5, Finding Spans in Text – Chunking*, for appropriate span-based evaluation techniques.

How to do it...

We will forgo running the code step and just get right into the source to put together a tokenizer evaluator. The source is in `src/com/lingpipe/chapter2/TestTokenizerFactory.java`. Perform the following steps:

1. The following code sets up a base tokenizer factory with a regular expression—look at the Javadoc for the class if you are not clear about what is being constructed:

    ```
    public static void main(String[] args) {
      String pattern = "[a-zA-Z]+|[0-9]+|\\S";
    ```

```
    TokenizerFactory tokFactory = new
      RegExTokenizerFactory(pattern);
    String[] tokens =
      {"Tokenizers","need","unit","tests","."};
    String text = "Tokenizers need unit tests.";
    checkTokens(tokFactory,text,tokens);
    String[] whiteSpaces = {" "," "," ","",""};
    checkTokensAndWhiteSpaces
      (tokFactory,text,tokens,whiteSpaces);
    System.out.println("All tests passed!");
  }
```

2. The `checkTokens` method takes `TokenizerFactory`, an array of `String` that is the desired tokenization, and `String` that is to be tokenized. It follows:

```
static void checkTokens(TokenizerFactory
  tokFactory, String string,
  String[] correctTokens) {
  Tokenizer tokenizer =
    tokFactory.tokenizer(input.toCharArray(),0,
    input.length());
  String[] tokens = tokenizer.tokenize();
  if (tokens.length != correctTokens.length) {
    System.out.println("Token list lengths do not match");
    System.exit(-1);
  }
  for (int i = 0; i < tokens.length; ++i) {
    if (!correctTokens[i].equals(tokens[i])) {
      System.out.println("Token mismatch:
        got |" + tokens[i] + "|");
      System.out.println(" expected |"
        + correctTokens[i] + "|" );
      System.exit(-1);
    }
  }
}
```

3. The method is quite intolerant of errors, because it exits the program if the token arrays are not of the same length or if any of the tokens are not equal. A proper unit test framework such as JUnit will be a better framework, but that is beyond the scope of the book. You can look at the LingPipe unit tests in `lingpipe.4.1.0/src/com/aliasi/test` for how JUnit is used.

4. The `checkTokensAndWhiteSpaces()` method checks white spaces as well as tokens. It follows the same basic ideas of `checkTokens()`, so we leave it unexplained.

Finding and Working with Words

Modifying tokenizer factories

In this recipe, we will describe a tokenizer that modifies the tokens in the token stream. We will extend the `ModifyTokenTokenizerFactory` class to return text that is rotated by 13 places in the English alphabet, also known as rot-13. Rot-13 is a very simple substitution cipher, which replaces a letter with the letter that follows after 13 places. For example, the letter `a` will be replaced by the letter `n`, and the letter `z` will be replaced by the letter `m`. This is a reciprocal cypher, which means that applying the same cypher twice recovers the original text.

How to do it...

We will invoke the `Rot13TokenizerFactory` class from the command line:

```
java -cp "lingpipe-cookbook.1.0.jar:lib/lingpipe-4.1.0.jar" com.lingpipe.cookbook.chapter2.Rot13TokenizerFactory

type a sentence below to see the tokens and white spaces:
Move along, nothing to see here.
Token:'zbir'
Token:'nybat'
Token:','
Token:'abguvat'
Token:'gb'
Token:'frr'
Token:'urer'
Token:'.'
Modified Output: zbir nybat, abguvat gb frr urer.
type a sentence below to see the tokens and white spaces:
zbir nybat, abguvat gb frr urer.
Token:'move'
Token:'along'
Token:','
Token:'nothing'
Token:'to'
Token:'see'
Token:'here'
Token:'.'
Modified Output: move along, nothing to see here.
```

You can see that the input text, which was mixed case and in normal English, has been transformed into its Rot-13 equivalent. You can see that the second time around, we passed the Rot-13 modified text as input and got the original text back, except that it was all lowercase.

How it works...

`Rot13TokenizerFactory` extends the `ModifyTokenTokenizerFactory` class. We will override the `modifyToken()` method, which operates a token at a time and, in this case, converts the token to its Rot-13 equivalent. There is a similar `modifyWhiteSpace` (String) method, which modifies the white spaces if required:

```java
public class Rot13TokenizerFactory
   extends ModifyTokenTokenizerFactory{

   public Rot13TokenizerFactory(TokenizerFactory f) {
      super(f);
   }

   @Override
   public String modifyToken(String tok) {
      return rot13(tok);
   }

   public static void main(String[] args) throws IOException {

   TokenizerFactory tokFactory =
      IndoEuropeanTokenizerFactory.INSTANCE;
   tokFactory = new LowerCaseTokenizerFactory(tokFactory);
   tokFactory = new Rot13TokenizerFactory(tokFactory);
```

The start and end offsets of the tokens themselves remain the same as that of the underlying tokenizer. Here, we will use an Indo-European tokenizer as our base tokenizer. Filter it once through `LowerCaseTokenizer` and then through `Rot13Tokenizer`.

The `rot13` method is:

```java
public static String rot13(String input) {
   StringBuilder sb = new StringBuilder();
   for (int i = 0; i < input.length(); i++) {
      char c = input.charAt(i);
      if      (c >= 'a' && c <= 'm') c += 13;
      else if (c >= 'A' && c <= 'M') c += 13;
      else if (c >= 'n' && c <= 'z') c -= 13;
      else if (c >= 'N' && c <= 'Z') c -= 13;
      sb.append(c);
   }
   return sb.toString();
}
```

Finding and Working with Words

Finding words for languages without white spaces

Languages such as Chinese do not have word boundaries. For example, 木卫三是围绕木星运转的一颗卫星，公转周期约为7天 from Wikipedia is a sentence in Chinese that translates roughly into "Ganymede is running around Jupiter's moons, orbital period of about seven days" as done by the machine translation service at `https://translate.google.com`. Notice the absence of white spaces.

Finding tokens in this sort of data requires a very different approach that is based on character-language models and our spell-checking class. This recipe encodes finding words by treating untokenized text as *misspelled* text, where the *correction* inserts a space to delimit tokens. Of course, there is nothing misspelled about Chinese, Japanese, Vietnamese, and other non-word delimiting orthographies, but we have encoded it in our spelling-correction class.

Getting ready

We will approximate non-word delimiting orthographies with de-white spaced English. This is sufficient to understand the recipe and can be easily modified to the actual language when needed. Get a 100,000 or so words of English and get them to the disk in UTF-8 encoding. The reason for fixing the encoding is that the input is assumed to be UTF-8—you can change it by changing the encoding and recompiling the recipe.

We used *A Connecticut Yankee in King Arthur's Court* by Mark Twain, downloaded from Project Gutenberg (`http://www.gutenberg.org/`). Project Gutenberg is an excellent source of texts that are in the public domain, and Mark Twain is fine writer—we highly recommend the book. Place your selected text in the cookbook directory or work with our default.

How to do it...

We will run a program, play with it a bit, and explain what it does and how it does it, using the following steps:

1. Type the following command:

   ```
   java -cp lingpipe-cookbook.1.0.jar:lib/lingpipe-4.1.0.jar com.lingpipe.cookbook.chapter2.TokenizeWithoutWhiteSpaces
   Type an Englese sentence (English without spaces like Chinese):
   TheraininSpainfallsmainlyontheplain
   ```

2. The following is the output:

   ```
   The rain in Spain falls mainly on the plain
   ```

3. You might not get the perfect output. How good is Mark Twain at recovering proper white space from the Java program that generated it? Let's find out:

   ```
   type an Englese sentence (English without spaces like Chinese)
   NGramProcessLMlm=newNGramProcessLM(nGram);
   NGram Process L Mlm=new NGram Process L M(n Gram);
   ```

4. The preceding way was not very good, but we are not being very fair; let's use the concatenated source of LingPipe as training data:

   ```
   java -cp lingpipe-cookbook.1.0.jar:lib/lingpipe-4.1.0.jar com.
   lingpipe.cookbook.chapter2.TokenizeWithoutWhiteSpaces data/
   cookbookSource.txt
   Compiling Spell Checker
   type an Englese sentence (English without spaces like Chinese)
   NGramProcessLMlm=newNGramProcessLM(nGram);
   NGramProcessLM lm = new NGramProcessLM(nGram);
   ```

5. This is the perfect space insertion.

How it works...

For all the fun and games, there is very little code involved. The cool thing is that we are building on the character-language models from *Chapter 1, Simple Classifiers*. The source is in `src/com/lingpipe/chapter2/TokenizeWithoutWhiteSpaces.java`:

```
public static void main (String[] args) throws IOException,
ClassNotFoundException {
  int nGram = 5;
  NGramProcessLM lm = new NGramProcessLM(nGram);
  WeightedEditDistance spaceInsertingEditDistance
    = CompiledSpellChecker.TOKENIZING;
  TrainSpellChecker trainer = new TrainSpellChecker(lm,
spaceInsertingEditDistance);
```

The `main()` method starts up with the creation of `NgramProcessLM`. Next up, we will access a class for edit distance that is designed to only add spaces to a character stream. That's it. `Editdistance` is typically a fairly crude measure of string similarity that scores how many edits need to happen to to `string1` to make it the same as `string2`. A lot of information on this is Javadoc `com.aliasi.spell`. For example, `com.aliasi.spell.EditDistance` has an excellent discussion of the basics.

> The `EditDistance` class implements the standard notion of edit distance, with or without transposition. The distance without transposition is known as the Levenshtein distance, and with transposition, it is known as the Damerau-Levenstein distance.

Finding and Working with Words

Read the Javadoc with LingPipe; it has a lot of useful of information that we don't have space for in this book.

So far we configured and constructed a `TrainSpellChecker` class. The next step is to naturally train it:

```
File trainingFile = new File(args[0]);
String training = Files.readFromFile(trainingFile, Strings.UTF8);
training = training.replaceAll("\\s+", " ");
trainer.handle(training);
```

We slurped up a text file, assuming it is UTF-8; if not, correct the character encoding and recompile. Then, we replaced all the multiple white spaces with a single one. This might not be the best move if multiple white spaces have meaning. This is followed by training, just like we trained language models in *Chapter 1*, *Simple Classifiers*.

Next up, we will compile and configure the spell checker:

```
System.out.println("Compiling Spell Checker");
CompiledSpellChecker spellChecker = (CompiledSpellChecker)
  AbstractExternalizable.compile(trainer);

spellChecker.setAllowInsert(true);
spellChecker.setAllowMatch(true);
spellChecker.setAllowDelete(false);
spellChecker.setAllowSubstitute(false);
spellChecker.setAllowTranspose(false);
spellChecker.setNumConsecutiveInsertionsAllowed(1);
```

The next interesting line compiles `spellChecker`, which translates all the counts in the underlying language model to precomputed probabilities, which is much faster. The compilation step can write to a disk, so it can be used later without training; however, visit the Javadoc for `AbstractExternalizable` on how to do this. The next lines configure `CompiledSpellChecker` to only consider the edits that insert characters and to check for the exact string matches, but it forbids deletions, substitutions, and transpositions. Finally, only one insert is allowed. It should be clear that we are using a very limited portion of the capabilities of `CompiledSpellChecker`, but this is exactly what is called for—insert a space or don't.

Last up is our standard I/O routine:

```
BufferedReader reader = new BufferedReader(new
InputStreamReader(System.in));
while (true) {
  System.out.println("type an Englese sentence
    (English " + "without spaces like Chinese)"));
  String input = reader.readLine();
  String result = spellChecker.didYouMean(input);
  System.out.println(result);
}
```

The mechanics of the `CompiledSpellChecker` and `WeightedEditDistance` classes are better described in either the Javadoc or the *Using edit distance and language models for spelling correction* recipe in *Chapter 6, String Comparison and Clustering*. However, the basic idea is that the string entered is compared to the language model just trained, resulting in a score that shows how good a fit this string is to the model. This string is going to be one huge word without any white spaces—but note that there is no tokenizer at work here, so the spell checker starts inserting spaces and reassessing the score of the resulting sequence. It keeps these sequences where insertion of spaces increases the score of the sequence.

Remember that the language model was trained on text with white spaces. The spell checker tries to insert a space everywhere it can and keeps a set of "best so far" insertions of white spaces. In the end, it returns the best scoring series of edits.

Note that to complete the tokenizer, the appropriate `TokenizerFactory` needs to be applied to the white space-modified text, but this is left as an exercise for the reader.

There's more...

`CompiledSpellChecker` allows for an *n*-best output as well; this allows for multiple possible analyses of the text. In a high-coverage/recall situation such as a research search engine, it might serve to allow the application of multiple tokenizations. Also, the edit costs can be manipulated by extending the `WeightedEditDistance` class directly to tune the system.

See also

It will be unhelpful to not actually provide non-English resources for this recipe. We built and evaluated a Chinese tokenizer using resources available on the web for research use. Our tutorial on Chinese word segmentation covers this in detail. You can find the Chinese word segmentation tutorial at `http://alias-i.com/lingpipe/demos/tutorial/chineseTokens/read-me.html`.

3
Advanced Classifiers

In this chapter, we will cover the following recipes:

- A simple classifier
- Language model classifier with tokens
- Naïve Bayes
- Feature extractors
- Logistic regression
- Multithreaded cross validation
- Tuning parameters in logistic regression
- Customizing feature extraction
- Combining feature extractors
- Classifier-building life cycle
- Linguistic tuning
- Thresholding classifiers
- Train a little, learn a little – active learning
- Annotation

Introduction

This chapter introduces more sophisticated classifiers that use different learning techniques as well as richer observations about the data (features). We will also address the best practices for building machine-learning systems as well as data annotation and approaches that minimize the amount of training data needed.

Advanced Classifiers

A simple classifier

This recipe is a thought experiment that should help make clear what machine learning does. Recall the *Training your own language model classifier* recipe in *Chapter 1*, *Simple Classifiers*, to train your own sentiment classifier in the recipe. Consider what a conservative approach to the same problem might be—build `Map<String,String>` from the inputs to the correct class. This recipe will explore how this might work and what its consequences might be.

How to do it...

Brace yourself; this will be spectacularly stupid but hopefully informative.

1. Enter the following in the command line:

   ```
   java -cp lingpipe-cookbook.1.0.jar:lib/lingpipe-
   4.1.0.jar:lib/opencsv-2.4.jar com.lingpipe.cookbook.chapter3.
   OverfittingClassifier
   ```

2. The usual anemic prompt appears, with some user input:

   ```
   Training
   Type a string to be classified. Empty string to quit.
   When all else fails #Disney
   Category is: e
   ```

3. It correctly gets the language as `e` or English. However, everything else is about to fail. Next, we will use the following code:

   ```
   Type a string to be classified. Empty string to quit.
   When all else fails #Disne
   Category is: n
   ```

   We just dropped the final `y` on `#Disney`, and as a result, we got a big confused classifier. What happened?

How it works...

This section should really be called *How it doesn't work*, but let's dive into the details anyway.

Just to be clear, this recipe is not recommended as an actual solution to a classification problem that requires any flexibility at all. However, it introduces a minimal example of how to work with LingPipe's `Classification` class as well as makes clear what an extreme case of overfitting looks like; this in turn, helps demonstrate how machine learning is different from most of standard computer engineering.

Starting with the `main()` method, we will get into standard code slinging that should be familiar to you from *Chapter 1, Simple Classifiers*:

```
String dataPath = args.length > 0 ? args[0] :
"data/disney_e_n.csv";
List<String[]> annotatedData =
  Util.readAnnotatedCsvRemoveHeader(new File(dataPath));

OverfittingClassifier classifier = new OverfittingClassifier();
System.out.println("Training");
for (String[] row: annotatedData) {
  String truth = row[Util.ANNOTATION_OFFSET];
  String text = row[Util.TEXT_OFFSET];
  classifier.handle(text,new Classification(truth));
}
Util.consoleInputBestCategory(classifier);
```

Nothing novel is going on here—we are just training up a classifier, as shown in *Chapter 1, Simple Classifiers*, and then supplying the classifier to the `Util.consoleInputBestCategory()` method. Looking at the class code reveals what is going on:

```
public class OverfittingClassifier implements
   BaseClassifier<CharSequence> {

  Map<String,Classification> mMap
        = new HashMap<String,Classification>();

  public void handle(String text,
                  Classification classification) {
    mMap.put(text, classification);
  }
```

So, the `handle()` method takes the `text` and `classification` pair and stuffs them in `HashMap`. The classifier does nothing else to learn from the data so training amounts to memorization of the data:

```
@Override
public Classification classify(CharSequence text) {
  if (mMap.containsKey(text)) {
    return mMap.get(text);
  }
  return new Classification("n");
}
```

Advanced Classifiers

The `classify()` method just does a lookup into `Map` and returns the value if there is one, otherwise, we will get the category `n` as the return classification.

What is good about the preceding code is that you have a minimalist example of a `BaseClassifier` implementation, and you can see how the `handle()` method adds data to the classifier.

What is bad about the preceding code is the utter rigidity of the mapping from training data to categories. If the exact example is not seen in training, then the `n` category is assumed.

This is an extreme example of overfitting, but it essentially conveys what it means to have an overfit model. An overfit model is tailored too close to the training data and cannot generalize well to new data.

Let's think a bit more about what is so wrong about the preceding classifier for language identification—the issue is that entire sentences/tweets are the wrong unit of processing. Words/tokens are a much better measure of what language is being used. Some improvements that will be borne out in the later recipes are:

- Break the text into words/tokens.
- Instead of a match/no-match decision, consider a more nuanced approach. A simple *which language matches more words* will be a huge improvement.
- As languages get closer, for example, British versus American English, probabilities can be called for that. Pay attention to likely discriminating words.

While this recipe might be comically inappropriate for the task at hand, consider trying a sentiment for an even more ludicrous example. It embodies a core assumption of much of computer science that the world of inputs is discrete and finite. Machine learning can be viewed as a response to a world where this is not the case.

There's more...

Oddly enough, we often have a need for such a classifier in commercial systems—we call it the management classifier; it runs preemptively on data. It has happened that a senior VP is unhappy with the system output for some example. This classifier then can be trained with the exact case that allows for immediate system fixing and satisfaction of the VP.

Language model classifier with tokens

Chapter 1, *Simple Classifiers*, covered classification without knowing what tokens/words were, with a language model per category—we used character slices or ngrams to model the text. *Chapter 2*, *Finding and Working with Words*, discussed at length the process of finding tokens in text, and now we can use them to build a classifier. Most of the time, we use tokenized input to classifiers, so this recipe is an important introduction to the concept.

How to do it...

This recipe will tell us how to train and use a tokenized language model classifier, but it will ignore issues such as evaluation, serialization, deserialization, and so on. You can refer to the recipes in *Chapter 1, Simple Classifiers*, for examples. This code of this recipe is in `com.lingpipe.cookbook.chapter3.TrainAndRunTokenizedLMClassifier`:

1. The exception of the following code is the same as found in the *Training your own language model classifier* recipe in *Chapter 1, Simple Classifiers*. The `DynamicLMClassifier` class provides a static method for the creation of a tokenized LM classifier. Some setup is required. The `maxTokenNgram` variable sets the largest size of token sequences used in the classifier—smaller datasets usually benefit from lower order (number of tokens) ngrams. Next, we will set up a `tokenizerFactory` method, selecting the workhorse tokenizer from *Chapter 2, Finding and Working with Words*. Finally, we will specify the categories that the classifier uses:

    ```
    int maxTokenNGram = 2;
    TokenizerFactory tokenizerFactory =
      IndoEuropeanTokenizerFactory.INSTANCE;
    String[] categories = Util.getCategories(annotatedData);
    ```

2. Next, the classifier is constructed:

    ```
    DynamicLMClassifier<TokenizedLM> classifier =
      DynamicLMClassifier.createTokenized
        (categories,tokenizerFactory,maxTokenNGram);
    ```

3. Run the code from the command line or your IDE:

    ```
    java -cp lingpipe-cookbook.1.0.jar:lib/lingpipe-
    4.1.0.jar:lib/opencsv-2.4.jar com.lingpipe.cookbook.chapter3.
    TrainAndRunTokenizedLMClassifier
    ```

There's more...

In application, the `DynamicLMClassifier` classifier does not see a great deal of use in commercial application. This classifier might be a good choice for an author-identification classifier (that is, one that classifies whether a given piece of text is written by an author or by someone else) that was highly sensitive to turns of phrase and exact word usage. The Javadoc is well worth consulting to better understand what this class does.

Naïve Bayes

Naïve Bayes is probably the world's most famous classification technology, and just to keep you on your toes, we provide two separate implementations with lots of configurability. One of the most well-known applications of a naïve Bayes classifier is for spam filtering in an e-mail.

Advanced Classifiers

The reason the word *naïve* is used is that the classifier assumes that words (features) occur independent of one another—this is clearly a naïve assumption, but lots of useful and not-so-useful technologies have been based on the approach. Some notable features of the traditional naïve Bayes include:

- Character sequences are converted to bags of tokens with counts. No whitespaces are considered, and the order of the tokens does not matter.
- Naïve Bayes classifiers require two or more categories into which input texts are categorized. These categories must be both exhaustive and mutually exclusive. This indicates that a document used for training must only belong to one category.
- The math is very simple: `p(category|tokens) = p(category,tokens)/p(tokens)`.
- The class is configurable for various kinds of unknown token models.

A naïve Bayes classifier estimates two things. First, it estimates the probability of each category, independent of any tokens. This is carried out based on the number of training examples presented for each category. Second, for each category, it estimates the probability of seeing each token in that category. Naïve Bayes is so useful and important that we will show you exactly how it works and plug through the formulas. The example we have is to classify hot and cold weather based on the text.

First, we will work out the math to calculate the probability of a category given a word sequence. Second, we will plug in an example and then verify it using the classifier we build.

Getting ready

Let's lay out the basic formula to calculate the probability of a category given a text input. A token-based naïve Bayes classifier computes the joint token count and category probabilities as follows:

```
p(tokens,cat) = p(tokens|cat) * p(cat)
```

1. Conditional probabilities are derived by applying Bayes's rule to invert the probability calculation:

   ```
   p(cat|tokens) = p(tokens,cat) / p(tokens)
                 = p(tokens|cat) * p(cat) / p(tokens)
   ```

2. Now, we will get to expand all these terms. If we look at `p(tokens|cat)`, this is where the naïve assumption comes into play. We assume that each token is independent, and thus, the probability of all the tokens is the product of the probability of each token:

   ```
   p(tokens|cat) = p(tokens[0]|cat) * p(tokens[1]|cat) * . . .
      * p(tokens[n]|cat)
   ```

The probability of the tokens themselves, that is, `p(tokens)`, the denominator in the preceding equation. This is just the sum of their probability in each category weighted by the probability of the category itself:

```
p(tokens) = p(tokens|cat1) * p(cat1) + p(tokens|cat2)
   * p(cat2) + . . . + p(tokens|catN) * p(catN)
```

> When building a naïve Bayes classifier, `p(tokens)` doesn't need to be explicitly calculated. Instead, we can use `p(tokens|cat) * p(cat)` and assign the tokens to the category with the higher product.

3. Now that we have laid out each element of our equation, we can look at how these probabilities are calculated. We can calculate both these probabilities using simple frequencies.

   The probability of a category is calculated by counting the number of times the category showed up in the training instances divided by the total number of training instances. As we know that Naïve Bayes classifiers have exhaustive and mutually-exclusive categories, the sum of the frequency of each category must equal the total number of training instances:

   ```
   p(cat) = frequency(cat) / (frequency(cat1) +
      frequency(cat2) + . . . + frequency(catN))
   ```

   The probability of a token in a category is computed by counting the number of times the token appeared in a category divided by the number of times all the other tokens appeared in this category:

   ```
   p(token|cat) = frequency(token,cat)/(frequency(token1,cat)
      + frequency(token2,cat) + . . . + frequency(tokenN,cat)
   ```

   These probabilities are calculated to provide what is called the **maximum likelihood estimate** of the model. Unfortunately, these estimates provide zero probability for tokens that were not seen during the training. You can see this very easily in the calculation of an unseen token probability. Since it wasn't seen, it will have a frequency count of 0, and the numerator of our original equation goes to 0.

   In order to overcome this, we will use a technique known as **smoothing** that assigns a prior and then computes a maximum a posteriori estimate rather than a maximum likelihood estimate. A very common smoothing technique is called additive smoothing, and it just involves adding a prior count to every count in the training data. Two sets of counts are added: the first is a token count added to all the token frequency calculations, and the second is a category count, which is added to all the category count calculations.

Advanced Classifiers

This obviously changes the `p(cat)` and the `p(token|cat)` values. Let's call the `alpha` prior that is added to the category count and the `beta` prior that is added to the token count. When we call the `alpha` prior, our previous calculations will change to:

```
p(cat) = frequency(cat) + alpha / [(frequency(cat1) +
   alpha) + (frequency(cat2)+alpha) + . . . +
     (frequency(catN) + alpha)]
```

When we call the `beta` prior, the calculations will change to:

```
p(token|cat) = (frequency(token,cat)+beta) /
   [(frequency(token1,cat)+beta) + frequency(token2,cat)+beta) + . . .
     + (frequency(tokenN,cat) + beta)]
```

4. Now that we have set up our equations, let's look at a concrete example.

   We'll build a classifier to classify whether the forecast calls for hot or cold weather based on a set of phrases:

   ```
   hot : super steamy today
   hot : boiling out
   hot : steamy out

   cold : freezing out
   cold : icy
   ```

   There are a total of seven tokens in these five training items:

   - super
   - steamy
   - today
   - boiling
   - out
   - freezing
   - icy

   Of these, all the tokens appear once, except `steamy`, which appears twice in the `hot` category and `out`, which appears once in each category. This is our training data. Now, let's calculate the probability of an input text being in the `hot` or `cold` category. Let's say our input is the word `super`. Let's set the category prior `alpha` to `1` and the token prior `beta` also to `1`.

5. So, we will calculate the probabilities of `p(hot|super)` and `p(cold|super)`:

   ```
   p(hot|super) = p(super|hot) * p(hot)/ p(super)

   p(super|hot) = (freq(super,hot) + beta) /
   ```

```
[(freq(super|hot)+beta) + (freq(steamy|hot) + beta) +
 . . . + (freq(freezing|hot)+beta)
```

We will take into consideration all the tokens, including the ones that haven't been seen in the hot category:

```
freq(super|hot) + beta = 1 + 1 = 2
freq(steamy|hot) + beta = 2 + 1 = 3
freq(today|hot) + beta = 1 + 1 = 2
freq(boiling|hot) + beta = 1 + 1 = 2
freq(out|hot) + beta = 1 + 1 = 2
freq(freezing|hot) + beta = 0 + 1 = 1
freq(icy|hot) + beta = 0 + 1 = 1
```

This will give us a denominator equal to a sum of these inputs:

```
2+3+2+2+2+1+1 = 13
```

6. Now, p(super|hot) = 2/13 is one part of the equation. We still need to calculate p(hot) and p(super):

```
p(hot) = (freq(hot) + alpha) /
              ((freq(hot) + alpha) +
               freq(cold)+alpha))
```

For the hot category, we have three documents or cases, and for the cold category, we have two documents in our training data. So, freq(hot) = 3 and freq(cold) = 2:

```
p(hot) = (3 + 1) / (3 + 1) + (2 +1) = 4/7
Similarly p(cold) = (2 + 1) / (3 + 1) + (2 +1) = 3/7
Please note that p(hot) = 1 - p(cold)

p(super) = p(super|hot) * p(hot) + p(super|cold) + p(cold)
```

To calculate p(super|cold), we need to repeat the same steps:

```
p(super|cold) = (freq(super,cold) + beta) /
[(freq(super|cold)+beta) + (freq(steamy|cold) + beta) + . . . +
(freq(freezing|cold)+beta)

freq(super|cold) + beta = 0 + 1 = 1
freq(steamy|cold) + beta = 0 + 1 = 1
freq(today|cold) + beta = 0 + 1 = 1
freq(boiling|cold) + beta = 0 + 1 = 1
freq(out|cold) + beta = 1 + 1 = 2
freq(freezing|cold) + beta = 1 + 1 = 2
freq(icy|cold) + beta = 1 + 1 = 2
```

Advanced Classifiers

```
p(super|cold) = freq(super|cold)+beta/sum of all terms above
              = 0 + 1 / (1+1+1+1+2+2+2) = 1/10
```

This gives us the probability of the token `super`:

```
P(super) = p(super|hot) * p(hot) + p(super|cold) * p(cold)
         = 2/13 * 4/7 + 1/10 * 3/7
```

We now have all the pieces together to calculate `p(hot|super)` and `p(cold|super)`:

```
p(hot|super) = p(super|hot) * p(hot) / p(super)
             = (2/13 * 4/7) / (2/13 * 4/7 + 1/10 * 3/7)

             = 0.6722
p(cold|super) = p(super|cold) * p(cold) /p(super)
              = (1/10 * 3/7) / (2/13 * 4/7 + 1/10 * 3/7)
              = 0.3277

Obviously, p(hot|super) = 1 - p(cold|super)
```

If we want to repeat this for the input stream `super super`, the following calculations can be used:

```
p(hot|super super) = p(super super|hot) * p(hot) / p(super super)
                   = (2/13 * 2/13 * 4/7) / (2/13 * 2/13 * 4/7 + 1/10 * 1/10 * 3/7)
                   = 0.7593
p(cold|super super) = p(super super|cold) * p(cold) /p(super super)
                    = (1/10 * 1/10 * 3/7) / (2/13 * 2/13 * 4/7 + 1/10 * 1/10 * 3/7)
                    = 0.2406
```

Remember our naïve assumption: the probability of the tokens is the product of the probabilities, since we assume that they are independent of each other.

Let's verify our calculations by training up the naïve Bayes classifier and using the same input.

How to do it...

Let's verify some of these calculations in code:

1. In your IDE, run the `TrainAndRunNaiveBayesClassifier` class in the code package of this chapter, or using the command line, type the following command:

   ```
   java -cp lingpipe-cookbook.1.0.jar:lib/lingpipe-
   4.1.0.jar:lib/opencsv-2.4.jar com.lingpipe.cookbook.chapter3.
   TrainAndRunNaiveBayesClassifier
   ```

2. In the prompt, let's use our first example, `super`:

   ```
   Type a string to be classified
   super
   h 0.67
   c 0.33
   ```

3. As we can see, our calculations were correct. For the case of a word, `hello`, that doesn't exist in our training; we will fall back to the prevalence of the categories modified by the category's prior counts:

   ```
   Type a string to be classified
   hello
   h 0.57
   c 0.43
   ```

4. Again, for the case of `super super`, our calculations were correct.

   ```
   Type a string to be classified
   super super

   h 0.76
   c 0.24
   ```

5. The source that generates the preceding output is in `src/com/lingpipe/chapter3/TrainAndRunNaiveBays.java`. The code should be straightforward, so we will not covering it in this recipe.

See also

- For more details on configuring naïve Bayes, including length normalizing, refer to the Javadoc at `http://alias-i.com/lingpipe/docs/api/index.html?com/aliasi/classify/TradNaiveBayesClassifier.html`
- You can refer to the expectation maximization tutorial at `http://alias-i.com/lingpipe/demos/tutorial/em/read-me.html`

Feature extractors

Up until now, we have been using characters and words to train our models. We are about to introduce a classifier (logistic regression) that allows for other observations about the data to inform the classifier—for example, whether a word is actually a date. Feature extractors are used in CRF taggers and K-means clustering. This recipe will introduce feature extractors independent of any technology that uses them.

Advanced Classifiers

How to do it...

There is not much to this recipe, but the upcoming *Logistic regression* recipe has many moving parts, and this is one of them.

1. Fire up your IDE or type in the command line:
   ```
   java -cp lingpipe-cookbook.1.0.jar:lib/lingpipe-4.1.0.jar com.lingpipe.cookbook.chapter3.SimpleFeatureExtractor
   ```

2. Type a string into our standard I/O loop:
   ```
   Type a string to see its features
   My first feature extraction!
   ```

3. Features are then produced:
   ```
   !=1
   My=1
   extraction=1
   feature=1
   first=1
   ```

4. Note that there is no order information here. Does it keep a count or not?
   ```
   Type a string to see its features
   My my my what a nice feature extractor.
   my=2
   .=1
   My=1
   a=1
   extractor=1
   feature=1
   nice=1
   what=1
   ```

5. The feature extractor keeps count with `my=2`, and it does not normalize the case (`My` is different from `my`). Refer to the later recipes in this chapter on how to modify feature extractors—they are very flexible.

How it works...

LingPipe provides solid infrastructure for the creation of feature extractors. The code for this recipe is in `src/com/lingipe/chapter3/SimpleFeatureExtractor.java`:

```
public static void main(String[] args) throws IOException {
  TokenizerFactory tokFact
    = IndoEuropeanTokenizerFactory.INSTANCE;
  FeatureExtractor<CharSequence> tokenFeatureExtractor
    = new TokenFeatureExtractor(tokFact);
```

The preceding code constructs `TokenFeatureExtractor` with `TokenizerFactory`. It is one of the 13 `FeatureExtractor` implementations provided in LingPipe.

Next, we will apply the I/O loop and print out the feature, which is `Map<String, ? extends Number>`. The `String` element is the feature name. In this case, the actual token is the name. The second element of the map is a value that extends `Number`, in this case, the count of how many times the token was seen in the text.

```
BufferedReader reader
  = new BufferedReader(new  InputStreamReader(System.in));
while (true) {
  System.out.println("\nType a string to see its features");
  String text = reader.readLine();
  Map<String, ? extends Number > features
    = tokenFeatureExtractor.features(text);
  System.out.println(features);
}
```

The feature name needs to only be a unique name—we could have prepended each feature name with `SimpleFeatExt_` to keep track of where the feature came from, which is helpful in complex feature-extraction scenarios.

Logistic regression

Logistic regression is probably responsible for the majority of industrial classifiers, with the possible exception of naïve Bayes classifiers. It almost certainly is one of the best performing classifiers available, albeit at the cost of slow training and considerable complexity in configuration and tuning.

Logistic regression is also known as maximum entropy, neural network classification with a single neuron, and others. So far in this book, the classifiers have been based on the underlying characters or tokens, but logistic regression uses unrestricted feature extraction, which allows for arbitrary observations of the situation to be encoded in the classifier.

This recipe closely follows a more complete tutorial at http://alias-i.com/lingpipe/demos/tutorial/logistic-regression/read-me.html.

How logistic regression works

All that logistic regression does is take a vector of feature weights over the data, apply a vector of coefficients, and do some simple math, which results in a probability for each class encountered in training. The complicated bit is in determining what the coefficients should be.

Advanced Classifiers

The following are some of the features produced by our training recipe for 21 tweets annotated for English `e` and non-English `n`. There are relatively few features because feature weights are being pushed to `0.0` by our prior, and once a weight is `0.0`, then the feature is removed. Note that one category, `n`, is set to `0.0` for all the features of the `n-1` category—this is a property of the logistic regression process that fixes once categories features to `0.0` and adjust all other categories features with respect to that:

```
FEATURE      e          n
I :        0.37       0.0
! :        0.30       0.0
Disney :   0.15       0.0
" :        0.08       0.0
to :       0.07       0.0
anymore :  0.06       0.0
isn :      0.06       0.0
' :        0.06       0.0
t :        0.04       0.0
for :      0.03       0.0
que :     -0.01       0.0
moi :     -0.01       0.0
_ :       -0.02       0.0
, :       -0.08       0.0
pra :     -0.09       0.0
? :       -0.09       0.0
```

Take the string, `I luv Disney`, which will only have two non-zero features: `I=0.37` and `Disney=0.15` for `e` and zeros for `n`. Since there is no feature that matches `luv`, it is ignored. The probability that the tweet is English breaks down to:

$$vectorMultiply(e,[I,Disney]) = \exp(.37*1 + .15*1) = 1.68$$

$$vectorMultiply(n,[I,Disney]) = \exp(0*1 + 0*1) = 1$$

We will rescale to a probability by summing the outcomes and dividing it:

$$p(e\,|\,[I,Disney]) = 1.68/(1.68 +1) = 0.62$$

$$p(e\,|\,[I,Disney]) = 1/(1.68 +1) = 0.38$$

This is how the math works on running a logistic regression model. Training is another issue entirely.

Getting ready

This recipe assumes the same framework that we have been using all along to get training data from `.csv` files, train the classifier, and run it from the command line.

Setting up to train the classifier is a bit complex because of the number of parameters and objects used in training. We will discuss all the 10 arguments to the training method as found in `com.lingpipe.cookbook.chapter3.TrainAndRunLogReg`.

The `main()` method starts with what should be familiar classes and methods—if they are not familiar, have a look at *How to train and evaluate with cross validation* and *Introduction to Introduction to tokenizer Factories – finding words in a character stream*, recipes from *Chapter 1*, *Simple Classifiers*, and *Chapter 2*, *Finding and Working with Words*, respectively:

```
public static void main(String[] args) throws IOException {
    String trainingFile = args.length > 0 ? args[0]
            : "data/disney_e_n.csv";
    List<String[]> training
        = Util.readAnnotatedCsvRemoveHeader(new File(trainingFile));

    int numFolds = 0;
    XValidatingObjectCorpus<Classified<CharSequence>> corpus
        = Util.loadXValCorpus(training,numFolds);

    TokenizerFactory tokenizerFactory
        = IndoEuropeanTokenizerFactory.INSTANCE;
```

Note that we are using `XValidatingObjectCorpus` when a simpler implementation such as `ListCorpus` will do. We will not take advantage of any of its cross-validation features, because the `numFolds` param as `0` will have training visit the entire corpus. We are trying to keep the number of novel classes to a minimum, and we tend to always use this implementation in real-world gigs anyway.

Now, we will start to build the configuration for our classifier. The `FeatureExtractor<E>` interface provides a mapping from data to features; this will be used to train and run the classifier. In this case, we are using a `TokenFeatureExtractor()` method, which creates features based on the tokens found by the tokenizer supplied during construction. This is similar to what naïve Bayes reasons over. The previous recipe goes into more detail about what the feature extractor is doing if this is not clear:

```
FeatureExtractor<CharSequence> featureExtractor
    = new TokenFeatureExtractor(tokenizerFactory);
```

The `minFeatureCount` item is usually set to a number higher than 1, but with small training sets, this is needed to get any performance. The thought behind filtering feature counts is that logistic regression tends to overfit low-count features that, just by chance, exist in one category of training data. As training data grows, the `minFeatureCount` value is adjusted usually by paying attention to cross-validation performance:

```
int minFeatureCount = 1;
```

Advanced Classifiers

The `addInterceptFeature` Boolean controls whether a category feature exists that models the prevalence of the category in training. The default name of the intercept feature is `*&^INTERCEPT%$^&**`, and you will see it in the weight vector output if it is being used. By convention, the intercept feature is set to `1.0` for all inputs. The idea is that if a category is just very common or very rare, there should be a feature that captures just this fact, independent of other features that might not be as cleanly distributed. This models the category probability in naïve Bayes in some way, but the logistic regression algorithm will decide how useful it is as it does with all other features:

```
boolean addInterceptFeature = true;
boolean noninformativeIntercept = true;
```

These Booleans control what happens to the intercept feature if it is used. Priors, in the following code, are typically not applied to the intercept feature; this is the result if this parameter is true. Set the Boolean to `false`, and the prior will be applied to the intercept.

Next is the `RegressionPrior` instance, which controls how the model is fit. What you need to know is that priors help prevent logistic regression from overfitting the data by pushing coefficients towards 0. There is a non-informative prior that does not do this with the consequence that if there is a feature that applies to just one category it will be scaled to infinity, because the model keeps fitting better as the coefficient is increased in the numeric estimation. Priors, in this context, function as a way to not be over confident in observations about the world.

Another dimension in the `RegressionPrior` instance is the expected variance of the features. Low variance will push coefficients to zero more aggressively. The prior returned by the static `laplace()` method tends to work well for NLP problems. For more information on what is going on here, consult the relevant Javadoc and the logistic regression tutorial referenced at the beginning of the recipe—there is a lot going on, but it can be managed without a deep theoretical understanding. Also, see the *Tuning parameters in logistic regression* recipe in this chapter.

```
double priorVariance = 2;
RegressionPrior prior
    = RegressionPrior.laplace(priorVariance,
        noninformativeIntercept);
```

Next, we will control how the algorithm searches for an answer.

```
AnnealingSchedule annealingSchedule
    = AnnealingSchedule.exponential(0.00025,0.999);
double minImprovement = 0.000000001;
int minEpochs = 100;
int maxEpochs = 2000;
```

`AnnealingSchedule` is best understood by consulting the Javadoc, but what it does is change how much the coefficients are allowed to vary when fitting the model. The `minImprovement` parameter sets the amount the model fit has to improve to not terminate the search, because the algorithm has converged. The `minEpochs` parameter sets a minimal number of iterations, and `maxEpochs` sets an upper limit if the search does not converge as determined by `minImprovement`.

Next is some code that allows for basic reporting/logging. `LogLevel.INFO` will report a great deal of information about the progress of the classifier as it tries to converge:

```
PrintWriter progressWriter = new PrintWriter(System.out,true);
progressWriter.println("Reading data.");
Reporter reporter = Reporters.writer(progressWriter);
reporter.setLevel(LogLevel.INFO);
```

Here ends the *Getting ready* section of one of our most complex classes—next, we will train and run the classifier.

How to do it...

It has been a bit of work setting up to train and run this class. We will just go through the steps to get it up and running; the upcoming recipes will address its tuning and evaluation:

1. Note that there is a more complex 14-argument train method as well the one that extends configurability. This is the 10-argument version:

   ```
   LogisticRegressionClassifier<CharSequence> classifier
       = LogisticRegressionClassifier.
           <CharSequence>train(corpus,
               featureExtractor,
               minFeatureCount,
               addInterceptFeature,
               prior,
               annealingSchedule,
               minImprovement,
               minEpochs,
               maxEpochs,
               reporter);
   ```

2. The `train()` method, depending on the `LogLevel` constant, will produce from nothing with `LogLevel.NONE` to the prodigious output with `LogLevel.ALL`.

Advanced Classifiers

3. While we are not going to use it, we show how to serialize the trained model to disk. The *How to serialize a LingPipe object – classifier example* recipe in *Chapter 1, Simple Classifiers*, explains what is going on:

   ```
   AbstractExternalizable.compileTo(classifier,
      new File("models/myModel.LogisticRegression"));
   ```

4. Once trained, we will apply the standard classification loop with:

   ```
   Util.consoleInputPrintClassification(classifier);
   ```

5. Run the preceding code in the IDE of your choice or use the command-line command:

   ```
   java -cp lingpipe-cookbook.1.0.jar:lib/lingpipe-4.1.0.jar:lib/opencsv-2.4.jar com.lingpipe.cookbook.chapter3.TrainAndRunLogReg
   ```

6. The result is a big dump of information about the training:

   ```
   Reading data.
   :00 Feature Extractor class=class com.aliasi.tokenizer.TokenFeatureExtractor
   :00 min feature count=1
   :00 Extracting Training Data
   :00 Cold start
   :00 Regression callback handler=null
   :00 Logistic Regression Estimation
   :00 Monitoring convergence=true
   :00 Number of dimensions=233
   :00 Number of Outcomes=2
   :00 Number of Parameters=233
   :00 Number of Training Instances=21
   :00 Prior=LaplaceRegressionPrior(Variance=2.0,
     noninformativeIntercept=true)
   :00 Annealing Schedule=Exponential(initialLearningRate=2.5E-4,
     base=0.999)
   :00 Minimum Epochs=100
   :00 Maximum Epochs=2000
   :00 Minimum Improvement Per Period=1.0E-9
   :00 Has Informative Prior=true
   :00 epoch=      0 lr=0.000250000 ll=    -20.9648 lp=
     -232.0139 llp=  -252.9787 llp*=  -252.9787
   :00 epoch=      1 lr=0.000249750 ll=    -20.9406 lp=
     -232.0195 llp=  -252.9602 llp*=  -252.9602
   ```

7. The `epoch` reporting goes on until either the number of epochs is met or the search converges. In the following case, the number of epochs was met:

   ```
   :00 epoch= 1998 lr=0.000033868 ll=    -15.4568 lp=
     -233.8125 llp=  -249.2693 llp*=  -249.2693
   :00 epoch= 1999 lr=0.000033834 ll=    -15.4565 lp=
     -233.8127 llp=  -249.2692 llp*=  -249.2692
   ```

8. Now, we can play with the classifier a bit:

   ```
   Type a string to be classified. Empty string to quit.
   I luv Disney
   Rank   Category   Score     P(Category|Input)
   0=e 0.626898085027528 0.626898085027528
   1=n 0.373101914972472 0.373101914972472
   ```

9. This should look familiar; it is exactly the same result as the worked example at the start of the recipe.

That's it! You have trained up and used the world's most relevant industrial classifier. However, there's a lot more to harnessing the power of this beast.

Multithreaded cross validation

Cross validation (refer to the *How to train and evaluate with cross validation* recipe in *Chapter 1, Simple Classifiers*) can be very slow, which interferes with tuning systems. This recipe will show you a simple but effective way to access all the available cores on your system to more quickly process each fold.

How to do it...

This recipe explains multi-threaded cross validation in the context of the next recipe, so don't be confused by the fact that the same class is repeated.

1. Engage your IDE or type in the command line:

   ```
   java -cp lingpipe-cookbook.1.0.jar:lib/lingpipe-4.1.0.jar:lib/
   opencsv-2.4.jar com.lingpipe.cookbook.chapter3.TuneLogRegParams
   ```

2. The system then responds with the following output (you might have to scroll to the top of the window):

   ```
   Reading data.
   RUNNING thread Fold 5 (1 of 10)
   RUNNING thread Fold 9 (2 of 10)
   RUNNING thread Fold 3 (3 of 10)
   RUNNING thread Fold 4 (4 of 10)
   RUNNING thread Fold 0 (5 of 10)
   RUNNING thread Fold 2 (6 of 10)
   RUNNING thread Fold 8 (7 of 10)
   RUNNING thread Fold 6 (8 of 10)
   RUNNING thread Fold 7 (9 of 10)
   RUNNING thread Fold 1 (10 of 10)
   reference\response
             \e,n,
          e 11,0,
          n 6,4,
   ```

Advanced Classifiers

3. The default training data is 21 tweets annotated for English `e` and non-English `n`. In the preceding output, we saw a report of each fold that runs as a thread and the resulting confusion matrix. That's it! We just did multithreaded cross validation. Let's see how this works.

How it works...

All the action happens in the `Util.xvalLogRegMultiThread()` method, which we invoke from `src/com/lingpipe/cookbook/chapter3/TuneLogRegParams.java`. The details of `TuneLogRegParams` are covered in the next recipe. This recipe will focus on the `Util` method:

```
int numThreads = 2;
int numFolds = 10;
Util.xvalLogRegMultiThread(corpus,
        featureExtractor,
        minFeatureCount,
        addInterceptFeature,
        prior,
        annealingSchedule,
        minImprovement,
        minEpochs,
        maxEpochs,
        reporter,
        numFolds,
        numThreads,
        categories);
```

All 10 parameters used to configure logistic regression are controllable (you can refer to the previous recipe for explanation), with the addition of `numFolds`, which controls how many folds there will be, `numThreads`, which controls how many threads can be run at the same time, and finally, `categories`.

If we look at the relevant method in `src/com/lingpipe/cookbook/Util.java`, we see:

```
public static <E> ConditionalClassifierEvaluator<E>
xvalLogRegMultiThread(
    final XValidatingObjectCorpus<Classified<E>> corpus,
    final FeatureExtractor<E> featureExtractor,
    final int minFeatureCount,
    final boolean addInterceptFeature,
    final RegressionPrior prior,
    final AnnealingSchedule annealingSchedule,
    final double minImprovement,
    final int minEpochs, final int maxEpochs,
    final Reporter reporter,
    final int numFolds,
```

```
      final int numThreads,
      final String[] categories) {
```

1. The method starts with the matching arguments for configuration information of logistic regression and running cross validation. Since cross validation is most often used in system tuning, all the relevant bits are exposed to modification. Everything is final because we are using an anonymous inner class to create threads.

2. Next, we will set up `crossFoldEvaluator` that will collect the results from each thread:

   ```
   corpus.setNumFolds(numFolds);
   corpus.permuteCorpus(new Random(11211));
   final boolean storeInputs = true;
   final ConditionalClassifierEvaluator<E> crossFoldEvaluator
       = new ConditionalClassifierEvaluator<E>(null, categories,
   storeInputs);
   ```

3. Now, we will get down to the business of creating threads for each fold, `i`:

   ```
   List<Thread> threads = new ArrayList<Thread>();
   for (int i = 0; i < numFolds; ++i) {
     final XValidatingObjectCorpus<Classified<E>> fold
       = corpus.itemView();
     fold.setFold(i);
   ```

   The `XValidatingObjectCorpus` class is set up for multithreaded access by creating a thread-safe version of the corpus for reads with the `itemView()` method. This method returns a corpus that can have the fold set, but no data can be added.

   Each thread is a `runnable` object, where the actual work of training and evaluating the fold is handled in the `run()` method:

   ```
   Runnable runnable
     = new Runnable() {
       @Override
       public void run() {
       try {
         LogisticRegressionClassifier<E> classifier
           = LogisticRegressionClassifier.<E>train(fold,
                   featureExtractor,
                   minFeatureCount,
                   addInterceptFeature,
                   prior,
                   annealingSchedule,
                   minImprovement,
                   minEpochs,
                   maxEpochs,
                   reporter);
   ```

Advanced Classifiers

In this code, we started with training the classifier, which, in turn, requires a `try/catch` statement to handle `IOException` thrown by the `LogisticRegressionClassifier.train()` method. Next, we will create `withinFoldEvaluator` that will be populated within the thread without a synchronization issue:

```
ConditionalClassifierEvaluator<E> withinFoldEvaluator
  = new ConditionalClassifierEvaluator<E>(classifier,
categories, storeInputs);
fold.visitTest(withinFoldEvaluator);
```

It is important that `storeInputs` be `true` so that the fold results can be added to `crossFoldEvaluator`:

```
addToEvaluator(withinFoldEvaluator,crossFoldEvaluator);
```

This method, also in `Util`, iterates over all the true positives and false negatives for each category and adds them to `crossFoldEvaluator`. Note that this is synchronized: this means that only one thread can access the method at a time, but given that classification has already been done, it should not be much of a bottleneck:

```
public synchronized static <E> void addToEvaluator(BaseClassifierE
valuator<E> foldEval, ScoredClassifierEvaluator<E> crossFoldEval)
{
  for (String category : foldEval.categories()) {
    for (Classified<E> classified : foldEval.
truePositives(category)) {
      crossFoldEval.addClassification(category,classified.
getClassification(),classified.getObject());
    }
    for (Classified<E> classified : foldEval.
falseNegatives(category)) {
      crossFoldEval.addClassification(category,classified.
getClassification(),classified.getObject());
    }
  }
}
```

The method takes the true positives and false negatives from each category and adds them to the `crossFoldEval` evaluator. These are essentially copy operations that do not take long to compute.

4. Returning to `xvalLogRegMultiThread`, we will handle the exception and add the completed `Runnable` to our list of `Thread`:

```
    catch (Exception e) {
      e.printStackTrace();
    }
  }
};
threads.add(new Thread(runnable,"Fold " + i));
```

5. With all the threads set up, we will invoke `runThreads()` as well as print the confusion matrix that results. We will not go into the source of `runThreads()`, because it is a straightforward Java management of threads, and `printConfusionMatrix` has been covered in *Chapter 1*, *Simple Classifiers*:

   ```
   runThreads(threads,numThreads);
   printConfusionMatrix(crossFoldEvaluator.confusionMatrix());
   }
   ```

That's it for really speeding up cross validation on multicore machines. It can make a big difference when tuning systems.

Tuning parameters in logistic regression

Logistic regression presents an intimidating array of parameters to tweak for better performance, and working with it is a bit of black art. Having built thousands of these classifiers, we are still learning how to do it better. This recipe will point you in the general right direction, but the topic probably deserves its own book.

How to do it...

This recipe involves extensive changes to the source of `src/com/lingpipe/chapter3/TuneLogRegParams.java`. We will just run one configuration of it here, with most of the exposition in the *How it works...* section.

1. Engage your IDE or type the following in the command line:

   ```
   java -cp lingpipe-cookbook.1.0.jar:lib/lingpipe-4.1.0.jar:lib/opencsv-2.4.jar com.lingpipe.cookbook.chapter3.TuneLogRegParams
   ```

2. The system then responds with cross-validation output confusion matrix for our default data in `data/disney_e_n.csv`:

   ```
   reference\response
         \e,n,
      e 11,0,
      n 6,4,
   ```

3. Next, we will report on false positives for each category—this will cover all the mistakes made:

   ```
   False Positives for e
   ES INSUPERABLE DISNEY !! QUIERO VOLVER:( : n
   @greenath_ t'as de la chance d'aller a Disney putain : n
   jamais été moi. : n
   @HedyHAMIDI au quartier pas a Disney moi: n
   ...
   ```

Advanced Classifiers

4. This output is followed by the features, their coefficients, and a count—remember that we will see n-1 categories, because one of the category's features is set to 0.0 for all features:

```
Feature coefficients for category e
I : 0.36688604
! : 0.29588525
Disney : 0.14954419
" : 0.07897427
to : 0.07378086
...
Got feature count: 113
```

5. Finally, we have our standard I/O that allows for examples to be tested:

```
Type a string to be classified
I luv disney
Rank  Category  Score              P(Category|Input)
0=e 0.5907060507161321 0.5907060507161321
1=n 0.40929394928386786 0.40929394928386786
```

6. This is the basic structure that we will work with. In the upcoming sections, we will explore the impact of varying parameters more closely.

How it works...

This recipe assumes that you are familiar with logistic regression training and configuration from two recipes back and cross validation, which is the previous recipe. The overall structure of the code is presented in an outline form, with the tuning parameters retained. Modifying each parameter will be discussed later in the recipe—below we start with the `main()` method ignoring some code as indicated by '...' and the tunable code shown for tokenization and feature extraction:

```
public static void main(String[] args) throws IOException {
    ...
    TokenizerFactory tokenizerFactory
        = IndoEuropeanTokenizerFactory.INSTANCE;
    FeatureExtractor<CharSequence> featureExtractor
        = new TokenFeatureExtractor(tokenizerFactory);
    int minFeatureCount = 1;
    boolean addInterceptFeature = false;
```

Next the priors are set up:

```
    boolean noninformativeIntercept = true;
    double priorVariance = 2 ;
    RegressionPrior prior
        = RegressionPrior.laplace(priorVariance,
                noninformativeIntercept);
```

Priors have a strong influence on the behavior coefficient assignment:

```
AnnealingSchedule annealingSchedule
   = AnnealingSchedule.exponential(0.00025,0.999);
double minImprovement = 0.000000001;
int minEpochs = 10;
int maxEpochs = 20;
```

The preceding code controls the search space of logistic regression:

```
Util.xvalLogRegMultiThread(corpus,…);
```

The preceding code runs cross validation to see how the system is doing—note the elided parameters with . . . .

In the following code, we will set the number of folds to 0, which will have the train method visit the entire corpus:

```
corpus.setNumFolds(0);
LogisticRegressionClassifier<CharSequence> classifier
   = LogisticRegressionClassifier.<CharSequence>train(corpus,…
```

Then, for each category, we will print out the features and their coefficients for the just trained classifier:

```
int featureCount = 0;
for (String category : categories) {
  ObjectToDoubleMap<String> featureCoeff
    = classifier.featureValues(category);
  System.out.println("Feature coefficients for category "
       + category);
  for (String feature : featureCoeff.keysOrderedByValueList()) {
    System.out.print(feature);
    System.out.printf(" :%.8f\n",featureCoeff.getValue(feature));
    ++featureCount;
  }
}
System.out.println("Got feature count: " + featureCount);
```

Finally, we will have the usual console classifier I/O:

```
Util.consoleInputPrintClassification(classifier);
```

Tuning feature extraction

The features that are fed into logistic regression have a huge impact on the performance of the system. We will cover feature extraction in greater detail in the later recipes, but we will bring to bear one of the most useful and somewhat counter-intuitive approaches here, because it is very easy to execute—use character ngrams instead of words/tokens. Let's look at an example:

```
Type a string to be classified. Empty string to quit.
The rain in Spain
Rank  Category  Score  P(Category|Input)
0=e 0.5 0.5
1=n 0.5 0.5
```

This output indicates that the classifier is tied between `e` English and `n` non-English as a decision. Scrolling back through the features, we will see that there are no matches for any of the words in the input. There are some substring matches on the English side. `The` has the substring `he` for the feature word `the`. For language ID, it makes sense to consider subsequences, but as a matter of experience, it can be a big help for sentiment and other problems as well.

Modifying the tokenizer to be two-to-four-character ngrams is done as follows:

```
int min = 2;
int max = 4;
TokenizerFactory tokenizerFactory
    = new NGramTokenizerFactory(min,max);
```

This results in the proper distinction being made:

```
Type a string to be classified. Empty string to quit.
The rain in Spain
Rank  Category  Score  P(Category|Input)
0=e 0.5113903651380305 0.5113903651380305
1=n 0.4886096348619695 0.4886096348619695
```

The overall performance on cross validation drops a bit. For very small training sets, such as 21 tweets, this is not unexpected. Generally, the cross-validation performance with a consultation of what the mistakes look like and a look at the false positives will help guide this process.

In looking at the false positives, it is clear that `Disney` is a source of problems, because the coefficients on features show it to be evidence for English. Some of the false positives are:

```
False Positives for e
@greenath_ t'as de la chance d'aller a Disney putain j'y ai jamais été
moi. : n
@HedyHAMIDI au quartier pas a Disney moi : n
```

```
Prefiro gastar uma baba de dinheiro pra ir pra cancun doq pra Disney
por exemplo : n
```

The following are the features for `e`:

```
Feature coefficients for category e
I : 0.36688604
! : 0.29588525
Disney : 0.14954419
" : 0.07897427
to : 0.07378086
```

In the absence of more training data, the features `!`, `Disney`, and `"` should be removed to help this classifier perform better, because none of these features are language specific, whereas `I` and `to` are, although not unique to English. This can be done by filtering the data or creating the appropriate tokenizer factory, but the best move is to probably get more data.

The `minFeature` count becomes useful when there is much more data, and you don't want logistic regression focusing on a very-low-count phenomenon because it tends to lead to overfitting.

Setting the `addInterceptFeature` parameter to `true` will add a feature that always fires. This will allow logistic regression to have a feature sensitive to the number of examples for each category. It is not the marginal likelihood of the category, as logistic regression will adjust the weight like any other feature—but the following priors show how it can be further tuned:

```
de : -0.08864114
( : -0.10818647
*&^INTERCEPT%$^&** : -0.17089337
```

The intercept is the strongest feature for `n` in the end, and the overall cross-validation performance suffered in this case.

Priors

The role of priors is to restrict the tendency of logistic regression to perfectly fit the training data. The ones we use try in varying degrees to push coefficients to zero. We will start with the `nonInformativeIntercept` prior, which controls whether the intercept feature is subject to the normalizing influences of the prior—if true, then the intercept is not subject to the prior, which was the case in the preceding example. Setting it to `false` moved it much closer to zero from `-0.17`:

```
*&^INTERCEPT%$^&** : -0.03874782
```

Advanced Classifiers

Next, we will adjust the variance of the prior. This sets an expected variation for the weights. A low variance means that coefficients are expected not to vary much from zero. In the preceding code, the variance was set to 2. This is the result of setting it to .01:

```
Feature coefficients for category e
' : -0.00003809
Feature coefficients for category n
```

This is a drop from 104 features with variance 2 to one feature for variance .01, because once a feature has dropped to 0, it is removed.

Increasing the variance changes our top e features from 2 to 4:

```
Feature coefficients for category e
I : 0.36688604
! : 0.29588525
Disney : 0.14954419

I : 0.40189501
! : 0.31387376
Disney : 0.18255271
```

This is a total of 119 features.

Consider a variance of 2 and a `gaussian` prior:

```
boolean noninformativeIntercept = false;
double priorVariance = 2;
RegressionPrior prior
   = RegressionPrior.gaussian(priorVariance,
     noninformativeIntercept);
```

We will get the following output:

```
I : 0.38866670
! : 0.27367013
Disney : 0.22699340
```

Oddly, we spend very little time worrying about which prior we use, but variance has a big role in performance, because it can cut down the feature space quickly. Laplace is a commonly accepted prior for NLP applications.

Consult the Javadoc and logistic regression tutorial for more information.

Annealing schedule and epochs

As logistic regression converges, the annealing schedule controls how the search space is explored and terminated:

```
AnnealingSchedule annealingSchedule
    = AnnealingSchedule.exponential(0.00025,0.999);
double minImprovement = 0.000000001;
int minEpochs = 10;
int maxEpochs = 20;
```

When tuning, we will increase the first parameter to the annealing schedule by order of magnitude (.0025,.025,..) if the search is taking too long—often, we can increase the training speed without impacting the cross-validation performance. Also, the `minImprovement` value can be increased to have the convergence end earlier, which can both increase the training speed and prevent the model from overfitting—this is called **early stopping**. Again, your guiding light in this situation is to look at the cross-validation performance when making changes.

The epochs required to achieve convergence can get quite high, so if the classifier is iterating to `maxEpochs -1`, this means that more epochs are required to converge. Be sure to set the `reporter.setLevel(LogLevel.INFO);` property or a more informative level to get the convergence report. This is another way to additionally force early stopping.

Parameter tuning is a black art that can only be learned through practice. The quality and quantity of training data is probably the dominant factor in classifier performance, but tuning can make a big difference as well.

Customizing feature extraction

Logistic regression allows for arbitrary features to be used. Features are any observations that can be made about data being classified. Some examples are as follows:

- Words/tokens from the text.
- We found that character ngrams work very well in lieu of words or stemmed words. For small data sets of less than 10,000 words of training, we will use 2-4 grams. Bigger training data can merit a longer gram, but we have never had good results above 8-gram characters.
- Output from another component can be a feature, for example, a part-of-speech tagger.
- Metadata known about the text, for example, the location of a tweet or time of the day it was created.
- Recognition of dates and numbers abstracted from the actual value.

Advanced Classifiers

How to do it...

The source for this recipe is in `src/com/lingpipe/cookbook/chapter3/ContainsNumberFeatureExtractor.java`.

1. Feature extractors are straightforward to build. The following is a feature extractor that returns a CONTAINS_NUMBER feature with weight 1:

    ```
    public class ContainsNumberFeatureExtractor implements
    FeatureExtractor<CharSequence> {
      @Override
      public Map<String,Counter> features(CharSequence text) {
            ObjectToCounterMap<String> featureMap
            = new ObjectToCounterMap<String>();
        if (text.toString().matches(".*\\d.*")) {
          featureMap.set("CONTAINS_NUMBER", 1);
        }
        return featureMap;  }
    ```

2. By adding a `main()` method, we can test the feature extractor:

    ```
    public static void main(String[] args) {
      FeatureExtractor<CharSequence> featureExtractor
            = new ContainsNumberFeatureExtractor();
      System.out.println(featureExtractor.features("I have a number 1"));
    }
    ```

3. Now run the following command:

    ```
    java -cp lingpipe-cookbook.1.0.jar:lib/lingpipe-4.1.0.jar:lib/opencsv-2.4.jar com.lingpipe.cookbook.chapter3.ContainsNumberFeatureExtractor
    ```

4. The preceding code yields the following output:

    ```
    CONTAINS_NUMBER=1
    ```

That's it. The next recipe will show you how to combine feature extractors.

There's more...

Designing features is a bit of an art. Logistic regression is supposed to be robust in the face of irrelevant features, but overwhelming it with really dumb features will likely detract from performance.

One way to think about what features you need is to wonder what evidence from the text or environment helps you, the human, decide what the correct classification is. Try and ignore your world knowledge when looking at the text. If world knowledge, that is, France is a country, is important, then try and model this world knowledge with a gazetteer to generate CONTAINS_COUNTRY_MENTION.

Be aware that features are strings, and the only notion of equivalence is the exact string match. The `12:01pm` feature is completely distinct from `12:02pm`, although, to a human, these strings are very close, because we understand time. To get the similarity of these two features, you must have something like a `LUNCH_TIME` feature that is computed using time.

Combining feature extractors

Feature extractors can be combined in much the same way as tokenizers in *Chapter 2, Finding and Working with Words*.

How to do it...

This recipe will show you how to combine the feature extractor from the previous recipe with a very common feature extractor over character ngrams.

1. We will start with a `main()` method in src/com/lingpipe/cookbook/chapter3/ CombinedFeatureExtractor.java that we will use to run the feature extractor. The following lines set up features that result from the tokenizer using the LingPipe class, `TokenFeatureExtractor`:

   ```
   public static void main(String[] args) {
     int min = 2;
     int max = 4;
     TokenizerFactory tokenizerFactory
         = new NGramTokenizerFactory(min,max);
     FeatureExtractor<CharSequence> tokenFeatures
   = new TokenFeatureExtractor(tokenizerFactory);
   ```

2. Then, we will construct the feature extractor from the previous recipe.

   ```
   FeatureExtractor<CharSequence> numberFeatures
   = new ContainsNumberFeatureExtractor();
   ```

3. Next, the LingPipe class joining feature extractors, `AddFeatureExtractor`, joins the two into a third:

   ```
   FeatureExtractor<CharSequence> joinedFeatureExtractors
      = new AddFeatureExtractor<CharSequence>(
            tokenFeatures,numberFeatures);
   ```

4. The remaining code gets the features and prints them out:

   ```
   String input = "show me 1!";
   Map<String,? extends Number> features
       = joinedFeatureExtractors.features(input);
   System.out.println(features);
   ```

Advanced Classifiers

5. Run the following command

   ```
   java -cp lingpipe-cookbook.1.0.jar:lib/lingpipe-
   4.1.0.jar:lib/opencsv-2.4.jar com.lingpipe.cookbook.chapter3.
   CombinedFeatureExtractor
   ```

6. The output looks like this:

   ```
   {me =1.0,   m=1.0, me 1=1.0, e =1.0, show=1.0,   me =1.0, ho=1.0,
   ow =1.0, e 1!=1.0, sho=1.0,   1=1.0, me=1.0, how =1.0, CONTAINS_
   NUMBER=1.0, w me=1.0,   me=1.0, how=1.0,   1!=1.0, sh=1.0, ow=1.0, e
   1=1.0, w m=1.0, ow m=1.0, w =1.0, 1!=1.0}
   ```

There's more...

The Javadoc references a broad range of feature extractors and combiners/filters to help manage the task of feature extraction. One slightly confusing aspect of the class is that the `FeatureExtractor` interface is in the `com.aliasi.util` package, and the implementing classes are all in `com.aliasi.features`.

Classifier-building life cycle

At the top-level building, a classifier usually proceeds as follows:

1. Create training data—refer to the following recipe for more about this.
2. Build training and evaluation infrastructure with sanity check.
3. Establish baseline performance.
4. Select optimization metric for classifier—this is what the classifier is trying to do and will guide tuning.
5. Optimize classifier via techniques such as:
   - Parameter tuning
   - Thresholding
   - Linguistic tuning
   - Adding training data
   - Refining classifier definition

This recipe will present the first four steps in concrete terms, and there are recipes in this chapter for the optimization step.

Getting ready

Nothing happens without training data for classifiers. Look at the *Annotation* recipe at the end of the chapter for tips on creating training data. You can also use an active learning framework to incrementally generate a training corpus (covered later in this chapter), which is the data used in this recipe.

Next, reduce the risk by starting with the dumbest possible implementation to make sure that the problem being solved is scoped correctly, and that the overall architecture makes sense. Connect the assumed inputs to assumed outputs with simple code. We promise that most of the time, one or the other will not be what you thought it would be.

This recipe assumes that you are familiar with the evaluation concepts in *Chapter 1*, *Simple Classifiers*, such as cross validation and confusion matrices, in addition to the logistic regression recipes covered so far.

The entire source is at `src/com/lingpipe/cookbook/chapter3/ClassifierBuilder.java`.

This recipe also assumes that you can compile and run the code within your preferred development environment. The result of all the changes we are making is in `src/com/lingpipe/cookbook/chapter3/ClassifierBuilderFinal.java`.

> Big caveat in this recipe—we are using a tiny dataset to make basic points on classifier building. The sentiment classifier we are trying to build would benefit from 10 times more data.

How to do it...

We start with a collection of tweets that have been deduplicated and are the result of the *Train a little, learn a little – active learning* recipe that will follow this recipe. The starting point of the recipe is the following code:

```java
public static void main(String[] args) throws IOException {
  String trainingFile = args.length > 0 ? args[0]
    : "data/activeLearningCompleted/"
    + "disneySentimentDedupe.2.csv";
  int numFolds = 10;
  List<String[]> training
    = Util.readAnnotatedCsvRemoveHeader(new File(trainingFile));
  String[] categories = Util.getCategories(training);
  XValidatingObjectCorpus<Classified<CharSequence>> corpus
    = Util.loadXValCorpus(training,numFolds);
  TokenizerFactory tokenizerFactory
    = IndoEuropeanTokenizerFactory.INSTANCE;
  PrintWriter progressWriter = new PrintWriter(System.out,true);
```

Advanced Classifiers

```
Reporter reporter = Reporters.writer(progressWriter);
reporter.setLevel(LogLevel.WARN);
boolean storeInputs = true;
ConditionalClassifierEvaluator<CharSequence> evaluator
    = new ConditionalClassifierEvaluator<CharSequence>(null,
    categories, storeInputs);
corpus.setNumFolds(0);
LogisticRegressionClassifier<CharSequence> classifier = Util.
trainLogReg(corpus, tokenizerFactory, progressWriter);
evaluator.setClassifier(classifier);
System.out.println("!!!Testing on training!!!");
Util.printConfusionMatrix(evaluator.confusionMatrix());
}
```

Sanity check – test on training data

The first thing to do is get the system running and test on training data:

1. We have left a print statement that advertises what is going on:

   ```
   System.out.println("!!!Testing on training!!!");
   corpus.visitTrain(evaluator);
   ```

2. Running `ClassifierBuilder` will yield the following:

   ```
   !!!Testing on training!!!
   reference\response
          \p,n,o,
         p 67,0,3,
         n 0,30,2,
         o 2,1,106,
   ```

3. The preceding confusion matrix is nearly a perfect system output, which validates that the system is basically working. This is the best system output you will ever see; never let management see it, or they will think this level of performance is either doable or done.

Establishing a baseline with cross validation and metrics

Now it is time to see what is really going on.

1. If you have small data, then set the number of folds to `10` so that 90 percent of the data is used for training. If you have large data or are in a huge rush, then set it to `2`:

   ```
   static int NUM_FOLDS = 10;
   ```

2. Comment out or remove the training on test code:

   ```
   //System.out.println("!!!Testing on training!!!");
   //corpus.visitTrain(evaluator);
   ```

3. Plumb in a cross-validation loop or just uncomment the loop in our source:

   ```
   corpus.setNumFolds(numFolds);
   for (int i = 0; i < numFolds; ++i) {
     corpus.setFold(i);
     LogisticRegressionClassifier<CharSequence> classifier
         = Util.trainLogReg(corpus, tokenizerFactory,
     progressWriter);
     evaluator.setClassifier(classifier);
     corpus.visitTest(evaluator);
   }
   ```

4. Recompiling and running the code will give us the following output:

   ```
   reference\response
           \p,n,o,
         p 45,8,17,
         n 16,13,3,
         o 18,3,88,
   ```

5. The classifier labels mean `p=positiveSentiment`, `n=negativeSentiment`, and `o=other`, which covered other languages or neutral sentiment. The first row of the confusion matrix indicates that the system gets 45 true positives, 8 false negatives that it thinks are `n`, and 17 false negatives that it thinks are `o`:

   ```
   reference\response
           \p,n,o,
       p 45,8,17,
   ```

6. To get the false positives for `p`, we need to look at the first column. We see that the system thought that 16 `n` annotations were `p` and 18 `o` annotations were `p`:

   ```
   reference\response
           \p,
         p 45
         n 16
         o 18
   ```

> The confusion matrix is the most honest and straightforward way to view/present results for classifiers. Performance metrics such as precision, recall, F-measure, and accuracy are all very slippery and often used incorrectly. When presenting results, always have a confusion matrix handy, because if we are in the audience or someone like us is, we will ask to see it.

7. Perform the same analysis for the other categories, and you will have an assessment of system performance.

Picking a single metric to optimize against

Perform the following steps:

1. While the confusion matrix establishes the overall performance of the classifier, it is too complex to use as a tuning guide. You don't want to have to digest the entire matrix every time you adjust a feature. You and your team must agree on a single number that, if it goes up, the system is considered better. The following metrics apply to binary classifiers; if there are more than two categories, then you will have to sum them somehow. Some common metrics we see are:

   - **F-measure**: F-measure is an attempt to reward reductions in false negatives and false positives at the same time:

     $$F\text{-measure} = 2*TP / (2*TP + FP + FN)$$

     It is mainly an academic measure to declare that one system is better than another. It sees little use in industry.

   - **Recall at 90 percent precision**: The goal is to provide as much coverage as possible while not making more than 10 percent false positives. This is when the system does not want to look bad very often; this applies to spell checkers, question answering systems, and sentiment dashboards.

   - **Precision at 99.9 percent recall**: This metric supports *needle in the haystack* or *needle in the needle stack* kind of problems. The user cannot afford to miss anything and is willing to perhaps slog through lots of false positives as long as they don't miss anything. The system is better if the false positive rate is lower. Use cases are intelligence analysts and medical researchers.

2. Determining this metric comes from a mixture of business/research needs, technical capability, available resources, and willpower. If a customer wants a high recall and high-precision system, our first question will be to ask what the budget is per document. If it is high enough, we will suggest hiring experts to correct system output, which is the best combination of what computers are good at (exhaustiveness) and what humans are good at (discrimination). Generally, budgets don't support this, so the balancing act begins, but we have deployed systems in just this way.

3. For this recipe, we will pick a maximizing recall at 50-percent precision for `n` (negative), because we want to be sure to intercept any negative sentiment and will tolerate false positives. We will choose 65 percent for a `p` positive, because the good news is less actionable, and who doesn't love Disney? We don't care what `o` (other performance) is—the category exists for linguistic reasons, independent of the business use. This metric a likely metric for a sentiment-dashboard application. This means that the system will produce one mistake for every two guesses of a negative-sentiment category and 13 out of 20 for positive sentiment.

Implementing the evaluation metric

Perform the following steps to implement the evaluation metric:

1. We will start with reporting precision/recall for all categories with the `Util.printPrecRecall` method after printing out the confusion matrix:

    ```
    Util.printConfusionMatrix(evaluator.confusionMatrix());
    Util.printPrecRecall(evaluator);
    ```

2. The output will now look like this:

    ```
    reference\response
              \p,n,o,
            p 45,8,17,
            n 16,13,3,
            o 18,3,88,
    Category p
    Recall: 0.64
    Prec  : 0.57
    Category n
    Recall: 0.41
    Prec  : 0.54
    Category o
    Recall: 0.81
    Prec  : 0.81
    ```

3. The precision for n exceeds our objective of .5–since we want to maximize recall at .5, we can make a few more mistakes before we get to the limit. You can refer to the *Thresholding classifiers* recipe to find out how to do this.

4. The precision for p is 57 percent, and this is too low for our business objective. Logistic regression classifiers, however, provide a conditional probability that might allow us to meet the precision needs just by paying attention to the probability. Adding the following line of code will allow us to see the results sorted by conditional probability:

    ```
    Util.printPRcurve(evaluator);
    ```

5. The preceding line of code starts by getting a `ScoredPrecisionRecallEvaluation` value from the evaluator. A double-scored curve (`[][]`) is gotten from that object with the Boolean interpolate set to false, because we want the curve to be unadulterated. You can look at the Javadoc for what is going on. Then, we will use a print route from the same class to print out the curve. The output will look like this:

    ```
    reference\response
              \p,n,o,
            p 45,8,17,
            n 16,13,3,
            o 18,3,88,
    ```

Advanced Classifiers

```
Category p
Recall: 0.64
Prec  : 0.57
Category n
Recall: 0.41
Prec  : 0.54
Category o
Recall: 0.81
Prec  : 0.81
PR Curve for Category: p
  PRECI.    RECALL    SCORE
0.000000 0.000000 0.988542
0.500000 0.014286 0.979390
0.666667 0.028571 0.975054
0.750000 0.042857 0.967286
0.600000 0.042857 0.953539
0.666667 0.057143 0.942158
0.571429 0.057143 0.927563
0.625000 0.071429 0.922381
0.555556 0.071429 0.902579
0.600000 0.085714 0.901597
0.636364 0.100000 0.895898
0.666667 0.114286 0.891566
0.615385 0.114286 0.888831
0.642857 0.128571 0.884803
0.666667 0.142857 0.877658
0.687500 0.157143 0.874135
0.647059 0.157143 0.874016
0.611111 0.157143 0.871183
0.631579 0.171429 0.858999
0.650000 0.185714 0.849296
0.619048 0.185714 0.845691
0.636364 0.200000 0.810079
0.652174 0.214286 0.807661
0.666667 0.228571 0.807339
0.640000 0.228571 0.799474
0.653846 0.242857 0.753967
0.666667 0.257143 0.753169
0.678571 0.271429 0.751815
0.655172 0.271429 0.747515
0.633333 0.271429 0.745660
0.645161 0.285714 0.744455
0.656250 0.300000 0.738555
0.636364 0.300000 0.736310
```

```
0.647059 0.314286 0.705090
0.628571 0.314286 0.694125
```

6. The output is sorted by score, in the third column, which in this case, happens to be a conditional probability, so the max value is 1 and min value is 0. Notice that the recall grows as correct cases are found (the second line), and it never goes down. However, when a mistake is made like in the fourth line, precision drops to `.6`, because 3 out of 5 cases are correct so far. The precision actually goes below `.65` before the last value is found—in bold, with a score of `.73`.

7. So, without any tuning, we can report that we can achieve 30 percent recall for `p` at our accepted precision limit of 65 percent. This requires that we threshold the classifier at `.73` for the category, which means if we reject scores less than `.73` for `p`, some comments are:

   - We got lucky. Usually, the first classifier runs do not reveal an immediately useful threshold with default values.
   - Logistic regression classifiers have a very nice property that they provide; they also provide conditional probability estimates for thresholding. Not all classifiers have this property—language models and naïve Bayes classifiers tend to push scores towards 0 or 1, making thresholding difficult.
   - As the training data is highly biased (this is from the *Train a little, learn a little – active learning* recipe that follows), we cannot trust this threshold. The classifier will have to be pointed at fresh data to set the threshold. Refer to the *Thresholding classifiers* recipe to see how this is done.
   - This classifier has seen very little data and will not be a good candidate for deployment despite the supporting evaluation. We would be more comfortable with at least 1,000 tweets from a diverse set of dates.

At this point in the process, we either accept the results by verifying that the performance is acceptable on fresh data or turn to improving the classifier by techniques covered by other recipes in this chapter. The final step of the recipe is to train up the classifier on all training data and write to disk:

```
corpus.setNumFolds(0);
LogisticRegressionClassifier<CharSequence> classifier
    = Util.trainLogReg(corpus, tokenizerFactory, progressWriter);
AbstractExternalizable.compileTo(classifier,
    new File("models/ClassifierBuilder.LogisticRegression"));
```

We will use the resulting model in the *Thresholding classifiers* recipe.

Advanced Classifiers

Linguistic tuning

This recipe will address issues around tuning the classifier by paying attention to the mistakes made by the system and making linguistic adjustments by adjusting parameters and features. We will continue with the sentiment use case from the previous recipe and work with the same data. We will start with a fresh class at `src/com/lingpipe/cookbook/chapter3/LinguisticTuning.java`.

We have very little data. In the real world, we will insist on more training data—at least 100 of the smallest category, negative, are needed with a natural distribution of positives and others.

How to do it...

We will jump right in and run some data—the default is `data/activeLearningCompleted/disneySentimentDedupe.2.csv`, but you can specify your own file in the command line.

1. Run the following in your command line or IDE equivalent:

   ```
   java -cp lingpipe-cookbook.1.0.jar:lib/lingpipe-4.1.0.jar:lib/opencsv-2.4.jar com.lingpipe.cookbook.chapter3.LinguisticTuning
   ```

2. For each fold, the features for the classifier will be printed. The output will look like the following for each category (just the first few features for each):

   ```
   Training on fold 0
   #####################Printing features for category p NON_ZERO
   ?: 0.52
   !: 0.41
   love: 0.37
   can: 0.36
   my: 0.36
   is: 0.34
   in: 0.29
   of: 0.28
   I: 0.28
   old: 0.26
   me: 0.25
   My: 0.25
   ?: 0.25
   wait: 0.24
   ?: 0.23
   an: 0.22
   out: 0.22
   movie: 0.22
   ?: 0.21
   movies: 0.21
   ```

114

```
shirt: 0.21
t: 0.20
again: 0.20
Princess: 0.19
i: 0.19
…
######################Printing features for category o NON_ZERO
:: 0.69
/: 0.52
*&^INTERCEPT%$^&**: 0.48
@: 0.41
*: 0.36
(: 0.35
…
######################Printing features for category n ZERO
```

3. Starting with the n category, note that there are no features. It is a property of logistic regression that one category's features are all set to 0.0, and the remaining n-1 category's features are offset accordingly. This cannot be controlled, which is a bit annoying because the n or negative category can be the focus of linguistic tuning given how badly it performs in the example. Not to be deterred, we will move on.

4. Note that the output is intended to make it easy to use a find command to locate feature output in the extensive reporting output. To find a feature search on category <feature name> to see if there is a nonzeroed report, search on category <feature name> NON_ZERO.

5. We are looking for a few things in these features. First of all, there are apparently odd features that are getting big scores—the output is ranked in positive to negative for the category. What we want to look for is some signal in the feature weights—so love makes sense as being associated with a positive sentiment. Looking at features like this can really be surprising and counter intuitive. The uppercase I and lowercase i suggest that the text should be downcased. We will make this change and see if it helps. Our current performance is:

```
Category p
Recall: 0.64
Prec  : 0.57
```

6. The code change is to add a LowerCaseTokenizerFactory item to the current IndoEuropeanTokenizerFactory class:

```
TokenizerFactory tokenizerFactory
   = IndoEuropeanTokenizerFactory.INSTANCE;
tokenizerFactory = new   LowerCaseTokenizerFactory(tokenizerFactory);
```

Advanced Classifiers

7. Run the code, and we will pick up some precision and recall:

   ```
   Category p
   Recall: 0.69
   Prec   : 0.59
   ```

8. The features are as follows:

   ```
   Training on fold 0
   #######################Printing features for category p NON_ZERO
   ?: 0.53
   my: 0.49
   love: 0.43
   can: 0.41
   !: 0.39
   i: 0.35
   is: 0.31
   of: 0.28
   wait: 0.27
   old: 0.25
   ▯: 0.24
   an: 0.22
   ```

9. What's the next move? The `minFeature` count is very low at `1`. Let's raise it to `2` and see what happens:

   ```
   Category p
   Recall: 0.67
   Prec   : 0.58
   ```

10. This hurts performance by a few cases, so we will return to `1`. However, experience dictates that the minimum count goes up as more data is found to prevent overfitting.

11. It is time for the secret sauce—change the tokenizer to `NGramTokenizer`; it tends to work better than standard tokenizers—we are now rolling with the following code:

    ```
    TokenizerFactory tokenizerFactory
       = new NGramTokenizerFactory(2,4);
    tokenizerFactory
    = new LowerCaseTokenizerFactory(tokenizerFactory);
    ```

12. This worked. We will pick up a few more cases:

    ```
    Category p
    Recall: 0.71
    Prec   : 0.64
    ```

13. However, the features are now pretty hard to scan:

    ```
    #########Printing features for category p NON_ZERO
    ea: 0.20
    !!: 0.20
    ov: 0.17
    n : 0.16
    ne: 0.15
     ?: 0.14
    al: 0.13
    rs: 0.13
    ca: 0.13
    ! : 0.13
    ol: 0.13
    lo: 0.13
     m: 0.13
    re : 0.12
    so: 0.12
    i : 0.12
    f : 0.12
     lov: 0.12
    ```

14. We have found over the course of time that character ngrams are the features of choice for text-classifier problems. They seem to nearly always help, and they helped here. Look at the features, and you can recover that `love` is still contributing but in little bits, such as `lov`, `ov`, and `lo`.

15. There is another approach that deserves a mention, which is some of the tokens produced by `IndoEuropeanTokenizerFactory` are most likely useless, and they are just confusing the issue. Using a stop-word list, focusing on more useful tokenization, and perhaps applying a stemmer such as the Porter stemmer might work as well. This has been the traditional approach to these kinds of problems—we have never had that much luck with them.

16. It is a good time to check on the performance of the n category; we have been messing about with the model and should check it:

    ```
    Category n
    Recall: 0.41
    Prec  : 0.72
    ```

17. The output also reports false positives for p and n. We really don't care much about o, except when it shows up as a false positive for the other categories:

    ```
    False Positives for p
    *<category> is truth category

    I was really excited for Disney next week until I just read that
    it's "New Jersey" week. #noooooooooo
    ```

Advanced Classifiers

```
     p 0.8434727204351016
     o 0.08488521562829848
    *n 0.07164206393660003
```

"Why worry? If you've done the best you can, worrying won't make anything better." ~Walt Disney
```
     p 0.4791823543407749
    *o 0.3278392260935065
     n 0.19297841956571868
```

18. Looking at false positives, we can suggest changes to feature extraction. Recognizing quotes from ~Walt Disney might help the classifier with IS_DISNEY_QUOTE.

19. Also, looking at errors can point out errors in annotation, one can argue that the following is actually positive:

Cant sleep so im watching.. Beverley Hills Chihuahua.. Yep thats right, I'm watching a Disney film about talking dogs.. FML!!!
```
     p 0.6045997587907997
     o 0.3113342571409484
    *n 0.08406598406825164
```

At this point, the system is somewhat tuned. The configuration should be saved someplace and the next steps are considered. They include the following:

- Declare victory and deploy. Before deploying, be sure to test on novel data using all training data to train. The *Thresholding classifiers* recipe will be very useful.

- Annotate more data. Use the active learning framework in the following recipe to help identify high-confidence cases that are wrong and right. This will likely help more than anything with performance, especially with low-count data such as the kind we have been working with.

- Looking at the epoch report, the system is never converging on its own. Increase the limit to 10,000 and see if this helps things.

The result of our tuning efforts was to improve the performance from:

```
reference\response
           \p,n,o,
         p 45,8,17,
         n 16,13,3,
         o 18,3,88;
Category p
Recall: 0.64
Prec  : 0.57
Category n
Recall: 0.41
Prec  : 0.54
Category o
```

```
Recall: 0.81
Prec  : 0.81
```
To the following:
```
reference\response
          \p,n,o,
         p 50,3,17,
         n 14,13,5,
         o 14,2,93,
Category p
Recall: 0.71
Prec  : 0.64
Category n
Recall: 0.41
Prec  : 0.72
Category o
Recall: 0.85
Prec  : 0.81
```

This is not a bad uptick in performance in exchange for looking at some data and thinking a bit about how to help the classifier do its job.

Thresholding classifiers

Logistic regression classifiers are often deployed with a threshold rather than the provided `classifier.bestCategory()` method. This method picks the category with the highest conditional probability, which, in a 3-way classifier, can be just above one-third. This recipe will show you how to adjust classifier performance by explicitly controlling how the best category is determined.

This recipe will consider the 3-way case with the p, n, and o labels and work with the classifier produced by the *Classifier-building life cycle* recipe earlier in this chapter. The cross-validation evaluation produced is:

```
Category p
Recall: 0.64
Prec  : 0.57
Category n
Recall: 0.41
Prec  : 0.54
Category o
Recall: 0.81
Prec  : 0.81
```

We will run novel data to set thresholds.

Advanced Classifiers

How to do it...

Our business use case is that recall be maximized while `p` has .65 precision and `n` has .5 precision for reasons discussed in the *Classifier-building life cycle* recipe. The `o` category is not important in this case. The `p` category appears to be too low with .57, and the `n` category can increase recall as the precision is above .5.

1. We cannot use the cross-validation results unless care has been taken to produce a proper distribution of annotations—the active learning approach used tends to not produce such distributions. Even with a good distribution, the fact that the classifier was likely tuned with cross validation means that it is most likely overfit to that dataset because tuning decisions were made to maximize performance of those sets that are not general to new data.

2. We need to point the trained classifier at new data—the rule of thumb is to train by hook or crook but always threshold on fresh. We followed the *Getting data from the Twitter API* recipe in *Chapter 1*, *Simple Classifiers*, and downloaded new data from Twitter with the `disney` query. Nearly a year has passed since our initial search, so the tweets are most likely non-overlapping. The resulting 1,500 tweets were put into `data/freshDisney.csv`.

3. Ensure that you don't run this code on data that is not backed up. The I/O is simple rather than robust. The code overwrites the input file.

4. Invoke `RunClassifier` on your IDE or run the following command:

   ```
   java -cp lingpipe-cookbook.1.0.jar:lib/lingpipe-4.1.0.jar:lib/opencsv-2.4.jar com.lingpipe.cookbook.chapter3/RunClassifier
   ```

   ```
   Data is: data/freshDisney.csv model is: models/ClassifierBuilder.LogisticRegression
   ```

   ```
   No annotations found, not evaluating
   ```

   ```
   writing scored output to data/freshDisney.csv
   ```

5. Open the `.csv` file in your favorite spreadsheet. All tweets should have a score and a guessed category in the standard annotation format.

6. Sort with the primary sort on the `GUESS` column in the ascending or descending order and then sort on `SCORE` in the descending order. The result should be each category with higher scores descending to lower scores. This is how we set up top-down annotations.

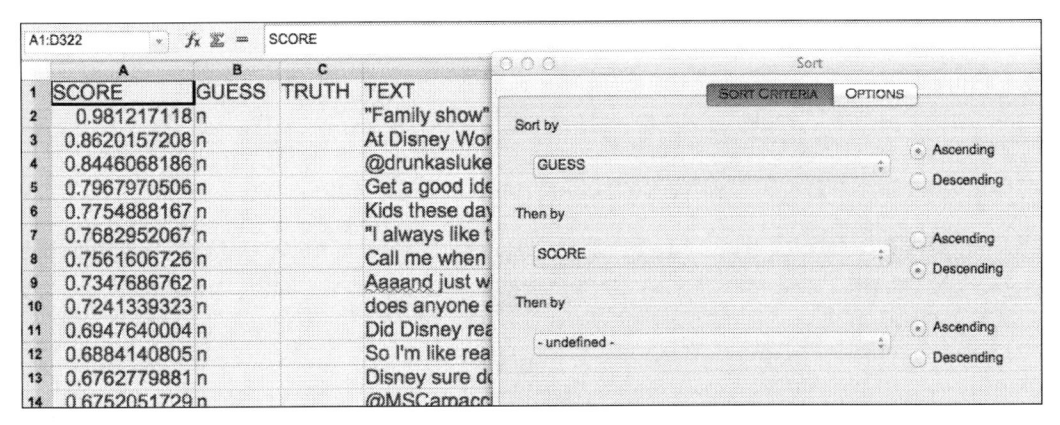

Setting up sort of data for top-down annotation. All categories are grouped together, and a descending sort of the score is established.

7. For the categories that you care about, in this case, p and n, annotate truth from the highest score to the lowest scores until it is likely that the precision goal has been broached. For example, annotate n until you either run out of n guesses, or you have enough mistakes that you have .50 precision. A mistake is when the truth is o or p. Do the same for p until you have a precision of .65, or you run out of number of p. For our canned example, we have put the annotations in data/freshDisneyAnnotated.csv.

8. Run the following command or the equivalent in your IDE (note that we are supplying the input file and not using the default):

```
java -cp lingpipe-cookbook.1.0.jar:lib/lingpipe-4.1.0.jar:lib/
opencsv-2.4.jar com.lingpipe.cookbook.chapter3/RunClassifier data/
freshDisneyAnnotated.csv
```

9. This command will produce the following output:

```
Data is: data/freshDisneyAnnotated.csv model is: models/
ClassifierBuilder.LogisticRegression
reference\response
         \p,n,o,
       p 141,25,0,
       n 39,37,0,
       o 51,28,0,
Category p
Recall: 0.85
Prec   : 0.61
Category n
Recall: 0.49
Prec   : 0.41
```

Advanced Classifiers

```
Category o
Recall: 0.00
Prec  : NaN
```

10. First off, this is a surprisingly good system performance for our minimally trained classifier. p is very close to the target precision of .65 without thresholding, and coverage is not bad: it is found as 141 true positives out of 1,500 tweets. As we have not annotated all 1,500 tweets, we cannot truly say what the recall of the classifier is, so the term is overloaded in common use. The n category is not doing as well, but it is still pretty good. Our annotation did no annotations for the o category, so the system column is all zeros.

11. Next, we will look at the precision/recall/score curve for thresholding guidance:

```
PR Curve for Category: p
  PRECI.    RECALL     SCORE
1.000000  0.006024  0.976872
1.000000  0.012048  0.965248
1.000000  0.018072  0.958461
1.000000  0.024096  0.947749
1.000000  0.030120  0.938152
1.000000  0.036145  0.930893
1.000000  0.042169  0.928653
...
0.829268  0.204819  0.781308
0.833333  0.210843  0.777209
0.837209  0.216867  0.776252
0.840909  0.222892  0.771287
0.822222  0.222892  0.766425
0.804348  0.222892  0.766132
0.808511  0.228916  0.764918
0.791667  0.228916  0.761848
0.795918  0.234940  0.758419
0.780000  0.234940  0.755753
0.784314  0.240964  0.755314
...
0.649746  0.771084  0.531612
0.651515  0.777108  0.529871
0.653266  0.783133  0.529396
0.650000  0.783133  0.528988
0.651741  0.789157  0.526603
0.648515  0.789157  0.526153
0.650246  0.795181  0.525740
0.651961  0.801205  0.525636
0.648780  0.801205  0.524874
```

12. Most values have been elided to save space in the preceding output. We saw that the point at which the classifier passes `.65` precision has a score of `.525`. This means that we can expect 65-percent precision if we threshold at `.525` with a bunch of caveats:

    - This is a single-point sample without a confidence estimate. There are more sophisticated ways to arrive at a threshold that is beyond the scope of this recipe.
    - Time is a big contributor to variance in performance.
    - 10-percent variance in performance for well-developed classifiers is not uncommon in practice. Factor this into performance requirements.

13. The nice thing about the preceding curve is that it looks like we can provide a `.80` precision classifier at a threshold of `.76` with nearly 30 percent of the coverage of the `.65` precision classifier if we decide that higher precision is called for.

14. The `n` case has a curve that looks like this:

    ```
    PR Curve for Category: n
       PRECI.    RECALL     SCORE
    1.000000  0.013158  0.981217
    0.500000  0.013158  0.862016
    0.666667  0.026316  0.844607
    0.500000  0.026316  0.796797
    0.600000  0.039474  0.775489
    0.500000  0.039474  0.768295
    ...
    0.468750  0.197368  0.571442
    0.454545  0.197368  0.571117
    0.470588  0.210526  0.567976
    0.485714  0.223684  0.563354
    0.500000  0.236842  0.552538
    0.486486  0.236842  0.549950
    0.500000  0.250000  0.549910
    0.487179  0.250000  0.547843
    0.475000  0.250000  0.540650
    0.463415  0.250000  0.529589
    ```

15. It looks like a threshold of `.549` gets the job done. The rest of the recipe will show how you to set up the thresholded classifier now that we have the thresholds.

The code behind `RunClassifier.java` offers nothing of novelty in the context of this chapter, so it is left to you to work through.

Advanced Classifiers

How it works...

The goal is to create a classifier that will assign p to a tweet if it scores above .525 for that category and n if scores above .549 for that category; otherwise, it gets o. Wrong.... management saw the p/r curve and now insists that p must be 80-percent precise, which means that the threshold will be .76.

The solution is very simple. If a score for p is below .76, then it will be rescored down to 0.0. Likewise, if a score for n is below .54, then it will be rescored down to 0.0. The effect of this is that o will be the best category for all below-threshold cases, because .75 p can at best be .25 n, which remains below the n threshold, and .53 n can at most be .47 p, which is below that category's threshold. This can get complicated if all categories are thresholded, or the thresholds are low.

Stepping back, we are taking a conditional classifier where all the category scores must sum to 1 and breaking this contract, because we will take any estimate for p that is below .76 and bust it down to 0.0. It is a similar story for n. The resulting classifier will now have to be `ScoredClassifier` because this is the next most specific contract in the LingPipe API that we can uphold.

The code for this class is in `src/com/lingpipe/cookbook/chapter3/ThresholdedClassifier`. At the top level, we have the class, relevant member variable, and constructor:

```
public class ThresholdedClassifier<E> implements
ScoredClassifier<E> {

  ConditionalClassifier<E> mNonThresholdedClassifier;

  public ThresholdedClassifier (ConditionalClassifier<E>
classifier) {
    mNonThresholdedClassifier = classifier;
  }
```

Next, we will implement the only required method for `ScoredClassification`, and this is where the magic happens:

```
@Override
public ScoredClassification classify(E input) {
  ConditionalClassification classification
    = mNonThresholdedClassifier.classify(input);
  List<ScoredObject<String>> scores
    = new ArrayList<ScoredObject<String>>();
  for (int i = 0; i < classification.size(); ++i) {
    String category = classification.category(i);
    Double score = classification.score(i);
      if (category.equals("p") && score < .76d) {
```

```
            score = 0.0;
        }
        if (category.equals("n") && score < .549d) {
            score = 0.0;
        }
        ScoredObject<String> scored
          = new ScoredObject<String>(category,score);
        scores.add(scored);
    }
    ScoredClassification thresholded
        = ScoredClassification.create(scores);
    return thresholded;
}
```

The complicated bit about scored classifications is that scores have to be assigned to all categories even if the score is `0.0`. The mapping from a conditional classification, where all scores sum to `1.0`, does not lend itself to a generic solution, which is why the preceding ad hoc implementation is used.

There is also a `main()` method that spools up the relevant bits for `ThresholdedClassifier` and applies them:

```
java -cp lingpipe-cookbook.1.0.jar:lib/lingpipe-4.1.0.jar:lib/opencsv-
2.4.jar com.lingpipe.cookbook.chapter3/ThresholdedClassifier data/
freshDisneyAnnotated.csv
Data is: data/freshDisneyAnnotated.csv model is: models/
ClassifierBuilder.LogisticRegression


reference\response
          \p,n,o,
        p 38,14,114,
        n 5,19,52,
        o 5,5,69,
Category p
Recall: 0.23
Prec  : 0.79
Category n
Recall: 0.25
Prec  : 0.50
Category o
Recall: 0.87
Prec  : 0.29
```

Advanced Classifiers

The thresholds are doing exactly as designed; `p` is `.79` precision, which is close enough for consulting, and `n` is spot on. The source for the `main()` method should be straightforward given the context of this chapter.

That's it. Almost never do we release a nonthresholded classifier, and best practices require that thresholds be set on held-out data, preferably from later epochs than the training data. Logistic regression is quite robust against skewed training data, but the ointment that cleanses the flaws of skewed data is novel data annotated top down to precision objectives. Yes, it is possible to threshold with cross validation, but it suffers from the flaws that overfit due to tuning, and you would screw up your distributions. Recall-oriented objectives are another matter.

Train a little, learn a little – active learning

Active learning is a super power to quickly develop classifiers. It has saved many a project in the real world. The idea is very simple and can be broken down as follows:

1. Assemble a packet of raw data that is way bigger than you can annotate manually.
2. Annotate an embarrassingly small amount of the raw data.
3. Train the classifier on the embarrassingly small amount of training data.
4. Run the trained classifier on all the data.
5. Put the classifier output into a `.csv` file ranked by confidence of best category.
6. Correct another embarrassingly small amount of data, starting with the most confident classifications.
7. Evaluate the performance.
8. Repeat the process until the performance is acceptable, or you run out of data.
9. If successful, be sure to evaluate/threshold on fresh data, because the active learning process can introduce biases to the evaluation.

What this process does is help the classifier distinguish the cases where it is making higher confidence mistakes and correcting it. It also works as a classification-driven search engine of sorts, where the positive training data functions as the query, and the remaining data functions as the index being searched.

Traditionally, active learning is applied to the near-miss cases where the classifier is unsure of the correct class. In this case, the corrections will apply to the lowest confidence classifications. We came up with the high-confidence correction approach because we were under pressure to increase precision with a thresholded classifier that only accepted high-confidence decisions.

Getting ready

What is going on here is that we are using the classifier to find more data that looks like what it knows about. For problems where the target classes are rare in the unannotated data, it can very quickly help the system identify more examples of the class. For example, in a binary-classification task with marginal probability of 1 percent for the target class in the raw data, this is almost certainly the way to go. You cannot ask annotators to reliably mark a 1-in-100 phenomenon over time. While this is the right way to do it, the end result is that it will not be done because of the effort involved.

Like most cheats, shortcuts, and super powers, the question to ask is what is the price paid. In the duality of precision and recall, recall suffers with this approach. This is because the approach biases annotation towards known cases. Cases that have very different wording are unlikely to be found, so coverage can suffer.

How to do it...

Let's get started with active learning:

1. Collect some training data in our `.csv` format from *Chapter 1*, *Simple Classifiers*, or use our example data in `data/activeLearning/disneyDedupe.0.csv`. Our data builds on the Disney tweets from *Chapter 1*, *Simple Classifiers*. Sentiment is a good candidate for active learning, because it benefits from quality training data and creating quality training data can be difficult. Use the `.csv` file format from the Twitter search downloader if you are using your own data.

2. Run the `.csv` deduplication routine from the *Eliminate near duplicates with Jaccard distance* recipe of *Chapter 1*, *Simple Classifiers* to get rid of near-duplicate tweets. We have already done this with our example data. We went from 1,500 tweets to 1,343.

3. If you have your own data, annotate around 25 examples in the TRUTH column according to the standard annotation:
    - p stands for positive sentiment
    - n stands for negative sentiment
    - o stands for other, which means that no sentiment is expressed, or the tweet is not in English
    - Be sure to get a few examples of each category

Advanced Classifiers

Our example data is already annotated for this step. If you are using your own data, be sure to use the format of the first file (that has the `0.csv` format), with no other . in the path.

	A	B	C	
1	SCORE	GUESS	TRUTH	TEXT
2			p	When all else fails #Disney
3			o	昨日の幸せな気持ちのまま今日はLANDにいっちゃうよ♡はあ、幸せ♡笑
4			p	Best part of having a neice now is having an excuse to relive all the old Disney movies #TheAristocat
5			p	I can't wait for Disney though
6			o	request now "let's get tricky" by @bellathorne and @ROSHON on @radiodisney!!! just call 1-877-870
7			o	100均のDisneyが可愛いよ ฅ~(/_;)ฅ帰る前に買っていこう。そしてプリンセスって、ラブちゃんが
8			p	I fully love the Disney Channel I do not care 🐭
9			o	@greenath_ t'as de la chance d'aller a Disney putain j'y ai jamais été moi.
10			p	AHH! What a talent! Love ya girl! @ShoshanaBean in Disney-Style Spell Block Tango! http://t.co/rmp
11			o	Prefiro gastar uma baba de dinheiro pra ir pra cancun doq pra Disney por exemplo
12			o	@meeelp mas que venha um filhinho mais fofo que o próprio pai, com covinha e amando a Disney k
13			p	"@rpdavlin: I want to go to a college in California so I can go to Disney Land whenever I want"
14			n	Cant sleep so im watching.. Beverley Hills Chihuahua.. Yep thats right, I'm watching a disney film abo
15			o	なんか、Twitterアップデートしたらさ…(^◇^;)
16			n	Miley isn't Hannah anymore, Demi isn't Sonny anymore, Selena isn't Alex anymore. Disney isn't Disn
17			o	ES INSUPERABLE DISNEY !! QUIERO VOLVER:(
18			o	Creo q fue lo peor q pude hacer mirar los videos de disney
19			o	Malisimos los nuevos dibujitos de disney, nickelodeon, cartoon, etc, no me gustannn
20			o	@Hukaaaa_disney ネオマウスという役で出てきてました（笑）聞いた瞬間マジフィニアスでした（笑
21			p	@FernandaAbarca_ how did you become an artist for Dream Works. I wanna do that for Disney!
22			n	Disney channel should have played "Mom's got a date with a vampire"
23			n	Some imagination, huh? #fantasmic #studios # glowwiththeshow #disney #disneynerd #disneyaddict.
24			o	@SolDominguez14 TE CONTE QUE SE ME PERDIERON CON LAS FOTOS DE DISNEY
25			o	@HedyHAMIDI au quartier pas a Disney moi
26			p	for Christmas break im going to Disney for 4 days then Naples (Florida) for 4 days and then south bea

Examples of tweets annotated. Note that all categories have examples.

4. Run the following command. Do not do this on your own annotated data without backing up the file. Our I/O routine is written for simplicity, not robustness. You have been warned:

   ```
   java -cp lingpipe-cookbook.1.0.jar:lib/lingpipe-4.1.0.jar:lib/
   opencsv-2.4.jar: com.lingpipe.cookbook.chapter3.ActiveLearner
   ```

5. Pointed at the supplied annotated data, this will print the following to the console with a final suggestion:

   ```
   reference\response
           \p,n,o,
            p 7,0,1,
            n 1,0,3,
            o 2,0,11,
   Category p
   Recall: 0.88
   Prec   : 0.70
   Category n
   Recall: 0.00
   Prec   : NaN
   Category o
   Recall: 0.85
   ```

```
Prec     : 0.73
Writing to file: data/activeLearning/disneySentimentDedupe.1.csv
Done, now go annotate and save with same file name
```

6. This recipe will show you how to make it better, mainly by making it bigger in smart ways. Let's see where we stand:

    - The data has been annotated a bit for three categories
    - Of 1,343 tweets, there have been 25 annotated, 13 of which are `o`, which we don't particularly care about given the use case, but they still are important because they are not `p` or `n`
    - This is not nearly enough annotated data to build a reliable classifier with, but we can use it to help annotate more data
    - The last line encourages more annotation and the name of a file to annotate

7. The precision and recall are reported for each category, that is, the result of cross validation over the training data. There is also a confusion matrix. At this point, we are not expecting very good performance, but `p` and `o` are doing quite well. The `n` category is not doing well at all.

    Next, fire up a spreadsheet, and import and view the indicated `.csv` file using a UTF-8 encoding. OpenOffice shows us the following:

	A	B	C	
1	SCORE	GUESS	TRUTH	TEXT
2	0.9471994630938778	o		@d_emi_1212 難しい！！(>_<) ショーバレなんかは、キャラに手振りたいし、踊りた
3	0.9419607496390708	o		@disney_pon ぽんちゃん、おはよう(^o^)こちらもいいお天気。昨日との温度差に(*_*)
4	0.9283149831857811	o		"@NurAyna_Diba: Disney ;) @anis_afiqah98 @syazafarzana3 @Miss_Thila @syeera
5	0.9203851660685771	o		@Izumisama ビックリしました(^◇^;)私も最終日にエントランスミッキーで参加しま
6	0.9117371628174511	o		@treasure_r4 めっちゃいやされます(((o(*´▽`*)o)))♡♡
7	0.8841236593075998	o		昨日は、初仮装してきた☆ でも、雨だったから動きにくかったけど(^_^;) ハピネスも
8	0.8757195792668063	o		@EntradaNumerada me lo han pasao, que estaba en el facebook de disney, pero no
9	0.8736601934881794	o		Me ha gustado un vídeo de @YouTube (http://t.co/xyKWyqkxpr - Personajes de disne
10	0.8724205561977442	p		I love October! I love all the Halloween movies on Disney. (: I don't think I'll ever get to
11	0.8722812346687495	o		なながくれた～(((o(*´▽`*)o))) lou若い～！ あ～ほんとありがとう大好き♡ http://t.co/O
12	0.8698138209417262	o		おはようございます('O ')♡ 今日から文化祭準備！ 頑張るぞーん(((o(*´▽`*)o)))
13	0.8641146493342046	o	p	AHH! What a talent! Love ya girl! @ShoshanaBean in Disney-Style Spell Block Tango
14	0.8579036427200295	o		"@_____LB: "@CallmeJroc: "@_____LB: What channel is TNT on Comcast?"I thin
15	0.8576209822092565	o		@z_103hr しおりんありがと(;_;)♡ これからもよろしくね(^o^)/ はやくDisney行こう

Initial output of the active learning approach

8. Reading from the left-hand side to the right-hand side, we will see the `SCORE` column, which reflects the classifier's confidence; its most likely category, shown in the `GUESS` column, is correct. The next column is the `TRUTH` class as determined by a human. The last `TEXT` column is the tweet being classified.

Advanced Classifiers

9. All 1,343 tweets have been classified in one of two ways:

    ❑ If the tweet had an annotation, that is, an entry in the TRUTH column, then the annotation was made when the tweet was in the test fold of a 10-fold cross validation. Line 13 is just such a case. In this case, the classification was o, but the truth was p, so it would be a false negative for p.

    ❑ If the tweet was not annotated, that is, no entry in the TRUTH column, then it was classified using all the available training data. All other examples in the shown spreadsheet are handled this way. They don't inform the evaluation at all. We will annotate these tweets to help improve classifier performance.

10. Next, we will annotate high-confidence tweets irrespective of category, as shown in the following screenshot:

	A	B	C	
1	SCORE	GUESS	TRUTH	TEXT
2	0.9471994630938778	o	o	@d_emi_1212 難しい！！(>_<)ショーバレなんかは、キャラに手振りたい
3	0.9419607496390708	o	o	@disney_pon ぽんちゃん、おはよう(^o^)こちらもいいお天気。昨日との温
4	0.9283149831857811	o	o	"@NurAyna_Diba: Disney ;) @anis_afiqah98 @syazafarzana3 @Miss_Th
5	0.9203851660685771	o	o	@Izumisama ビックリしました(^◇^;)私も最終日にエントランスミッキー
6	0.9117371628174511	o	o	@treasure_r4 めっちゃいやされます(((o(*ﾟ▽ﾟ*)o)))♡♡♡
7	0.8841236593075998	o	o	昨日は、初仮装してきた☆ でも、雨だったから動きにくかったけど(^_^;)
8	0.8757195792668063	o	o	@EntradaNumerada me lo han pasao, que estaba en el facebook de disn
9	0.8736601934881794	o	o	Me ha gustado un vídeo de @YouTube (http://t.co/xyKWyqkxpr - Personaj
10	0.8724205561977442	p	p	I love October! I love all the Halloween movies on Disney. (: I don't think I'l
11	0.8722812346687495	o	o	ななかくれた~(((o(*ﾟ▽ﾟ*)o))) lou若い~！ あ~ほんとありがとう大好き♡
12	0.8698138209417262	o	o	おはようございます('O ')♪ 今日から文化祭準備！ 頑張るぞ~(((o(*ﾟ▽ﾟ
13	0.8641146493342046	o	p	AHH! What a talent! Love ya girl! @ShoshanaBean in Disney-Style Spell B
14	0.8579036427200295	o	o	"@____LB: "@CallmeJroc: "@____LB: What channel is TNT on Com
15	0.8576209822092565	o	o	@z_103hr しおりんありがと(; ;)♪ これからもよろしくね(ˆoˆ)♥ はやくD
16	0.8542441393721144	o	o	@tobimori_disney 最初、ナタリー姉さんを厳選してたのですが…マリー姉
17	0.8485044944794032	p	p	Omg this lady came up to me & she told me that I'm beautiful & I wanted t
18	0.8483696756024185	o	o	@nachiyoooooo ありがとう~！！！(*^o^*)ごめんね…！着いたら地蔵交代
19	0.8472430644312434	o	o	@sa_disney_ki じゃあ何聞いてるのって言われたらちゃんと答える (ˆ O
20	0.8462310752023967	o		@ANfxxx え…宮田さんの悪役…!？聴いてみたいです//////// あと先ほどの

Corrected output for active learning output. Note the dominance of the o category.

11. Annotating down to line 19, we will notice that most of the tweets are o and are dominating the process. There are only three p and no n. We need to get some n annotations.

12. We can focus on likely candidate n annotations by selecting the entire sheet, except for the headers, and sorting by column **B** or GUESS. Scrolling to the n guesses, we should see the highest confidence examples. In the following screenshot, we have annotated all the n guesses because the category needs data. Our annotations are in data/activeLearningCompleted/disneySentimentDedupe.1.csv. If you want to exactly duplicate the recipe, you will have to copy this file to the activeLearning directory.

	A	B	C	
1	SCORE	GUESS	TRUTH	TEXT
2	0.7703571400075279	n	n	Stay High. #mickeymouse #mickey #disney #drawing #draw #graffiti #art #skillz #high
3	0.6179962361514403	n	p	Donald is a joy to draw :) #sketch #donald #disney #kingdomhearts #draw #drawing #
4	0.5991773762077569	n	o	The #buffalo is watching you #disney #disneyworld #magickingdom #wishes #mickey
5	0.5817997687434362	n	o	#happyhalloween#disney#zombies#pirate#japan#makeup http://t.co/ZJaMWMWnI6
6	0.5713388940277104	n	p	What's your #favoritefairytaleprincess? #OnceUponATime #OnceWonderland #Disney
7	0.5483527336780735	n	o	More East Coast #fantasmic #wdw #dhs #florida #disney http://t.co/vbQjh0VzTV
8	0.5273008556659156	n	o	Hoy tenía el #Woody'sMode #ToyStory #Disney #son #instapic #Happy http://t.co/xK2
9	0.5267176567154189	n	o	Am I the only one who has seen the Mickey's Nutcracker? #disney #mickey #nutcrack
10	0.5261349424313857	n	p	Milk & cookies and dumbo ♥ #bigkid #missedthis #disney #cadbury #malk http://t.co/s
11	0.5142050312904649	n	p	These disney songs at campus candy > #cinderella #aladdin #awholenewworld #inne
12	0.5011808358524934	n	o	I've never seen a human this close before. Oh... he's very handsome, isn't he? #Littlel
13	0.497765755803829	n	o	Finished product. #mickey #disney #pumpkin #family http://t.co/tnfRA1oqFf
14	0.4936319509041913	n	o	Parent Trap was right, Oreos and peanut butter are the bomb #amazing #supersnack
15	0.49267706505085745	n	o	I just entered to win a #LeSportSac #ItsASmallWorld bag from http://t.co/FRcZLOjmbr
16	0.4894013180786297	n	o	#Ratatouille BY ME #art #pixar #drawing #Paris #Disney #instavideo @ Saltde
17	0.48421603087720827	n	p	My Disney Blu-ray collection continues to grow! #disney #bluray #movies #monsters #
18	0.4840113274689928	n	p	#rafiki #lionking #disney #bitchdontkillmyvibe Lol love this. There is no one out there t
19	0.483219491957155	n	p	My Babysitter is a Vampire <3 #Love #Disney #NeverTooOld #Perfection #Popcorn #T
20	0.47129503081075874	n	o	#Shopping #Sewing #5: Crayola Color Wonder Disney Preschool Coloring Pad: Crayo
21	0.470168053626517	n	p	Who wishes they were eating a #wildernesslodge #wildernesssalad right now? #disne
22	0.4635340209179496	n	o	Mi sueño era ir a disney, cosa que ya lo hice :D haora mi sueño es ir a Europa :D #Es
23	0.4611524197316742	n	n	Our boyfriends are better than these princes, but maybe not as animated ;) http://t.co/
24	0.4505007354069556	n	o	#Disney: MY LIFE ME, #Playhouse: PICCOLO GRANDE TIMMY, #Rai4: MONGA, #R
25	0.4276291517303308	n	o	our @danielle_bunday's pumpkin creation #theLionKing #prideRock #simba #disney h

Annotations sorted by category with very few n or negative categories.

13. Scrolling to the p guesses, we annotated a bunch as well.

	A	B	C	
949	0.8724205561977442	p	p	I love October! I love all the Halloween movies on Disney. (: I don't think I'll ever get to
950	0.8485044944794032	p	p	Omg this lady came up to me & she told me that I'm beautiful & I wanted to be on Disi
951	0.8310584005730502	p	p	All the seniors scored I the last game of the season.....this feels like the end of a Disn
952	0.7965840744832615	p	p	Holy crap I want to go back to Disney so damn bad I can't stand it #disneycrew
953	0.7958127325812825	p	p	I mean I could write a speech and an essay, or I could sing Disney songs. I think the c
954	0.7891010786490208	p	n	I feel bad for kids that have to grow up watching the new Disney and Nickelodeon sho
955	0.7883925341519806	p	p	Who's more excited than their 4 yr old to go to Disney??? This girl!!!!!
956	0.7717185818498742	p	p	I need to find someone to go with me to Disney on ice again. Kaitlin and I are going o
957	0.7712570586117128	p	o	I hope you will forgive me @JosephMorgan for not watching The Originals tonight but
958	0.7661168825901645	p	n	I hate all the shows that are on Disney channel now so much. They make me want to
959	0.7528778351867063	p	p	That speaker made me want to be an Imagineer, but I'm not into engineering and I ca
960	0.743508993345372	p	p	My dear Disney friends. I can't just pick one of you. I love you all so much! Happy #na
961	0.7362033673515557	p	n	The Kardashians rented a Disney park for the day& had it closed down to the public fo
962	0.7320019124025289	p	n	Oh! And one day I'll get to meet @blizzardfox and take him to Disney land and preten
963	0.7312837337891654	p	n	I need two people to be Selena and Demi for Halloween so we can be the x stars of D
964	0.7300676805695224	p	o	@amylouisej4 NFL was brilliant, so much cheap American beer. I'm going to get to a g
965	0.7279650119184519	p	p	"@rpdavlin: I want to go to a college in California so I can go to Disney Land wheneve
966	0.7251422293969907	p	n	Next time I become overly emotional @ school, I'm going to start singing Disney song
967	0.7246156359194971	p	p	I always get excited knowing I'm going to Disney it's like can we just fast fwd please!!!
968	0.7237282570730921	p	o	Giveaway Time! Those who get the chance to go to Disney are fortunate to do so. Tri
969	0.7234869546564598	p	n	I wish my kids would have the opportunity to watch the Disney movies I did as a kid
970	0.7174808233919484	p	p	One of my lifetime goals is to collect all of Disney's and Pixar's animated movies. I wa
971	0.7038309765050552	p	o	I love breaking my toe 3 days before I go to Disney...
972	0.7035828185939226	p	n	In another life I'd like to come back having the job of poorly singing kids jingles for Dis
973	0.7016215010019654	p	o	As a child I was offered an acting job for Disney, but I turned this enormous opportunit

Positive labels with corrections and surprising number of negatives

14. There are eight negative cases that we found in the p guesses mixed in with lots of p and some o annotations.

Advanced Classifiers

15. We will save the file without changing the filename and run the same program as we did earlier:

    ```
    java -cp lingpipe-cookbook.1.0.jar:lib/lingpipe-4.1.0.jar:lib/
    opencsv-2.4.jar: com.lingpipe.cookbook.chapter3.ActiveLearner
    ```

16. The output will be as follows:

    ```
    First file: data/activeLearning2/disneySentimentDedupe.0.csv
    Reading from file data/activeLearning2/disneySentimentDedupe.1.csv
    reference\response
              \p,n,o,
             p 17,1,20,
             n 9,1,5,
             o 9,1,51,
    Category p
    Recall: 0.45
    Prec   : 0.49
    Category n
    Recall: 0.07
    Prec   : 0.33
    Category o
    Recall: 0.84
    Prec   : 0.67
    Corpus is: 114
    Writing to file: data/activeLearning2/disneySentimentDedupe.2.csv
    Done, now go annotate and save with same file name
    ```

17. This is a fairly typical output early in the annotation process. Positive `p`, the easy category, is dragging along at 49-percent precision and 45-percent recall. Negative `n` is even worse. Undaunted, we will do another round of annotation on the output file indicating focus on `n` guesses to help that category improve performance. We will save and rerun the file:

    ```
    First file:  data/activeLearning2/disneySentimentDedupe.0.csv
    Reading from file data/activeLearning2/disneySentimentDedupe.2.csv
    reference\response
              \p,n,o,
             p 45,8,17,
             n 16,13,3,
             o 18,3,88,
    Category p
    Recall: 0.64
    Prec   : 0.57
    Category n
    Recall: 0.41
    Prec   : 0.54
    ```

```
       Category o
         Recall: 0.81
         Prec   : 0.81
```

18. This last round of annotation got us over the edge (remember to copy over our annotation from `activeLearningCompleted/disneySentimentDedupe.2.csv` if you are mirroring the recipe exactly). We annotated high-confidence examples from both p and n, adding nearly 100 examples. The first best annotation for n is above 50-percent precision with 41-percent recall. We assume that there will be a tunable threshold that meets our 80-percent requirement for p and declares victory in 211 moves, which is much less than the total 1,343 annotations.

19. That's it. This is a real-world example and the first example we have tried for the book, so the data is not cooked. The approach tends to work, although no promises; some data resists even the most focused efforts of a well-equipped computational linguist.

20. Be sure to store the final `.csv` file some place safe. It would be a shame to lose all that directed annotation.

21. Before releasing this classifier we would want to run the classifier, which trains on all annotated data, on new text to verify performance and set thresholds. This annotation process introduces biases over the data that will not be reflected in the real world. In particular, we have biased annotation for n and p and added o as we saw them. This is not the actual distribution.

How it works...

This recipe has some subtlety because of the simultaneous evaluation and creation of ranked output for annotation. The code starts with constructs that should be familiar to you:

```
public static void main(String[] args) throws IOException {
  String fileName = args.length > 0 ? args[0]
    : "data/activeLearning/disneySentimentDedupe.0.csv";
  System.out.println("First file:  " + fileName);
  String latestFile = getLatestEpochFile(fileName);
```

The `getLatestEpochFile` method looks for the highest numbered file that ends with `csv`, shares the root with the filename, and returns it. On no account will we use this routine for anything serious. The method is standard Java, so we won't cover it.

Advanced Classifiers

Once we have the latest file, we will do some reporting, read it in our standard `.csv` annotated files, and load a cross-validating corpus. All these routines are explained elsewhere in locations specified in the `Util` source. Finally, we will get the categories that were found in the `.csv` annotated file:

```
List<String[]> data
   = Util.readCsvRemoveHeader(new File(latestFile));
int numFolds = 10;
XValidatingObjectCorpus<Classified<CharSequence>> corpus
   = Util.loadXValCorpus(data,numFolds);
String[] categories = Util.getCategoryArray(corpus);
```

Next, we will configure some standard logistic-regression-training parameters and create the evaluator for cross-fold evaluation. Note that the Boolean for `storeInputs` is `true`, which will facilitate recording results. The *How to train and evaluate with cross validation* recipe in *Chapter 1, Simple Classifiers*, has a complete explanation:

```
PrintWriter progressWriter = new PrintWriter(System.out,true);
boolean storeInputs = true;
ConditionalClassifierEvaluator<CharSequence> evaluator
   = new ConditionalClassifierEvaluator<CharSequence>(null,
categories, storeInputs);
TokenizerFactory tokFactory
   = IndoEuropeanTokenizerFactory.INSTANCE;
```

Then, we will execute standard cross validation:

```
for (int i = 0; i < numFolds; ++i) {
  corpus.setFold(i);
   final LogisticRegressionClassifier<CharSequence> classifier
     = Util.trainLogReg(corpus,tokFactory, progressWriter);
   evaluator.setClassifier(classifier);
   corpus.visitTest(evaluator);
}
```

At the end of cross validation, the evaluator has all the classifications stored in `visitTest()`. Next, we will transfer this data to an accumulator, which creates and stores rows that will be put into the output spreadsheet and redundantly stores the score; this score will be used in a sort to control the order of annotations printed out:

```
final ObjectToDoubleMap<String[]> accumulator
   = new ObjectToDoubleMap<String[]>();
```

Then, we will iterate over each category and create a list of the false negatives and true positives for the category—these are the cases that the truth category is the category label:

```
for (String category : categories) {
List<Classified<CharSequence>> inCategory
   = evaluator.truePositives(category);
inCategory.addAll(evaluator.falseNegatives(category));
```

Next, all the in-category test cases are used to create rows for the accumulator:

```
for (Classified<CharSequence> testCase : inCategory) {
   CharSequence text = testCase.getObject();
   ConditionalClassification classification
      = (ConditionalClassification)                testCase.
getClassification();
   double score = classification.conditionalProbability(0);
   String[] xFoldRow = new String[Util.TEXT_OFFSET + 1];
   xFoldRow[Util.SCORE] = String.valueOf(score);
   xFoldRow[Util.GUESSED_CLASS] = classification.bestCategory();
   xFoldRow[Util.ANNOTATION_OFFSET] = category;
   xFoldRow[Util.TEXT_OFFSET] = text.toString();
   accumulator.set(xFoldRow,score);
}
```

Next, the code will print out some standard evaluator output:

```
Util.printConfusionMatrix(evaluator.confusionMatrix());
Util.printPrecRecall(evaluator);
```

All the mentioned steps only apply to annotated data. We will now turn to getting best category and scores for all the unannotated data in the .csv file.

First, we will set the number of folds on the cross-validating corpus to 0, which means that vistTrain() will visit the entire corpus of annotations—unannotated data is not contained in the corpus. The logistic regression classifier is trained in the usual way:

```
corpus.setNumFolds(0);
final LogisticRegressionClassifier<CharSequence> classifier
   = Util.trainLogReg(corpus,tokFactory,progressWriter);
```

Armed with a classifier, the code iterates over all the data items, one row at a time. The first step is to check for an annotation. If the value is not the empty string, then the data was in the aforementioned corpus and used as training data so that the loop skips to the next row:

```
for (String[] csvData : data) {
   if (!csvData[Util.ANNOTATION_OFFSET].equals("")) {
    continue;
   }
   ScoredClassification classification = classifier.
classify(csvData[Util.TEXT_OFFSET]);
   csvData[Util.GUESSED_CLASS] = classification.category(0);
   double estimate = classification.score(0);
   csvData[Util.SCORE] = String.valueOf(estimate);
   accumulator.set(csvData,estimate);
}
```

Advanced Classifiers

If the row is unannotated, then the score and `bestCategory()` method is added at the appropriate points, and the row is added to the accumulator with the score.

The rest of the code increments the index of the filename and writes out the accumulator data with a bit of reporting:

```
String outfile = incrementFileName(latestFile);
Util.writeCsvAddHeader(accumulator.keysOrderedByValueList(),
        new File(outfile));
System.out.println("Corpus size: " + corpus.size());
System.out.println("Writing to file: " + outfile);
System.out.println("Done, now go annotate and save with same"
        + " file name");
```

This is how it works. Remember that the biases that can be introduced by this approach invalidate evaluation numbers. Always run on fresh held-out data to get a proper sense of the classifier's performance.

Annotation

One of the most valuable services we provide is teaching our customers how to create gold-standard data, also known as training data. Nearly every successful-driven NLP project we have done has involved a good deal of customer-driven annotation. The quality of the NLP is entirely dependent on the quality of the training data. Creating training data is a fairly straightforward process, but it requires attention to detail and significant resources. From a budget perspective, you can expect to spend as much as the development team on annotation, if not more.

How to do it...

We will use sentiment over tweets as our example, and we will assume a business context, but even academic efforts will have similar dimensions.

1. Get 10 examples of what you expect the system to do. For our example, this means getting 10 tweets that reflect the scope of what the system is expected to do.

2. Make some effort to pick from the range of what you expect as inputs/outputs. Feel free to cherry-pick strong examples, but do not make up examples. Humans are terrible at creating example data. Seriously, don't do it.

3. Annotate these tweets for the expected categories.

4. Have a meeting with all the stakeholders in the annotation. This includes user-experience designers, business folks, developers, and end users. The goal of this meeting is to expose all the relevant parties to what the system will actually do—the system will take the 10 examples and produce the category label. You will be amazed at how much clarity this step establishes. Here are the kinds of clarity:
   - Upstream/downstream users of the classifier will have a clear idea of what they are expected to produce or consume. For example, the system consumes UTF-8-encoded English tweets and produces an ASCII single character of p, n, or u.
   - For a sentiment, people tend to want a severity score, which is very hard to get. You can expect annotation costs to double at least. Is it worth it? A score of confidence can be provided, but that is confidence that the category is correct *not* the severity of the sentiment. This meeting will force the discussion.
   - During this meeting explain that each category will likely need at least 100 examples, if not 500, to do a reasonable job. Also explain that switching domains might require new annotations. NLP is extremely easy for your human colleagues, and as a result, they tend to underestimate what it takes to build systems.
   - Don't neglect to include whoever is paying for all this. I suppose you should not have your parents involved if this is your undergraduate thesis.

5. Write down an annotation standard that explains the intention behind each category. It doesn't need to be very complex, but it needs to exist. The annotation standard should be circulated around the stakeholders. Bonus points if you have one at the mentioned meetings; if so, it will likely be different at the end, but this is fine. An example is:
   - A tweet is positive p if the sentiment is unambiguously positive about Disney. A positive sentiment that applies to a non-Disney tweet is not p but u. An example is the n tweet indicates clearly negative intent towards Disney. Examples include that all other tweets are u.
   - Examples in the annotation standard do the best job of communicating the intent. Humans do a better job with examples rather than descriptions in our experience.

6. Create your collection of unannotated data. The best practice here is for the data to be random from the expected source. This works fine for categories with noticeable prevalence in data, say 10 percent or more, but we have built classifiers that occur at a rate of 1/2,000,000 for question-answering systems. For rare categories, you can use a search engine to help find instances of the category—for example, search for luv to find positive tweets. Alternatively, you can use a classifier trained on a few examples, run it on data, and look at the high-scoring positives—we covered this in the previous recipe.

Advanced Classifiers

7. Recruit at least two annotators to annotate data. The reason we need at least two is that the task has to be shown to be reproducible by humans. If people can't reliably do the task, then you can't expect a computer to do it. This is where we execute some code. Type in the following command in the command line or invoke your annotators in you IDE—this will run with our default files:

```
java -cp lingpipe-cookbook.1.0.jar:lib/lingpipe-
4.1.0.jar:lib/opencsv-2.4.jar com.lingpipe.cookbook.chapter3.
InterAnnotatorAgreement

data/disney_e_n.csv treated as truth

data/disney1_e_n.csv treated as response

Disagreement: n x e for: When all else fails #Disney

Disagreement: e x n for: 昨日の幸せな気持ちのまま今日はLANDにいっ

reference\response
        \e,n,
        e 10,1,
        n 1,9,
Category: e Precision: 0.91, Recall: 0.91
Category: n Precision: 0.90, Recall: 0.90
```

8. The code reports disagreements and prints out a confusion matrix. Precision and recall are useful metrics as well.

How it works...

There is little novel data in the code in `src/com/lingpipe/cookbook/chapter3/InterAnnotatorAgreement.java`. One slight twist is that we used `BaseClassifierEvaluator` to do the evaluation work without a classifier ever being specified—the creation is as follows:

```
BaseClassifierEvaluator<CharSequence> evaluator
    = new BaseClassifierEvaluator<CharSequence>(null,
              categories, storeInputs);
```

The evaluator is populated with classifications directly rather than the usual `Corpus.visitTest()` method, as done elsewhere in the book:

```
evaluator.addClassification(truthCategory,
          responseClassification, text);
```

If the recipe requires further explanation, consult the *Evaluation of classifiers—the confusion matrix* recipe in *Chapter 1, Simple Classifiers*.

There's more...

Annotation is a very complex area that deserves its own book, and fortunately, there is a good one, *Natural Language Annotation for Machine Learning*, *James Pustejovsky and Amber Stubbs*, *O'Reilly Media*. To get annotations done, there is Amazon's Mechanical Turk service as well as companies that specialize in the creation of training data such as CrowdFlower. However, be careful of outsourcing because classifiers are very dependent on the quality of data.

Conflict resolution between annotators is a challenging area. Many errors will be due to attention lapses, but some will persist as legitimate areas of disagreement. Two easy resolution strategies are either to throw out the data or keep both annotations.

4
Tagging Words and Tokens

In this chapter, we will cover the following recipes:

- Interesting phrase detection
- Foreground- or background-driven interesting phrase detection
- Hidden Markov Models (HMM) – part-of-speech
- N-best word tagging
- Confidence-based tagging
- Training word tagging
- Word-tagging evaluation
- Conditional random fields (CRF) for word/token tagging
- Modifying CRFs

Introduction

Words and tokens are the focus of this chapter. The more common extraction technologies, such as named entity recognition, are actually encoded into the concepts presented here, but this will have to wait until *Chapter 5, Finding Spans in Text – Chunking*. We will start easy with finding interesting sets of tokens. Then, we will move on to HMM and finish with one of the most complex components of LingPipe—CRF. As usual, we show you how to evaluate tagging and train your own taggers.

Tagging Words and Tokens

Interesting phrase detection

Imagine that a program can take a bunch of text data and automatically find the interesting parts, where "interesting" means that the word or phrase occurs more often than expected. It has a very nice property—no training data is needed, and it works for any language that we have tokens for. You have seen this most often in tag clouds such as the one in the following figure:

> javadoc models textbook LingPipe 3.9.3 Home Page
> bugs license install sandbox home citations Services
> demos competition contact customers about alias-i
> lingpipe core tutorials

The preceding figure shows a tag cloud generated for the `lingpipe.com` home page. However, be aware that tag clouds are considered to be the "mullets of the Internet" as noted by Jeffery Zeldman in `http://www.zeldman.com/daily/0405d.shtml`, so you will be on shaky ground if you deploy such a feature on a website.

How to do it...

To get the interesting phrases from a small dataset with tweets about Disney, perform the following steps:

1. Fire up the command line and type:

   ```
   java -cp lingpipe-cookbook.1.0.jar:lib/lingpipe-4.1.0.jar:lib/
   opencsv-2.4.jar com.lingpipe.cookbook.chapter4.InterestingPhrases
   ```

2. The program should respond with something like:

   ```
   Score 42768.0 : Crayola Color
   Score 42768.0 : Bing Rewards
   Score 42768.0 : PassPorter Moms
   Score 42768.0 : PRINCESS BATMAN
   Score 42768.0 : Vinylmation NIB
   Score 42768.0 : York City
   Score 42768.0 : eternal damnation
   Score 42768.0 : ncipes azules
   Score 42768.0 : diventare realt
   Score 42768.0 : possono diventare
   ….
   ```

```
Score 42768.0 : Pictures Releases
Score 42768.0 : SPACE MOUNTAIN
Score 42768.0 : DEVANT MOI
Score 42768.0 : QUOI DEVANT
Score 42768.0 : Lindsay Lohan
Score 42768.0 : EPISODE VII
Score 42768.0 : STAR WARS
Score 42768.0 : Indiana Jones
Score 42768.0 : Steve Jobs
Score 42768.0 : Smash Mouth
```

3. You can also supply a `.csv` file in our standard format as an argument to see different data.

The output tends to be tantalizingly useless. Tantalizingly useless means that some useful phrases show up, but with a bunch of less interesting phrases that you will never want in your summary of what is interesting in the data. On the interesting side, we can see `Crayola Color`, `Lindsey Lohan`, `Episode VII`, and so on. On the junk side, we can see `ncipes azules`, `pictures releases`, and so on. There are lots of ways to address the junk output—the obvious first step will be to use a language ID classifier to throw out non-English.

How it works...

Here, we will go through the source in its entirety, broken by explanatory text:

```
package com.lingpipe.cookbook.chapter4;

import java.io.FileReader;
import java.io.IOException;
import java.util.List;
import java.util.SortedSet;
import au.com.bytecode.opencsv.CSVReader;
import com.aliasi.lm.TokenizedLM;
import com.aliasi.tokenizer.IndoEuropeanTokenizerFactory;
import com.aliasi.util.ScoredObject;

public class InterestingPhrases {
  static int TEXT_INDEX = 3;
  public static void main(String[] args) throws IOException {
    String inputCsv = args.length > 0 ? args[0]
      : "data/disney.csv";
```

Tagging Words and Tokens

Here, we see the path, imports, and the `main()` method. Our ternary operator that supplies a default file name or reads from the command line is the last line:

```
List<String[]> lines = Util.readCsv(new File(inputCsv));
int ngramSize = 3;
TokenizedLM languageModel = new
  TokenizedLM(IndoEuropeanTokenizerFactory.INSTANCE,
  ngramSize);
```

After collecting the input data, the first interesting code constructs a tokenized language model which differs in significant ways from the character language models used in *Chapter 1*, *Simple Classifiers*. A tokenized language model operates over tokens created by `TokenizerFactory`, and the `ngram` parameter dictates the number of tokens used instead of the number of characters. A subtlety of `TokenizedLM` is that it can also use character language models to make predictions for tokens it has not seen before. See the *Foreground- or background-driven interesting phrase detection* recipe to understand how this works in practice; don't use the preceding constructor unless there are no unknown tokens when estimating. Also, the relevant Javadoc provides more details on this. In the following code snippet, the language model is trained:

```
for (String [] line: lines) {
   languageModel.train(line[TEXT_INDEX]);
}
```

The next relevant step is the creation of collocations:

```
int phraseLength = 2;
int minCount = 2;
int maxReturned = 100;
SortedSet<ScoredObject<String[]>> collocations =
  languageModel.collocationSet(phraseLength,
  minCount, maxReturned);
```

The parameterization controls the phrase length in tokens; it also sets a minimum count of how often the phrase can be seen and how many phrases to return. We can look at phrases of length 3 as we have a language model that stores 3 grams. Next, we will visit the results:

```
for (ScoredObject<String[]> scoredTokens : collocations) {
   double score = scoredTokens.score();
   StringBuilder sb = new StringBuilder();
   for (String token : scoredTokens.getObject()) {
     sb.append(token + " ");
   }
   System.out.printf("Score %.1f : ", score);
   System.out.println(sb);
}
```

The `SortedSet<ScoredObject<String[]>>` collocation is sorted from a high score to a low score. The intuition behind the score is that a higher score is given when the tokens are seen together more than one would expect, given their singleton frequency in the training data. In other words, phrases are scored depending on how much they vary from the independence assumption based on the tokens. See the Javadoc at `http://alias-i.com/lingpipe/docs/api/com/aliasi/lm/TokenizedLM.html` for the exact definitions—an interesting exercise will be to create your own score and compare it with what is done in LingPipe.

There's more...

Given that this code is close to being usable on a website, it is worth discussing tuning. Tuning is the process of looking at system output and making changes based on the mistakes the system makes. Some changes that we would immediately consider include:

- A language ID classifier that will be handy to filter out non-English texts
- Some thought around how to better tokenize the data
- Varying token lengths to include 3 grams and unigrams in the summary
- Using named entity recognition to highlight proper nouns

Foreground- or background-driven interesting phrase detection

Like the previous recipe, this recipe finds interesting phrases, but it uses another language model to determine what is interesting. Amazon's statistically improbable phrases (**SIP**) work this way. You can get a clear view from their website at `http://www.amazon.com/gp/search-inside/sipshelp.html`:

> "Amazon.com's Statistically Improbable Phrases, or "SIPs", are the most distinctive phrases in the text of books in the Search Inside!™ program. To identify SIPs, our computers scan the text of all books in the Search Inside! program. If they find a phrase that occurs a large number of times in a particular book relative to all Search Inside! books, that phrase is a SIP in that book.
>
> SIPs are not necessarily improbable within a particular book, but they are improbable relative to all books in Search Inside!."

The foreground model will be the book being processed, and the background model will be all the other books in Amazon's Search Inside!™ program. While Amazon has probably introduced tweaks that differ, it is the same basic idea.

Tagging Words and Tokens

Getting ready

There are a few sources of data worth looking at to get interesting phrases with two separate language models. The key is you want the background model to function as the source of expected word/phrase distributions that will help highlight interesting phrases in the foreground model. Some examples include:

- **Time-separated Twitter data**: The examples of time-separated Twitter data are as follows:
    - **Background model**: This refers to a year worth of tweets about Disney World up to yesterday.
    - **Foreground model**: Tweets for today.
    - **Interesting phrases**: What's new in Disney World today on Twitter.

- **Topic-separated Twitter data**: The examples of topic-separated Twitter data are as follows:
    - **Background model**: Tweets about Disneyland
    - **Foreground model**: Tweets about Disney World
    - **Interesting phrases**: What is said about Disney World that is not said about Disneyland

- **Books on very similar topics**: The examples of books on similar topics are as follows:
    - **Background model**: A pile of early sci-fi novels
    - **Foreground model**: Jules Verne's *War of the Worlds*
    - **Interesting phrases**: The unique phrases and concepts of "War of the Worlds"

How to do it...

Here are the steps to run a foreground or background model on tweets about Disneyland versus tweets about Disney World:

1. In the command line, type:

   ```
   java -cp  lingpipe-cookbook.1.0.jar:lib/lingpipe-
   4.1.0.jar:lib/opencsv-2.4.jar com.lingpipe.cookbook.chapter4.
   InterestingPhrasesForegroundBackground
   ```

2. The output will look something like:

   ```
   Score 989.621859 : [sleeping, beauty]
   Score 989.621859 : [california, adventure]
   Score 521.568529 : [winter, dreams]
   Score 367.309361 : [disneyland, resort]
   ```

```
Score 339.429700 : [talking, about]
Score 256.473825 : [disneyland, during]
```

3. The foreground model consists of tweets for the search term, `disneyland`, and the background model consists of tweets for the search term, `disneyworld`.
4. The top tied results are for unique features of California-based Disneyland, namely, the name of the castle, Sleeping Beauty's Castle, and a theme park built in the parking lot of Disneyland, California Adventure.
5. The next bigram is for *Winter Dreams*, which refers to a premier for a film.
6. Overall, not a bad output to distinguish between the tweets of the two resorts.

How it works...

The code is in `src/com/lingpipe/cookbook/chapter4/InterestingPhrasesForegroundBackground.java`. The exposition starts after we loaded the raw `.csv` data for the foreground and background models:

```
TokenizerFactory tokenizerFactory
    = IndoEuropeanTokenizerFactory.INSTANCE;
tokenizerFactory
    = new LowerCaseTokenizerFactory(tokenizerFactory);
int minLength = 5;
tokenizerFactory
    = new LengthFilterTokenizerFactoryPreserveToken(tokenizerFactory,
    minLength);
```

One can be excused for wondering why we dedicated all of *Chapter 2, Finding and Working with Words*, to tokenization, but it turns out that most NLP systems are very sensitive to how the character stream is broken up into words or tokens. In the preceding code snippet, we saw a stack of three tokenizer factories doing useful violence to the character sequence. The first two are covered adequately in *Chapter 2, Finding and Working with Words*, but the third one is a customized factory that bears some examination. The intent behind the `LengthFilterTokenizerFactoryPreserveToken` class is to filter short tokens but at the same time not lose adjacency information. The goal is to take the phrase, "Disney is my favorite resort", and produce tokens (`disney, _234, _235, favorite, resort`), because we don't want short words in our interesting phrases—they tend to sneak past simple statistical models and mess up the output. Please refer to `src/come/lingpipe/cookbook/chapter4/LengthFilterTokenizerFactoryPreserveToken.java` for the source of the third tokenizer. Also, refer to *Chapter 2, Finding and Working with Words* for exposition. Next is the background model:

```
int nGramOrder = 3;
TokenizedLM backgroundLanguageModel = new
TokenizedLM(tokenizerFactory, nGramOrder);
for (String [] line: backgroundData) {
  backgroundLanguageModel.train(line[Util.TEXT_OFFSET]);
}
```

Tagging Words and Tokens

What is being built here is the model that is used to judge the novelty of phrases in the foreground model. Then, we will create and train the foreground model:

```
TokenizedLM foregroundLanguageModel = new TokenizedLM
(tokenizerFactory,nGramOrder);
for (String [] line: foregroundData) {
   foregroundLanguageModel.train(line[Util.TEXT_OFFSET]);
}
```

Next, we will access the `newTermSet()` method from the foreground model. The parameters and `phraseSize` determine how long the token sequences are; `minCount` specifies a minimum number of instances of the phrase to be considered, and `maxReturned` controls how many results to return:

```
int phraseSize = 2;
int minCount = 3;
int maxReturned = 100;
SortedSet<ScoredObject<String[]>> suprisinglyNewPhrases
    = foregroundLanguageModel.newTermSet(phraseSize, minCount,
maxReturned,backgroundLanguageModel);
for (ScoredObject<String[]> scoredTokens : suprisinglyNewPhrases) {
    double score = scoredTokens.score();
    String[] tokens = scoredTokens.getObject();
    System.out.printf("Score %f : ", score);
    System.out.println(java.util.Arrays.asList(tokens));
}
```

The preceding `for` loop prints out the phrases in order of the most surprising phrase to the least surprising one.

The details of what is going on here are beyond the scope of the recipe, but the Javadoc again starts us down the road to enlightenment.

The exact scoring used is the z-score, as defined in `BinomialDistribution.z(double ,int,int)`, with the success probability defined by the n-grams probability estimate in the background model, the number of successes being the count of the n-gram in this model, and the number of trials being the total count in this model.

There's more...

This recipe is the first place where we have faced unknown tokens, which can have very bad properties if not handled correctly. It is easy to see why this is a problem with a maximum likelihood of a token-based language model, which is a fancy name for a language model that provides an estimate of some unseen tokens by multiplying the likelihoods of each token. Each likelihood is the number of times the token was seen in training divided by the number of tokens seen in data. For example, consider training on the following data from *A Connecticut Yankee in King Arthur's Court*:

"The ungentle laws and customs touched upon in this tale are historical, and the episodes which are used to illustrate them are also historical."

This is very little training data, but it is sufficient for the point being made. Consider how we will get an estimate for the phrase, "The ungentle inlaws" using our language model. There are 24 words with "The" occurring once; we will assign a probability of 1/24 to this. We will assign a probability of 1/24 to "ungentle" as well. If we stop here, we can say that the likelihood of "The ungentle" is 1/24 * 1/24. However, the next word is "inlaws", which does not exist in the training data. If this token is assigned a value of 0/24, it will make the likelihood of the entire string 0 (1/24 * 1/24 * 0/20). This means that whenever there is an unseen token for which the estimate is likely going to be zero, this is generally an unhelpful property.

The standard response to this issue is to substitute and approximate the value to stand in for data that has not been seen in training. There are a few approaches to solving this problem:

- Provide a low but non-zero estimate for unknown tokens. This is a very common approach.
- Use character language models with the unknown token. There are provisions for this in the class—refer to the Javadoc.
- There are lots of other approaches and substantial research literature. Good search terms are "back off" and "smoothing".

Hidden Markov Models (HMM) – part-of-speech

This recipe brings in the first hard-core linguistic capability of LingPipe; it refers to the grammatical category for words or **part-of-speech** (**POS**). What are the verbs, nouns, adjectives, and so on in text?

How to do it...

Let's jump right in and drag ourselves back to those awkward middle-school years in English class or our equivalent:

1. As always, head over to your friendly command prompt and type the following:
   ```
   java -cp lingpipe-cookbook.1.0.jar:lib/lingpipe-4.1.0.jar: com.lingpipe.cookbook.chapter9.PosTagger
   ```

2. The system will respond with a prompt to which we will add a Jorge Luis Borges quote:
   ```
   INPUT> Reality is not always probable, or likely.
   ```

Tagging Words and Tokens

3. The system will respond delightfully to this quote with:

   ```
   Reality_nn is_bez not_* always_rb probable_jj ,_, or_cc likely_jj
   ._.
   ```

Appended to each token is _ with a part-of-speech tag; `nn` is noun, `rb` is adverb, and so on. The complete tag set and description of the corpus of the tagger can be found at http://en.wikipedia.org/wiki/Brown_Corpus. Play around with it a bit. POS tagger was one of the first breakthrough machine-learning applications in NLP back in the '90s. You can expect this one to perform at better than 90-percent accuracy, although it might suffer a bit on Twitter data given that that the underlying corpus was collected in 1961.

How it works...

As appropriate for a recipe book, we are not revealing the fundamentals of how part-of-speech taggers are built. There is Javadoc, the Web, and the research literature to help you understand the underlying technology—in the recipe for training an HMM, there is a brief discussion of the underlying HMM. This is about how to use the API as presented:

```java
public static void main(String[] args) throws ClassNotFoundException,
IOException {
  TokenizerFactory tokFactory = IndoEuropeanTokenizerFactory.INSTANCE;
  String hmmModelPath = args.length > 0 ? args[0]
    : "models/pos-en-general-brown.HiddenMarkovModel";
  HiddenMarkovModel hmm = (HiddenMarkovModel) AbstractExternalizable.readObject(new File(hmmModelPath));
  HmmDecoder decoder
    = new HmmDecoder(hmm);
  BufferedReader bufReader
    = new BufferedReader(new InputStreamReader(System.in));
  while (true) {
    System.out.print("\n\nINPUT> ");
    System.out.flush();
    String input = bufReader.readLine();
    Tokenizer tokenizer =
      tokFactory.tokenizer(input.toCharArray(),0,input.length());
    String[] tokens = tokenizer.tokenize();
    List<String> tokenList = Arrays.asList(tokens);
    firstBest(tokenList,decoder);
  }
}
```

The code starts by setting up `TokenizerFactory`, which makes sense because we need to know what the words that are going to get the parts of speech are. The next line reads in a previously trained part-of-speech tagger as `HiddenMarkovModel`. We will not go into too much detail; you just need to know that an HMM assigns a part-of-speech tag for token *n* as a function of the tag assignments that preceded it.

The fact that these tags are not directly observed in data makes the Markov model hidden. Usually, one or two tokens back are looked at. There is a lot going on with HMMs that is worth understanding.

The next line with HmmDecoder decoder wraps the HMM in code to tag provided tokens. Our standard interactive `while` loop is up next with all the interesting bits happening in the firstBest(tokenList,decoder) method at the end. The method is as follows:

```
static void firstBest(List<String> tokenList, HmmDecoder decoder) {
  Tagging<String> tagging = decoder.tag(tokenList);
    System.out.println("\nFIRST BEST");
    for (int i = 0; i < tagging.size(); ++i){
      System.out.print(tagging.token(i) + "_" +
        tagging.tag(i) + " ");
    }
  System.out.println();
}
```

Note the `decoder.tag(tokenList)` call that produces a `Tagging<String>` tagging. Tagging does not have an iterator or useful encapsulation of the tag/token pair, so the information is accessed by incrementing an index i.

N-best word tagging

The certainty-driven nature of Computer Science is not reflected in the vagaries of linguistics where reasonable PhDs can agree or disagree at least until Chomsky's henchmen show up. This recipe uses the same HMM trained in the preceding recipe but provides a ranked list of possible tags for each word.

Where might this be helpful? Imaging a search engine that searched for words and a tag—not necessarily part-of-speech. The search engine can index the word and the top *n*-best tags that will allow a match into a non-first best tag. This can help increase recall.

How to do it...

N-best analyses push the sophistication boundaries of NLP developers. What used to be a singleton is now a ranked list, but it is where the next level of performance occurs. Let's get started by performing the following steps:

1. Put away your copy of *Syntactic Structures* face down and type out the following:
   ```
   java -cp lingpipe-cookbook.1.0.jar:lib/lingpipe-4.1.0.jar: com.lingpipe.cookbook.chapter4.NbestPosTagger
   ```

2. Then, enter the following:

   ```
   INPUT> Colorless green ideas sleep furiously.
   ```

3. It yields the following output:

   ```
   N BEST
   #    JointLogProb         Analysis
   0     -91.141   Colorless_jj   green_jj   ideas_nns   sleep_vb
   furiously_rb    ._.
   1     -93.916   Colorless_jj   green_nn   ideas_nns   sleep_vb
   furiously_rb    ._.
   2     -95.494   Colorless_jj   green_jj   ideas_nns   sleep_rb
   furiously_rb    ._.
   3     -96.266   Colorless_jj   green_jj   ideas_nns   sleep_nn
   furiously_rb    ._.
   4     -98.268   Colorless_jj   green_nn   ideas_nns   sleep_rb
   furiously_rb    ._.
   ```

The output lists from most likely to least likely the estimate of the entire sequence of tokens given the estimates from the HMM. Remember that the joint probabilities are log 2 based. To compare joint probabilities subtract -93.9 from -91.1 for a difference of 2.8. So, the tagger thinks that option 1 is 2 ^ 2.8 = 7 times less likely to occur than option 0. The source of this difference is in assigning green to noun rather than adjective.

How it works...

The code to load the model and command I/O is the same as that of the previous recipe. The difference is in the method used to get and display the tagging:

```
static void nBest(List<String> tokenList, HmmDecoder decoder, int maxNBest) {
  System.out.println("\nN BEST");
  System.out.println("#    JointLogProb         Analysis");
  Iterator<ScoredTagging<String>> nBestIt =
    decoder.tagNBest(tokenList,maxNBest);
  for (int n = 0; nBestIt.hasNext(); ++n) {
    ScoredTagging<String> scoredTagging = nBestIt.next();
    System.out.printf(n + "    %9.3f   ",scoredTagging.score());
    for (int i = 0; i < tokenList.size(); ++i){
      System.out.print(scoredTagging.token(i) + "_" +
        pad(scoredTagging.tag(i),5));
    }
    System.out.println();
  }
}
```

There is nothing much to it other than working out the formatting issues as the taggings are being iterated over.

Confidence-based tagging

There is another view into the tagging probabilities; this reflects the probability assignments at the level of word. The code reflects the underlying `TagLattice` and offers insights into whether the tagger is confident or not.

How to do it...

This recipe will focus the probability estimates on the individual token. Perform the following steps:

1. Type in the following on the command line or IDE equivalent:

   ```
   java -cp lingpipe-cookbook.1.0.jar:lib/lingpipe-4.1.0.jar: com.lingpipe.cookbook.chapter4.ConfidenceBasedTagger
   ```

2. Then, enter the following:

   ```
   INPUT> Colorless green ideas sleep furiously.
   ```

3. It yields the following output:

   ```
   CONFIDENCE
   #    Token          (Prob:Tag)*
   0    Colorless      0.991:jj       0.006:np$      0.002:np
   1    green          0.788:jj       0.208:nn       0.002:nns
   2    ideas          1.000:nns      0.000:rb       0.000:jj
   3    sleep          0.821:vb       0.101:rb       0.070:nn
   4    furiously      1.000:rb       0.000:ql       0.000:jjr
   5    .              1.000:.        0.000:np       0.000:nn
   ```

This view of the data distributes the joint probabilities of the tag and word. We can see that there is .208 chance that `green` should be tagged as `nn` or a singular noun, but the correct analysis is still .788 with adjective `jj`.

How it works...

We are still using the same old HMM from the *Hidden Markov Models (HMM) – part-of-speech* recipe but using different parts of it. The code to read in the model is exactly the same, with a major difference in how we report results. `src/com/lingpipe/cookbook/chapter4/ConfidenceBasedTagger.java` the method:

```
static void confidence(List<String> tokenList, HmmDecoder decoder) {
  System.out.println("\nCONFIDENCE");
  System.out.println("#    Token          (Prob:Tag)*");
```

```
        TagLattice<String> lattice = decoder.tagMarginal(tokenList);

     for (int tokenIndex = 0; tokenIndex < tokenList.size();
        ++tokenIndex) {
        ConditionalClassification tagScores =
          lattice.tokenClassification(tokenIndex);
        System.out.print(pad(Integer.toString(tokenIndex),4));
        System.out.print(pad(tokenList.get(tokenIndex),15));

        for (int i = 0; i < 3; ++i) {
          double conditionalProb = tagScores.score(i);
          String tag = tagScores.category(i);
          System.out.printf(" %9.3f:" + pad(tag,4),conditionalProb);

        }
        System.out.println();
     }
  }
```

The method demonstrates the underlying lattice of tokens to the probabilities explicitly, which is at the heart of the HMM. Change the termination condition on the `for` loop to see more or fewer tags.

Training word tagging

Word tagging gets much more interesting when you can create your own models. The realm of annotating part-of-speech tagging corpora is a bit too much for a mere recipe book—annotation of the part-of-speech data is very difficult because it requires considerable linguistic knowledge to do well. This recipe will directly address the machine-learning component of the HMM-based sentence detector.

As this is a recipe book, we will minimally explain what an HMM is. The token language models that we have been working with do their previous context calculations on some number of words/tokens that precede the current word being estimated. HMMs take into account some length of the previous tags while calculating estimates for the current token's tag. This allows for seemingly disparate neighbors such as of and in to be similar, because they are both prepositions.

In the *Sentence detection* recipe, from *Chapter 5, Finding Spans in Text – Chunking*, a useful but not very flexible sentence detector is based on the `HeuristicSentenceModel` in LingPipe. Rather than mucking about with modifying/extending the `HeuristicSentenceModel`, we will build a machine-learning-based sentence system with the data that we annotate.

How to do it...

The steps here describe how to run the program in `src/com/lingpipe/cookbook/chapter4/HMMTrainer.java`:

1. Either create a new corpus of the sentence-annotated data or use the following default data, which is in `data/connecticut_yankee_EOS.txt`. If you are rolling your own data, simply edit some text with `[` and `]` to mark the sentence boundaries. Our example looks like the following:

   ```
   [The ungentle laws and customs touched upon in this tale are
   historical, and the episodes which are used to illustrate them
   are also historical.] [It is not pretended that these laws and
   customs existed in England in the sixth century; no, it is only
   pretended that inasmuch as they existed in the English and other
   civilizations of far later times, it is safe to consider that it
   is
   no libel upon the sixth century to suppose them to have been in
   practice in that day also.] [One is quite justified in inferring
   that whatever one of these laws or customs was lacking in that
   remote time, its place was competently filled by a worse one.]
   ```

2. Go to the command prompt and run the program with the following command:

   ```
   java -cp lingpipe-cookbook.1.0.jar:lib/lingpipe-4.1.0.jar com.lingpipe.cookbook.chapter4.HmmTrainer
   ```

3. It will give the following output:

   ```
   Training The/BOS ungentle/WORD laws/WORD and/WORD customs/WORD touched/WORD...
   done training, token count: 123
   Enter text followed by new line
   > The cat in the hat. The dog in a bog.
   The/BOS cat/WORD in/WORD the/WORD hat/WORD ./EOS The/BOS dog/WORD in/WORD a/WORD bog/WORD ./EOS
   ```

4. The output is a tokenized text with one of the three tags: BOS for the beginning of a sentence, EOS for the end of a sentence, and WORD for all other tokens.

Tagging Words and Tokens

How it works...

Like many span-based markups, the `span` annotation is translated into a token-level annotation, as shown earlier in the recipe's output. So, the first order of business is to collect the annotated text, set up `TokenizerFactory`, and then call a parsing subroutine to add to `List<Tagging<String>>`:

```
public static void main(String[] args) throws IOException {
  String inputFile = args.length > 0 ? args[0] :
    "data/connecticut_yankee_EOS.txt";
  char[] text = Files.readCharsFromFile(new File(inputFile),
    Strings.UTF8);
  TokenizerFactory tokenizerFactory =
    IndoEuropeanTokenizerFactory.INSTANCE;
  List<Tagging<String>> taggingList = new
    ArrayList<Tagging<String>>();
  addTagging(tokenizerFactory,taggingList,text);
```

The subroutine to parse the preceding format works by first tokenizing the text with `IndoEuropeanTokenizer`, which has the desirable property of treating the `['` and `']` sentence delimiters as separate tokens. It does not check whether the sentence delimiters are well formed—a more robust solution will be needed to do this. The tricky bit is that we want to ignore this markup in the resulting token stream, but we want to use it to have the token following `['` be a `BOS` and the token preceding `']` be `EOS`. Other tokens are just `WORD`. The subroutine builds a parallel `Lists<String>` instance for tags and tokens, which is then used to create `Tagging<String>` and is added to `taggingList`. The tokenization recipes in *Chapter 2, Finding and Working with Words*, cover what is going on with the tokenizer. Have a look at the following code snippet:

```
static void addTagging(TokenizerFactory tokenizerFactory,
List<Tagging<String>> taggingList, char[] text) {
  Tokenizer tokenizer =
    tokenizerFactory.tokenizer(text, 0, text.length);
  List<String> tokens = new ArrayList<String>();
  List<String> tags = new ArrayList<String>();
  boolean bosFound = false;
  for (String token : tokenizer.tokenize()) {
    if (token.equals("[")) {
      bosFound = true;
    }
    else if (token.equals("]")) {
      tags.set(tags.size() - 1,"EOS");
    }
    else {
      tokens.add(token);
      if (bosFound) {
```

```
          tags.add("BOS");
          bosFound = false;
        }
        else {
          tags.add("WORD");
        }
      }
    }
    if (tokens.size() > 0) {
      taggingList.add(new Tagging<String>(tokens,tags));
    }
  }
```

There is a subtlety with the preceding code. The training data is treated as a single tagging—this will emulate what the input will look like when we use the sentence detector on novel data. If more than one document/chapter/paragraph is being used for training, then we will call this subroutine for each block of text.

Returning to the `main()` method, we will set up `ListCorpus` and add the tagging to the training side of the corpus, one tagging at a time. There is an `addTest()` method as well, but this recipe is not concerned with evaluation; if it was, we would most likely use `XValidatingCorpus` anyway:

```
ListCorpus<Tagging<String>> corpus =
  new ListCorpus<Tagging<String>> ();
for (Tagging<String> tagging : taggingList) {
  System.out.println("Training " + tagging);
  corpus.addTrain(tagging);
}
```

Next, we will create `HmmCharLmEstimator`, which is our HMM. Note that there are constructors that allow for customized parameters that affect performance—see the Javadoc. Next, the estimator is trained against the corpus, and `HmmDecoder` is created, which will actually tag tokens, as shown in the following code snippet:

```
HmmCharLmEstimator estimator = new HmmCharLmEstimator();
corpus.visitTrain(estimator);
System.out.println("done training, token count: " +
  estimator.numTrainingTokens());
HmmDecoder decoder = new HmmDecoder(estimator);
```

In the following code snippet, our standard I/O loop gets invoked for some user feedback. Once we get some text from the user, it is tokenized with the same tokenizer we used for training, and the decoder is presented with the resulting tokens.

Tagging Words and Tokens

Note that there is no requirement that the training tokenizer be the same as the production tokenizer, but one must be careful to not tokenize in a radically different way; otherwise, the HMM will not be seeing the tokens it was trained with. The back-off model will then be used, which will likely degrade performance. Have a look at the following code snippet:

```
BufferedReader reader = new BufferedReader(new
InputStreamReader(System.in));
while (true) {
  System.out.print("Enter text followed by new line\n>");
  String evalText = reader.readLine();
  Tokenizer tokenizer = tokenizerFactory.tokenizer(evalText.
toCharArray(),0,evalText.length());
  List<String> evalTokens = Arrays.asList(tokenizer.tokenize());
  Tagging<String> evalTagging = decoder.tag(evalTokens);
  System.out.println(evalTagging);
}
```

That's it! To truly wrap this as a proper sentence detector, we will need to map back to the character offsets in the original text, but this is covered in *Chapter 5*, *Finding Spans in Text – Chunking*. This is sufficient to show how to work with HMMs. A more full-featured approach will make sure that each BOS has a matching EOS and the other way around. The HMM has no such requirement.

There's more...

We have a small and easy-to-use corpus of the part-of-speech tags; this allows us to show how training the HMM for a very different problem works out to be the same thing. It is like our *How to classify a sentiment – simple version* recipe, in *Chapter 1*, *Simple Classifiers*; the only difference between the language ID and sentiment is the training data. We will start with a hard-coded corpus for simplicity—it is in `src/com/lingpipe/cookbook/chapter4/TinyPosCorus.java`:

```
public class TinyPosCorpus extends Corpus<ObjectHandler<Tagging<
String>>> {

  public void visitTrain(ObjectHandler<Tagging<String>> handler) {
    for (String[][] wordsTags : WORDS_TAGSS) {
      String[] words = wordsTags[0];
      String[] tags = wordsTags[1];
      Tagging<String> tagging = new
        Tagging<String>(Arrays.asList(words),
        Arrays.asList(tags));
      handler.handle(tagging);
    }
  }
```

```java
  public void visitTest(ObjectHandler<Tagging<String>> handler) {
    /* no op */
  }

  static final String[][][] WORDS_TAGSS = new String[][][] {
    { { "John", "ran", "." },{ "PN", "IV", "EOS" } },
    { { "Mary", "ran", "." },{ "PN", "IV", "EOS" } },
    { { "John", "jumped", "!" },{ "PN", "IV", "EOS" } },
    { { "The", "dog", "jumped", "!" },{ "DET", "N", "IV", "EOS" } },
    { { "The", "dog", "sat", "." },{ "DET", "N", "IV", "EOS" } },
    { { "Mary", "sat", "!" },{ "PN", "IV", "EOS" } },
    { { "Mary", "likes", "John", "." },{ "PN", "TV", "PN", "EOS" } },
    { { "The", "dog", "likes", "Mary", "." }, { "DET", "N", "TV",
"PN", "EOS" } },
    { { "John", "likes", "the", "dog", "." }, { "PN", "TV", "DET",
"N", "EOS" } },
    { { "The", "dog", "ran", "." },{ "DET", "N", "IV", "EOS", } },
    { { "The", "dog", "ran", "." },{ "DET", "N", "IV", "EOS", } }
  };
```

The corpus manually creates tokens as well as the tags for the tokens in the static `WORDS_TAGS` and creates `Tagging<String>` for each sentence; `Tagging<String>` consists of two aligned `List<String>` instances in this case. The taggings are then sent to the `handle()` method for the `Corpus` superclass. Swapping in this corpus looks like the following:

```java
/*
List<Tagging<String>> taggingList = new
  ArrayList<Tagging<String>>();
addTagging(tokenizerFactory,taggingList,text);
ListCorpus<Tagging<String>> corpus = new
  ListCorpus<Tagging<String>> ();
for (Tagging<String> tagging : taggingList) {
  System.out.println("Training " + tagging);
  corpus.addTrain(tagging);
}
*/

Corpus<ObjectHandler<Tagging<String>>> corpus = new TinyPosCorpus();
HmmCharLmEstimator estimator = new HmmCharLmEstimator();
corpus.visitTrain(estimator);
```

Tagging Words and Tokens

We just commented out the code that loads the corpus with sentence detection and features in `TinyPosCorpus` in its place. It doesn't need data to be added so we will just train the HMM with it. To avoid confusion we have created a separate class `HmmTrainerPos.java`. Running it results in the following:

```
java -cp lingpipe-cookbook.1.0.jar:lib/lingpipe-4.1.0.jar
done training, token count: 42
Enter text followed by new line
> The cat in the hat is back.
The/DET cat/N in/TV the/DET hat/N is/TV back/PN ./EOS
```

The only mistake is that `in` is a transitive verb `TV`. The training data is very small so mistakes are to be expected. Like the difference in language ID and sentiment classification in *Chapter 1, Simple Classifiers*, the HMM is used to learn a very different phenomenon just by changing what the training data is.

Word-tagging evaluation

Word tagging evaluation drives developments in downstream technologies such as named entity detection, which, in turn, drives high-end applications such as coreference. You will notice that much of the evaluation resembles the evaluation from our classifiers except that each tag is evaluated like its own classifier category.

This recipe should serve to get you started on evaluation, but be aware that there is a very good tutorial on tagging evaluation on our website at `http://alias-i.com/lingpipe/demos/tutorial/posTags/read-me.html`; this recipe goes into greater detail on how to best understand tagger performance.

This recipe is short and easy to use, so you have no excuses to not evaluate your tagger.

Getting ready

The following is the class source for our evaluator located at `src/com/lingpipe/cookbook/chapter4/TagEvaluator.java`:

```
public class TagEvaluator {
  public static void main(String[] args) throws
    ClassNotFoundException, IOException {
    HmmDecoder decoder = null;
    boolean storeTokens = true;
    TaggerEvaluator<String> evaluator = new
      TaggerEvaluator<String>(decoder,storeTokens);
    Corpus<ObjectHandler<Tagging<String>>>
      smallCorpus = new TinyPosCorpus();
```

```
    int numFolds = 10;
    XValidatingObjectCorpus<Tagging<String>> xValCorpus =
      new XValidatingObjectCorpus<Tagging<String>>(numFolds);
    smallCorpus.visitCorpus(xValCorpus);
    for (int i = 0; i < numFolds; ++i) {
      xValCorpus.setFold(i);
      HmmCharLmEstimator estimator = new HmmCharLmEstimator();
      xValCorpus.visitTrain(estimator);
      System.out.println("done training " +
         estimator.numTrainingTokens());
      decoder = new HmmDecoder(estimator);
      evaluator.setTagger(decoder);
      xValCorpus.visitTest(evaluator);
    }
    BaseClassifierEvaluator<String> classifierEval =
      evaluator.tokenEval();
    System.out.println(classifierEval);
  }
}
```

How to do it...

We will call out the interesting bits of the preceding code:

1. First off, we will set up `TaggerEvaluator` with a null `HmmDecoder` and `boolean` that controls whether the tokens are stored or not. The `HmmDecoder` object will be set in the cross-validation code later in the code:

   ```
   HmmDecoder decoder = null;
   boolean storeTokens = true;
   TaggerEvaluator<String> evaluator = new TaggerEvaluator<String>
   (decoder,storeTokens);
   ```

2. Next, we will load `TinyPosCorpus` from the previous recipe and use it to populate `XValididatingObjectCorpus`—a pretty neat trick that allows for easy conversion between corpus types. Note that we pick 10 folds—the corpus only has 11 training examples, so we want to maximize the amount of training data per fold. See the *How to train and evaluate with cross validation* recipe in *Chapter 1, Simple Classifiers*, if you are new to this concept. Have a look at the following code snippet:

   ```
   Corpus<ObjectHandler<Tagging<String>>> smallCorpus
      = new TinyPosCorpus();
   int numFolds = 10;
   XValidatingObjectCorpus<Tagging<String>> xValCorpus
      = new XValidatingObjectCorpus<Tagging<String>>(numFolds);
   smallCorpus.visitCorpus(xValCorpus);
   ```

3. The following code snippet is a `for()` loop that iterates over the number of folds. The first half of the loop handles training:

```
for (int i = 0; i < numFolds; ++i) {
  xValCorpus.setFold(i);
  HmmCharLmEstimator estimator = new HmmCharLmEstimator();
  xValCorpus.visitTrain(estimator);
  System.out.println("done training " +
    estimator.numTrainingTokens());
```

4. The rest of the loop first creates a decoder for the HMM, sets the evaluator to use this decoder, and then applies the appropriately configured evaluator to the test portion of the corpus:

```
decoder = new HmmDecoder(estimator);
evaluator.setTagger(decoder);
xValCorpus.visitTest(evaluator);
```

5. The last lines apply after all folds of the corpus have been used for training and testing. Notice that the evaluator is `BaseClassifierEvaluator`! It reports on each tag as a category:

```
BaseClassifierEvaluator<String> classifierEval =
  evaluator.tokenEval();
System.out.println(classifierEval);
```

6. Brace yourself for the torrent of evaluation. The following is a small bit of it, namely, the confusion matrix that you should be familiar with from *Chapter 1, Simple Classifiers*:

```
Confusion Matrix
reference \ response
  ,DET,PN,N,IV,TV,EOS
  DET,4,2,0,0,0,0
  PN,0,7,0,1,0,0
  N,0,0,4,1,1,0
  IV,0,0,0,8,0,0
  TV,0,1,0,0,2,0
  EOS,0,0,0,0,0,11
```

That's it. You have an evaluation setup that is strongly related to the classifier evaluation from *Chapter 1, Simple Classifiers*.

There's more...

There are evaluation classes for the n-best word tagging, that is, `NBestTaggerEvaluator` and `MarginalTaggerEvaluator`, for the confidence ranked. Again, look at the more detailed tutorial on part-of-speech tagging for a quite thorough presentation on evaluation metrics and some example software to help tune the HMM.

Conditional random fields (CRF) for word/token tagging

Conditional random fields (**CRF**) are an extension of the *Logistic regression* recipe in *Chapter 3*, *Advanced Classifiers*, but are applied to word tagging. At the end of *Chapter 1*, *Simple Classifiers*, we discussed various ways to encode a problem into a classification problem. CRFs treat the sequence tagging problem as finding the best category where each category (C) is one of the C*T tag (T) assignments to tokens.

For example, if we have the tokens `The` and `rain` and tag `d` for determiner and `n` for noun, then the set of categories for the CRF classifier are:

- **Category 1**: d d
- **Category 2**: n d
- **Category 3**: n n
- **Category 4**: d d

Various optimizations are applied to keep this combinatoric nightmare computable, but this is the general idea. Crazy, but it works.

Additionally, CRFs allow random features to be used in training in the exact same way that logistic regression does for classification. Additionally, it has data structures optimized for HMM style observations against context. Its use for part-of-speech tagging is not very exciting, because our current HMMs are pretty close to state of the art. Where CRFs really make a difference is in use cases like named entity detection which are covered in *Chapter 5*, *Finding Spans in Text – Chunking*, but we wanted to address the pure CRF implementation before complicating the presentation with a chunking interface.

There is an excellent detailed tutorial on CRFs at `http://alias-i.com/lingpipe/demos/tutorial/crf/read-me.html`; this recipe follows this tutorial fairly closely. You will find more information and proper references there.

How to do it...

All of the technologies we have been presenting up to now were invented in the previous millennium; this is a technology from the new millennium. Perform the following steps:

1. In the command line, type:

   ```
   java -cp lingpipe-cookbook.1.0.jar:lib/lingpipe-4.1.0.jar: com.lingpipe.cookbook.chapter4.CRFTagger
   ```

2. The console continues with the convergence results that should be familiar from the *Logistic regression* recipe of *Chapter 3*, *Advanced Classifiers*, and we will get the standard command prompt:

   ```
   Enter text followed by new line
   >The rain in Spain falls mainly on the plain.
   ```

Tagging Words and Tokens

3. In response to this, we will get some fairly confused output:

   ```
   The/DET rain/N in/TV Spain/PN falls/IV mainly/EOS on/DET the/N
   plain/IV ./EOS
   ```

4. This is an awful output, but the CRF has been trained on 11 sentences. So, let's not be too harsh—particularly since this technology mostly reigns supreme for word tagging and span tagging when given sufficient training data to do its work.

How it works...

Like logistic regression, there are many configuration-related tasks that we need to perform to get this class up and running. This recipe will address the CRF-specific aspects of the code and refer to *the Logistic regression* recipe of *Chapter 3, Advanced Classifiers* for the logistic-regression aspects of the configuration.

Starting at the top of the `main()` method, we will get our corpus, which was discussed in the earlier three recipes:

```
Corpus<ObjectHandler<Tagging<String>>> corpus
  = new TinyPosCorpus();
```

Next up is the feature extractor, which is the actual input to the CRF trainer. The only reason it is final is that an anonymous inner class will access it to demonstrate how feature extraction works in the next recipe:

```
final ChainCrfFeatureExtractor<String> featureExtractor
  = new SimpleCrfFeatureExtractor();
```

We will address how this class works later in the recipe.

The next block of configuration is for the underlying logistic-regression algorithm. Refer to the *logistic regression* recipe in *Chapter 3, Advanced Classifiers*, for more information on this. Have a look at the following code snippet:

```
boolean addIntercept = true;
int minFeatureCount = 1;
boolean cacheFeatures = false;
boolean allowUnseenTransitions = true;
double priorVariance = 4.0;
boolean uninformativeIntercept = true;
RegressionPrior prior = RegressionPrior.gaussian(priorVariance,
  uninformativeIntercept);
int priorBlockSize = 3;
double initialLearningRate = 0.05;
double learningRateDecay = 0.995;
AnnealingSchedule annealingSchedule =
  AnnealingSchedule.exponential(initialLearningRate,
```

```
    learningRateDecay);
double minImprovement = 0.00001;
int minEpochs = 2;
int maxEpochs = 2000;
Reporter reporter = Reporters.stdOut().setLevel(LogLevel.INFO);
```

Next up, the CRF is trained with:

```
System.out.println("\nEstimating");
ChainCrf<String> crf = ChainCrf.estimate(corpus,
  featureExtractor,
  addIntercept,
  minFeatureCount,
  cacheFeatures,
  allowUnseenTransitions,
  prior,
  priorBlockSize,
  annealingSchedule,
  minImprovement,
  minEpochs,
  maxEpochs,
  reporter);
```

The rest of the code just uses the standard I/O loop. Refer to *Chapter 2, Finding and Working with Words*, for how the `tokenizerFactory` works:

```
TokenizerFactory tokenizerFactory = IndoEuropeanTokenizerFactory.INSTANCE;
BufferedReader reader = new BufferedReader(new
  InputStreamReader(System.in));
while (true) {
  System.out.print("Enter text followed by new line\n>");
  System.out.flush();
  String text = reader.readLine();
  Tokenizer tokenizer = tokenizerFactory.tokenizer(
    text.toCharArray(),0,text.length());
  List<String> evalTokens = Arrays.asList(tokenizer.tokenize());
  Tagging<String> evalTagging = crf.tag(evalTokens);
  System.out.println(evalTagging);
```

SimpleCrfFeatureExtractor

Now, we will get to the feature extractor. The provided implementation closely mimics the features of a standard HMM. The class at `com/lingpipe/cookbook/chapter4/SimpleCrfFeatureExtractor.java` starts with:

```
public class SimpleCrfFeatureExtractor implements ChainCrfFeatureExtractor<String> {
```

```
public ChainCrfFeatures<String> extract(List<String> tokens,
  List<String> tags) {
  return new SimpleChainCrfFeatures(tokens,tags);
}
```

The `ChainCrfFeatureExtractor` interface requires an `extract()` method with the tokens and associated tags that get converted into `ChainCrfFeatures<String>` in this case. This is handled by an inner class below `SimpleChainCrfFeatures`; this inner class extends `ChainCrfFeatures` and provides implementations of the abstract methods, `nodeFeatures()` and `edgeFeatures()`:

```
static class SimpleChainCrfFeatures extends ChainCrfFeatures<String> {
```

The following constructor access passes the tokens and tags to the super class, which will do the bookkeeping to support looking up `tags` and `tokens`:

```
public SimpleChainCrfFeatures(List<String> tokens, List<String> tags)
{
  super(tokens,tags);
}
```

The node features are computed as follows:

```
public Map<String,Double> nodeFeatures(int n) {
  ObjectToDoubleMap<String> features =
    new ObjectToDoubleMap<String>();
  features.increment("TOK_" + token(n),1.0);
  return features;
}
```

The tokens are indexed by their position in the sentence. The node feature for the word/token in position n is the `String` value returned by the base class method `token(n)` from `ChainCrfFeatures` with the prefix `TOK_`. The value here is `1.0`. Feature values can be usefully adjusted to values other than 1.0, which is handy for more sophisticated approaches to CRFs, such as using the confidence estimates of other classifiers. Take a look at the following recipe for an example of this.

Like HMMs, there are features that are dependent on other positions in the input—these are called **edge features**. The edge features take two arguments: one for the position that features are being generated for n and k, which will apply to all other positions in the sentence:

```
public Map<String,Double> edgeFeatures(int n, int k) {
  ObjectToDoubleMap<String> features = new
    ObjectToDoubleMap<String>();
  features.increment("TAG_" + tag(k),1.0);
  return features;
}
```

The next recipe will address how to modify feature extraction.

There's more...

There is an extensive research literature referenced in the Javadoc and a much more exhaustive tutorial on the LingPipe website.

Modifying CRFs

The power and appeal of CRFs comes from rich feature extraction—proceed with an evaluation harness that provides feedback on your explorations. This recipe will detail how to create more complex features.

How to do it...

We will not train and run a CRF; instead, we will print out the features. Substitute this feature extractor for the one in the previous recipe to see them at work. Perform the following steps:

1. Go to a command line and type:

   ```
   java -cp lingpipe-cookbook.1.0.jar:lib/lingpipe-4.1.0.jar: com.lingpipe.cookbook.chapter4.ModifiedCrfFeatureExtractor
   ```

2. The feature extractor class outputs for each token in the training data the truth tagging that is being used to learn:

   ```
   -------------------
   Tagging:   John/PN
   ```

3. This reflects the training tagging for the token `John` as determined by `src/com/lingpipe/cookbook/chapter4/TinyPosCorpus.java`.

4. The node features follow the top-three POS tags from our Brown corpus HMM tagger and the `TOK_John` feature:

   ```
   Node Feats:{nps=2.0251355582754984E-4, np=0.9994337160349874, nn=2.994165140854113E-4, TOK_John=1.0}
   ```

5. Next, the edge features are displayed for the other tokens in the sentence, "John ran":

   ```
   Edge Feats:{TOKEN_SHAPE_LET-CAP=1.0, TAG_PN=1.0}
   Edge Feats:{TAG_IV=1.0, TOKEN_SHAPE_LET-CAP=1.0}
   Edge Feats:{TOKEN_SHAPE_LET-CAP=1.0, TAG_EOS=1.0}
   ```

6. The rest of the output are the features for the remaining tokens in the sentence and then the remaining sentences in `TinyPosCorpus`.

Tagging Words and Tokens

How it works...

Our feature extraction code occurs in `src/com/lingpipe/cookbook/chapter4/ModifiedCrfFeatureExtractor.java`. We will start with the `main()` method that loads a corpus, runs the contents past the feature extractor, and prints it out:

```
public static void main(String[] args) throws IOException,
ClassNotFoundException {

  Corpus <ObjectHandler<Tagging<String>>> corpus
    = new TinyPosCorpus();
  final ChainCrfFeatureExtractor<String> featureExtractor
    = new ModifiedCrfFeatureExtractor();
```

We will tee up `TinyPosCorpus` from the previous recipe as our corpus, and then, we will create a feature extractor from the containing class. The use of `final` is required by referencing the variable in the anonymous inner class that follows.

Apologies for the anonymous inner class, but it is just the easiest way to access what is stored in the corpus for various reasons such as copying and printing. In this case, we are just generating and printing the features found for the training data:

```
corpus.visitCorpus(new ObjectHandler<Tagging<String>>() {
  @Override
  public void handle(Tagging<String> tagging) {
    ChainCrfFeatures<String> features =
      featureExtractor.extract(tagging.tokens(), tagging.tags());
```

The corpus contains `Tagging` objects, and they, in turn, contain a `List<String>` of tokens and tags. Then, this information is used to create a `ChainCrfFeatures<String>` object by applying the `featureExtractor.extract()` method to the tokens and tags. This will involve substantial computation, as will be shown.

Next, we will do reporting of the training data with tokens and the expected tagging:

```
for (int i = 0; i < tagging.size(); ++i) {
  System.out.println("---------");
  System.out.println("Tagging:  " + tagging.token(i) + "/" + tagging.tag(i));
```

Then, we will follow with the features that will be used to inform the CRF model in attempting to produce the preceding tagging for nodes:

```
System.out.println("Node Feats:" + features.nodeFeatures(i));
```

Then, the edge features are produced by the following iteration of relative positions to the source node `i`:

```
for (int j = 0; j < tagging.size(); ++j) {
  System.out.println("Edge Feats:"
      + features.edgeFeatures(i, j));
}
```

This is it to print out the features. Now, we will address how the feature extractor is constructed. We assume that you are familiar with the previous recipe. First, the constructor that brings in the Brown corpus POS tagger:

```
HmmDecoder mDecoder;

public ModifiedCrfFeatureExtractor() throws IOException,
  ClassNotFoundException {
  File hmmFile = new File("models/pos-en-general-"
    + "brown.HiddenMarkovModel");
  HiddenMarkovModel hmm
    = (HiddenMarkovModel)
    AbstractExternalizable.readObject(hmmFile);
  mDecoder = new HmmDecoder(hmm);
}
```

The constructor brings in some external resources for feature generation, namely, a POS tagger trained on the Brown corpus. Why involve another POS tagger for a POS tagger? We will call the role of the Brown POS tagger a "feature tagger" to distinguish it from the tagger we are trying to build. A few reasons to use the feature tagger are:

- We are using a stupidly small corpus for training, and a more robust generalized POS feature tagger will help things out. `TinyPosCorpus` is too small for even this benefit, but with a bit more data, the fact that there is a feature `at` that unifies `the`, `a`, and `some` will help the CRF recognize that `some dog` is `'DET' 'N'`, even though it has never seen `some` in training.

- We have had to work with tag sets that are not aligned with POS feature taggers. The CRF can use these observations in the foreign tag set to better reason about the desired tagging. The simplest case is that `at`, from the Brown corpus tag set, maps cleanly onto `DET` in this tag set.

- There can be performance improvements to run multiple taggers that are either trained on different data or use different technologies to tag. The CRF can then, hopefully, recognize contexts where one tagger outperforms others and use this information to guide the analysis. Back in the day, our MUC-6 system featured 3 POS taggers that voted for the best output. Letting the CRF sort it out will be a superior approach.

Tagging Words and Tokens

The guts of feature extraction are accessed with the `extract` method:

```
public ChainCrfFeatures<String>
    extract(List<String> tokens, List<String> tags) {
  return new ModChainCrfFeatures(tokens,tags);
}
```

`ModChainCrfFeatures` is created as an inner class just to keep the proliferation of classes to a minimum, and the enclosing class is very lightweight:

```
class ModChainCrfFeatures extends ChainCrfFeatures<String> {

  TagLattice<String> mBrownTaggingLattice;

  public ModChainCrfFeatures(List<String> tokens,
      List<String> tags) {
    super(tokens,tags);
    mBrownTaggingLattice =
      mDecoder.tagMarginal(tokens);
  }
```

The preceding constructor hands off the tokens and tags to the super class, which handles bookkeeping of this data. Then, the "feature tagger" is applied to the tokens, and the resulting output is assigned to the member variable, `mBrownTaggingLattice`. The code will access the tagging, one token at a time, so it must be computed now.

The feature creation step happens with two methods: `nodeFeatures` and `edgeFeatures`. We will start with a simple enhancement of `edgeFeatures` from the previous recipe:

```
public Map<String,? extends Number> edgeFeatures(int n, int k) {
  ObjectToDoubleMap<String> features = new
    ObjectToDoubleMap<String>();
  features.set("TAG_" + tag(k), 1.0d);
  String category = IndoEuropeanTokenCategorizer
    .CATEGORIZER
    .categorize(token(n));
  features.set("TOKEN_SHAPE_" + category,1.0d);
  return features;
}
```

The code adds a token-shaped feature that generalizes 12 and 34 into 2-DIG and many other generalizations. To CRF, the similarity of 12 and 34 as two-digit numbers is non-existent unless feature extraction says otherwise. Refer to the Javadoc for the complete categorizer output.

Candidate-edge features

CRFs allow random features to be applied, so the question is what features make sense to use. Edge features are used in conjunction with node features, so another issue is whether a feature should be applied to edges or nodes. Edge features will be used to reason about relationships between the current word/token to those around it. Some possible edge features are:

- The token shape (all caps, starts with a number, and so on) of the previous token as done earlier.
- Recognition of iambic pentameter that requires a correct ordering of stressed and unstressed syllables. This will require a syllable-stress tokenizer as well.
- It often happens that text contains one or more languages—this is called code switching. It is a common occurrence in tweets. A reasonable edge feature will be the language of surrounding tokens; this language will better model that the next word is likely to be of the same language as the previous word.

Node features

The node features tend to be where the action is in CRFs, and they can get very rich. The *Named entity recognition using CRFs with better features* recipe in *Chapter 5, Finding Spans in Text – Chunking*, is an example. We will add part-of-speech tags in this recipe to the token feature of the previous recipe:

```
public Map<String,? extends Number> nodeFeatures(int n) {
  ObjectToDoubleMap<String> features
    = new ObjectToDoubleMap<String>();
  features.set("TOK_" + token(n), 1);
  ConditionalClassification tagScores
    = mBrownTaggingLattice.tokenClassification(n);
  for (int i = 0; i < 3; ++ i) {
    double conditionalProb = tagScores.score(i);
    String tag = tagScores.category(i);
    features.increment(tag, conditionalProb);
  }
  return features;
}
```

Then as in the previous recipe the token feature is added with:

```
features.set("TOK_" + token(n), 1);
```

This results in the token string being prepended with `TOK_` and a count of `1`. Note that while `tag(n)` is available in training, it doesn't make sense to use this information, as that is what the CRF is trying to predict.

Tagging Words and Tokens

Next, the top-three tags are extracted from the POS feature tagger and added with the associated conditional probability. CRFs will be able to work with the varying weights productively.

There's more...

When generating new features, some thought about the sparseness of data is worth considering. If dates were likely to be an important feature for the CRF, it would probably not be a good idea to do the standard Computer Science thing and convert the date to milliseconds since Jan 1, 1970 GMT. The reason is that the `MILLI_1000000000` feature will be treated as completely different from `MILLI_1000000001`. There are a few reasons:

- The underlying classifier does not know that the two values are nearly the same
- The classifier does not know that the `MILLI_` prefix is the same—the common prefix is only there for human convenience
- The feature is unlikely to occur in training more than once and will likely be pruned by a minimum feature count

Instead of normalizing dates to milliseconds, consider an abstraction over the dates that will likely have many instances in training data, such as the `has_date` feature that ignores the actual date but notes the existence of the date. If the date is important, then compute all the important information about the date. If it is a day of the week, then map to days of the week. If temporal order matters, then map to coarser measurement that is likely to have many measurements. Generally speaking, CRFs and the underlying logistic regression classifier are robust against ineffective features, so feel free to be creative—you are unlikely to make accuracy worse by adding features.

5
Finding Spans in Text – Chunking

This chapter covers the following recipes:

- Sentence detection
- Evaluation of sentence detection
- Tuning sentence detection
- Marking embedded chunks in a string – sentence chunk example
- Paragraph detection
- Simple noun phrases and verb phrases
- Regular expression-based chunking for NER
- Dictionary-based chunking for NER
- Translating between word tagging and chunks – BIO codec
- HMM-based NER
- Mixing the NER sources
- CRFs for chunking
- NER using CRFs with better features

Finding Spans in Text – Chunking

Introduction

This chapter will tell us how to work with spans of text that typically cover one or more words/tokens. The LingPipe API represents this unit of text as a chunk with corresponding chunkers that produce chunkings. The following is some text with character offsets indicated:

```
LingPipe is an API. It is written in Java.
01234567890123456789012345678901234567890 1
          1         2         3         4
```

Chunking the preceding text into sentences will give us the following output:

```
Sentence start=0, end=18
Sentence start =20, end=41
```

Adding in a chunking for named entities adds entities for LingPipe and Java:

```
Organization start=0, end=7
Organization start=37, end=40
```

We can define the named-entity chunkings with respect to their offsets from the sentences that contain them; this will make no difference to LingPipe, but Java will be:

```
Organization start=17, end=20
```

This is the basic idea of chunks. There are lots of ways to make them.

Sentence detection

Sentences in written text roughly correspond to a spoken utterance. They are the standard unit of processing words in industrial applications. In almost all mature NLP applications, sentence detection is a part of the processing pipeline even in the case of tweets, which can have more than one sentence in the allotted 140 characters.

How to do it...

1. As usual, we will play with some data first. Enter the following command in the console:

   ```
   java -cp lingpipe-cookbook.1.0.jar:lib/lingpipe-4.1.0.jar: com.lingpipe.cookbook.chapter5.SentenceDetection
   ```

2. The program will provide a prompt for your sentence-detection experimentation. A new line / return terminates the text to be analyzed:

   Enter text followed by new line

   >A sentence. Another sentence.

```
SENTENCE 1:
A sentence.
SENTENCE 2:
Another sentence.
```

3. It is worth playing around a bit with different inputs. The following are some examples that explore the properties of the sentence detector. Drop the capitalized beginning of a sentence; this will prevent the detection of the second sentence:

```
>A sentence. another sentence.
SENTENCE 1:
A sentence. another sentence.
```

4. The detector does not require a final period—this is configurable:

```
>A sentence. Another sentence without a final period
SENTENCE 1:A sentence.
SENTENCE 2:Another sentence without a final period
```

5. The detector balances parentheses, which will not allow sentences to break inside parentheses—this is also configurable:

```
>(A sentence. Another sentence.)
SENTENCE 1: (A sentence. Another sentence.)
```

How it works...

This sentence detector is a heuristic-based or rule-based sentence detector. A statistical sentence detector would be a reasonable approach as well. We will get through the entire source to run the detector, and later, we will discuss the modifications:

```
package com.lingpipe.cookbook.chapter5;

import com.aliasi.chunk.Chunk;
import com.aliasi.chunk.Chunker;
import com.aliasi.chunk.Chunking;
import com.aliasi.sentences.IndoEuropeanSentenceModel;
import com.aliasi.sentences.SentenceChunker;
import com.aliasi.sentences.SentenceModel;
import com.aliasi.tokenizer.IndoEuropeanTokenizerFactory;
import com.aliasi.tokenizer.TokenizerFactory;
import java.io.BufferedReader;
import java.io.IOException;
import java.io.InputStreamReader;
import java.util.Set;
```

```
public class SentenceDetection {

public static void main(String[] args) throws IOException {
  boolean endSent = true;
  boolean parenS = true;
  SentenceModel sentenceModel = new
    IndoEuropeanSentenceModel(endSent,parenS);
```

Working from the top of the `main` class, the Boolean `endSent` parameter controls whether the string that is sentence detected is assumed to end with a sentence, no matter what—this means that the last character is a sentence boundary always—it does not need to be a period or other typical sentence-ending mark. Change it and try a sentence without a final period, and the result will be that no sentence is detected.

The next Boolean `parenS` declaration gives priority to parentheses over sentence makers when finding sentences. Next, the actual sentence chunker will be set up:

```
TokenizerFactory tokFactory =
  IndoEuropeanTokenizerFactory.INSTANCE;
Chunker sentenceChunker =
  new SentenceChunker(tokFactory,sentenceModel);
```

The `tokFactory` should be familiar to you from *Chapter 2, Finding and Working with Words*. The `sentenceChunker` then can be constructed. Following is the standard I/O code for command-line interaction:

```
BufferedReader reader =
  new BufferedReader(new InputStreamReader(System.in));
while (true) {
  System.out.print("Enter text followed by new line\n>");
  String text = reader.readLine();
```

Once we have the text, then the sentence detector is applied:

```
Chunking chunking = sentenceChunker.chunk(text);
Set<Chunk> sentences = chunking.chunkSet();
```

The chunking provides a `Set<Chunk>` parameter, which will noncontractually provide an appropriate ordering of `Chunks`; they will be added as per the `ChunkingImpl` Javadoc. The truly paranoid programmer might impose the proper sort order, which we will cover later in the chapter when we have to handle overlapping chunks.

Next, we will check to see if any sentences were found, and if we don't find them, we will report to the console:

```
if (sentences.size() < 1) {
  System.out.println("No sentence chunks found.");
  return;
}
```

The following is the first exposure to the `Chunker` interface in the book, and a few comments are in order. The `Chunker` interface generates the `Chunk` objects, which are typed and scored contiguous-character sequences over `CharSequence`—usually, `String`. Chunks can overlap. The `Chunk` objects are stored in `Chunking`:

```
String textStored = chunking.charSequence().toString();
for (Chunk sentence : sentences) {
  int start = sentence.start();
  int end = sentence.end();
  System.out.println("SENTENCE :"
    + textStored.substring(start,end));
}
}
```

First, we recovered the underlying text string `textStored` that the chunks are based on. It is the same string as `text`, but we wanted to illustrate this potentially useful method of the `Chunking` class, which can come up in recursive or other contexts when the chunking is far removed from where `CharSequence` that it uses is unavailable.

The remaining `for` loop iterates over the sentences and prints them out with the `substring()` method of `String`.

There's more...

Before moving on to how to roll your own sentence detector, it is worth mentioning that LingPipe has `MedlineSentenceModel`, which is oriented towards the kind of sentences found in the medical research literature. It has seen a lot of data and should be a starting place for your own sentence-detection efforts over these kinds of data.

Nested sentences

Sentences, particularly in literature, can contain nested sentences. Consider the following:

```
John said "this is a nested sentence" and then shut up.
```

The preceding sentence will be marked up properly as:

```
[John said "[this is a nested sentence]" and then shut up.]
```

This sort of nesting is different from a linguist's concept of a nested sentence, which is based on grammatical role. Consider the following example:

```
[[John ate the gorilla] and [Mary ate the burger]].
```

This sentence consists of two linguistically complete sentences joined by `and`. The difference between the two is that the former is determined by punctuation and the latter by a grammatical function. Whether this distinction is significant or not can be debated. However, the former case is much easier to recognize programmatically.

Finding Spans in Text – Chunking

However, we have rarely needed to model nested sentences in industrial contexts, but we took it on in our MUC-6 system and various coreference resolution systems in research contexts. This is beyond the scope of a recipe book, but be aware of the issue. LingPipe has no out-of-the-box capabilities for nested sentence detection.

Evaluation of sentence detection

Like most of the things we do, we want to be able to evaluate the performance of our components. Sentence detection is no different. Sentence detection is a span annotation that differs from our previous evaluations for classifiers and tokenization. As text can have characters that are not in any sentence, there is a notion of sentence start and sentence end. An example of characters that don't belong in a sentence will be JavaScript from an HTML page.

The following recipe will take you through the steps of creating evaluation data and running it past an evaluation class.

How to do it...

Perform the following steps to evaluate sentence detection:

1. Open a text editor and copy and paste some literary gem that you want to evaluate sentence detection with, or you can go with our supplied default text, which is used if you don't provide your own data. It is easiest if you stick to plain text.

2. Insert balanced [and] to indicate the beginnings and ends of sentences in the text. If the text already contains either [or], pick another character that is not in the text as a sentence delimiter—curly brackets or slashes are a good choice. If you use different delimiters, you will have to modify the source appropriately and recreate the JAR file. The code assumes a single-character text delimiter. An example of a sentence-annotated text from *The Hitchhiker's Guide to the Galaxy* is as follows—note that not every character is in a sentence; some whitespaces are between sentences:

   ```
   [The Guide says that the best drink in existence is the Pan
   Galactic Gargle Blaster.] [It says that the effect of a Pan
   Galactic Gargle Blaster is like having your brains smashed out by
   a slice of lemon wrapped round a large gold brick.]
   ```

3. Get yourself a command line and run the following command:

   ```
   java -cp lingpipe-cookbook.1.0.jar:lib/lingpipe-4.1.0.jar: com.
   lingpipe.cookbook.chapter5.EvaluateAnnotatedSentences
   ```

   ```
   TruePos: 0-83/The Guide says that the best drink in existence is
   the Pan Galactic Gargle Blaster.:S
   ```

   ```
   TruePos: 84-233/It says that the effect of a Pan Galactic Gargle
   Blaster is like having your brains smashed out by a slice of lemon
   wrapped round a large gold brick.:S
   ```

4. For this data, the code will display two sentences that match perfectly with the sentences annotated with [], as indicated by the `TruePos` label.

5. A good exercise is to modify the annotation a bit to force errors. We will move the first sentence boundary one character in:

   T[he Guide says that the best drink in existence is the Pan Galactic Gargle Blaster.] [It says that the effect of a Pan Galactic Gargle Blaster is like having your brains smashed out by a slice of lemon wrapped round a large gold brick.]

6. Rerunning the modified annotation file after saving it yields:

   TruePos: 84-233/It says that the effect of a Pan Galactic Gargle Blaster is like having your brains smashed out by a slice of lemon wrapped round a large gold brick.:S

   FalsePos: 0-83/The Guide says that the best drink in existence is the Pan Galactic Gargle Blaster.:S

   FalseNeg: 1-83/he Guide says that the best drink in existence is the Pan Galactic Gargle Blaster.:S

   By changing the truth annotation, a false negative is produced, because the sentence span was missed by one character. In addition, a false positive is created by the sentence detector that recognizes the 0-83 character sequence.

7. It is a good idea to play around with the annotation and various kinds of data to get a feel of how evaluation works and the capabilities of the sentence detector.

How it works...

The class starts by digesting the annotated text and storing the sentence chunks in an evaluation object. Then, the sentence detector is created, just as we did in the previous recipe. The code finishes by applying the created sentence detector to the text, and the results are printed.

Parsing annotated data

Given text annotated with [] for sentence boundaries means that the correct offsets of the sentences have to be recovered, and the original unannotated text must be created, that is, without any []. Span parsers can be a bit tricky to code, and the following is offered for simplicity rather than efficiency or proper coding technique:

```
String path = args.length > 0 ? args[0]
              : "data/hitchHikersGuide.sentDetected";
char[] chars
  = Files.readCharsFromFile(new File(path), Strings.UTF8);
StringBuilder rawChars = new StringBuilder();
int start = -1;
int end = 0;
Set<Chunk> sentChunks = new HashSet<Chunk>();
```

Finding Spans in Text – Chunking

The preceding code reads in the entire file as a single `char[]` array with an appropriate character encoding. Also, note that for large files, a streaming approach will be more memory friendly. Next, an accumulator for unannotated chars is setup as a `StringBuilder` object with the `rawChars` variable. All characters encountered that are not either a `[` or `]` will be appended to the object. The remaining code sets up counters for sentence starts and ends that are indexed into the unannotated character array and an accumulator for `Set<Chunk>` for annotated sentence segments.

The following `for` loop advances one character at a time over the annotated character sequence:

```
for (int i=0; i < chars.length; ++i) {
  if (chars[i] == '[') {
    start = rawChars.length();
  }
  else if (chars[i] == ']') {
    end = rawChars.length();

    Chunk chunk = ChunkFactory.createChunk(start,end,
      SentenceChunker.SENTENCE_CHUNK_TYPE);
    sentChunks.add(chunk);}
  else {
    rawChars.append(chars[i]);
  }
}
String originalText = rawChars.toString();
```

The first `if (chars[i] == '[')` tests for starts of sentences in the annotation and sets the start variable to the length of `rawChars`. The iteration variable `i` includes the length added by the annotations. The corresponding `else if (chars[i] == ']')` statement handles the end of sentence case. Note that there are no error checks for this parser—this is a very bad idea because annotation errors are very likely if entered with a text editor. However, this is motivated by keeping the code as simple as possible. Later in the recipe, we will provide an example with some minimal error checking. Once the end of a sentence is found, a chunk is created for the sentence with `ChunkFactory.createChunk` with offsets and for the standard LingPipe sentence type `SentenceChunker.SENTENCE_CHUNK_TYPE`, which is required for the upcoming evaluation classes to work properly.

The remaining `else` statement applies for all the characters that are not sentence boundaries, and it simply adds the character to the `rawChars` accumulator. The result of this accumulator can be seen outside the `for` loop when `String unannotatedText` is created. Now, we have sentence chunks indexed correctly into a text string. Next, we will create a proper `Chunking` object:

```
ChunkingImpl sentChunking = new ChunkingImpl(unannotatedText);
for (Chunk chunk : sentChunks) {
  sentChunking.add(chunk);
}
```

The `ChunkingImpl` implementing class (`Chunking` is an interface) requires the underlying text on construction, which is why we didn't just populate it in the preceding loop. LingPipe generally tries to make object construction complete. If Chunkings can be created without the underlying `CharSequence` method, then what will be returned when the `charSequence()` method is called? An empty string is actively misleading. Alternatively, returning `null` needs to be caught and dealt with. Better to just force the object to make sense of construction.

Moving on, we will see the standard configuration of the sentence chunker from the previous recipe:

```
boolean eosIsSentBoundary = false;
boolean balanceParens = true;
SentenceModel sentenceModel = new
  IndoEuropeanSentenceModel(eosIsSentBoundary, balanceParens);
TokenizerFactory tokFactory =
  IndoEuropeanTokenizerFactory.INSTANCE;
SentenceChunker sentenceChunker =
  new SentenceChunker(tokFactory,sentenceModel);
```

The interesting stuff follows with an evaluator that takes `sentenceChunker` as being evaluated as a parameter:

```
SentenceEvaluator evaluator =
  new SentenceEvaluator(sentenceChunker);
```

Next up, the `handle(sentChunking)` method will take the text we just parsed into `Chunking` and run the sentence detector on `CharSequence` supplied in `sentChunking` and set up the evaluation:

```
evaluator.handle(sentChunking);
```

Then, we will just get the evaluation data and work our way through the differences between the truth sentence detection and what the system did:

```
SentenceEvaluation eval = evaluator.evaluation();
ChunkingEvaluation chunkEval = eval.chunkingEvaluation();
for (ChunkAndCharSeq truePos : chunkEval.truePositiveSet()) {
  System.out.println("TruePos: " + truePos);
}
for (ChunkAndCharSeq falsePos : chunkEval.falsePositiveSet()) {
  System.out.println("FalsePos: " + falsePos);
}
for (ChunkAndCharSeq falseNeg : chunkEval.falseNegativeSet()){
  System.out.println("FalseNeg: " + falseNeg);
}
```

Finding Spans in Text – Chunking

This recipe does not cover all the evaluation methods—check out the Javadoc—but it does provide what a sentence detection tuner will likely be most in need of; this is a listing of what the sentence detector got right (true positives), sentences it found but were wrong (false positives), and sentences it missed (false negatives). Note that true negatives don't make much sense in span annotations, because they will be the set of all the possible spans that are not in the truth sentence detection.

Tuning sentence detection

Lots of data will resist the charms of `IndoEuropeanSentenceModel`, so this recipe will provide a starting place to modify sentence detection to meet new kinds of sentences. Unfortunately, this is a very open-ended area of system building, so we will focus on techniques rather than likely formats for sentences.

How to do it...

This recipe will follow a well-worn pattern: create evaluation data, set up evaluation, and start hacking. Here we go:

1. Haul out your favorite text editor and mark up some data—we will stick to the [and] markup approach. The following is an example that runs afoul of our standard `IndoEuropeanSentenceModel`:

   ```
   [All decent people live beyond their incomes nowadays, and those
   who aren't respectable live beyond other people's.]  [A few gifted
   individuals manage to do both.]
   ```

2. We will put the preceding sentence in `data/saki.sentDetected.txt` and run it:

   ```
   java -cp lingpipe-cookbook.1.0.jar:lib/lingpipe-4.1.0.jar: com.
   lingpipe.cookbook.chapter5.EvaluateAnnotatedSentences data/saki.
   sentDetected
   ```

   ```
   FalsePos: 0-159/All decent people live beyond their incomes
   nowadays, and those who aren't respectable live beyond other
   people's.  A few gifted individuals manage to do both.:S

   FalseNeg: 0-114/All decent people live beyond their incomes
   nowadays, and those who aren't respectable live beyond other
   people's.:S

   FalseNeg: 116-159/A few gifted individuals manage to do both.:S
   ```

There's more...

The single false positive corresponds to the one sentence found, and the two false negatives are the two sentences not found that we annotated here. What happened? The sentence model missed `people's.` as a sentence end. If the apostrophe is removed, the sentence is detected properly—what is going on?

First, let's look at the code running in the background. `IndoEuropeanSentenceModel` extends `HeuristicSentenceModel` by configuring several categories of tokens from the Javadoc for `HeuristicSentenceModel`:

- **Possible stops**: These are tokens that are allowed to be the final ones in a sentence. This set typically includes sentence-final punctuation tokens, such as periods (.) and double quotes (").
- **Impossible penultimates**: These are tokens that might not be the penultimate (second-to-last) token in a sentence. This set is typically made up of abbreviations or acronyms, such as `Mr`.
- **Impossible starts**: These are tokens that might not be the first ones in a sentence. This set typically includes punctuation characters that should be attached to the previous sentence, such as end quotes (").

`IndoEuropeanSentenceModel` is not configurable, but from the Javadoc, it is clear that all single characters are considered impossible penultimates. The words `people's` is tokenized into `people`, `'`, `s`, and `.`. The single character `s` is penultimate to the `.` and is thus blocked. How to fix this?

A few options present themselves:

- Ignore the mistake assuming that it won't happen frequently
- Fix by creating a custom sentence model
- Fix by modifying the tokenizer to not separate apostrophes
- Write a complete sentence-detection model for the interface

The second option, create a custom sentence model, is handled most easily by copying the source from `IndoEuropeanSentenceModel` into a new class and modifying it, as the relevant data structures are private. This is done to simplify the serialization of the class—very little configuration needs to be written to disk. In the example classes, there is a `MySentenceModel.java` file that differs by obvious changes in the package name and imports:

```
IMPOSSIBLE_PENULTIMATES.add("R");
//IMPOSSIBLE_PENULTIMATES.add("S"); breaks on "people's."
//IMPOSSIBLE_PENULTIMATES.add("T"); breaks on "didn't."
IMPOSSIBLE_PENULTIMATES.add("U");
```

The preceding code just comments out two of the likely single-letter cases of penultimate tokens that are a single-word character. To see it at work, change the sentence model to `SentenceModel sentenceModel = new MySentenceModel();` in the `EvaluateAnnotatedSentences.java` class and recompile and run it.

Finding Spans in Text – Chunking

If you see the preceding code as a reasonable balancing of finding sentences that end in likely contractions versus non-sentence cases such as `[Hunter S. Thompson is a famous fellow.]`, which will detect `S.` as a sentence boundary.

Extending `HeuristicSentenceModel` can work well for many sorts of data. Mitzi Morris built `MedlineSentenceModel.java`, which is designed to work well with the abstracts provided in the MEDLINE research index.

One way to look at the preceding problem is that contractions should not be broken up into tokens for the purpose of sentence detection. `IndoEuropeanTokenizerFactory` should be tuned up to keep "people's" and other contractions together. While it initially seems slightly better that the first solution, it might well run afoul of the fact that `IndoEuropeanSentenceModel` was tuned with a particular tokenization in mind, and the consequences of the change are unknown in the absence of an evaluation corpus.

The other option is to write a completely novel sentence-detection class that supports the `SentenceModel` interface. Faced with a highly novel data collection such as Twitter feeds, we will consider using a machine-learning-driven span-annotation technique such as HMMs or CRFs covered in *Chapter 4, Tagging Words and Tokens*, and at the end of this chapter.

Marking embedded chunks in a string – sentence chunk example

The method of displaying chunkings in the previous recipes is not well suited for applications that need to modify the underlying string. For example, a sentiment analyzer might want to highlight only sentences that are strongly positive and not mark up the remaining sentences while still displaying the entire text. The slight complication in producing the marked-up text is that adding markups changes the underlying string. This recipe provides working code to insert the chunking by adding chunks in reverse.

How to do it...

While this recipe may not be technically complex it is useful to get span annotations into a text without out having to invent the code from whole cloth. The `src/com/lingpipe/coobook/chapter5/WriteSentDetectedChunks` class has the referenced code:

1. The sentence chunking is created as per the first sentence-detection recipe. The following code extracts the chunks as `Set<Chunk>` and then sorts them by `Chunk.LONGEST_MATCH_ORDER_COMPARITOR`. In the Javadoc, the comparator is defined as:

    Compares two chunks based on their text position. A chunk is greater if it starts later than another chunk, or if it starts at the same position and ends earlier.

There is also `TEXT_ORDER_COMPARITOR`, which is as follows:

```
String textStored = chunking.charSequence().toString();
Set<Chunk> chunkSet = chunking.chunkSet();
System.out.println("size: " + chunkSet.size());
Chunk[] chunkArray = chunkSet.toArray(new Chunk[0]);
Arrays.sort(chunkArray,Chunk.LONGEST_MATCH_ORDER_COMPARATOR);
```

2. Next, we will iterate over the chunks in the reverse order, which eliminates having to keep an offset variable for the changing length of the `StringBuilder` object. Offset variables are a common source of bugs, so this recipe avoids them as much as possible but does non-standard reverse loop iteration, which might be worse:

```
StringBuilder output = new StringBuilder(textStored);
int sentBoundOffset = 0;
for (int i = chunkArray.length -1; i >= 0; --i) {
  Chunk chunk = chunkArray[i];
  String sentence = textStored.substring(chunk.start(), chunk.end());
  if (sentence.contains("like")) {
    output.insert(chunk.end(),"}");
    output.insert(chunk.start(),"{");
  }
}
System.out.println(output.toString());
```

3. The preceding code does a very simple sentiment analysis by looking for the string `like` in the sentence and marking that sentence if `true`. Note that this code cannot handle overlapping chunks or nested chunks. It assumes a single, non-overlapping chunk set. Some example output is:

   `java -cp lingpipe-cookbook.1.0.jar:lib/lingpipe-4.1.0.jar: com.lingpipe.cookbook.chapter5.WriteSentDetectedChunks`

   `Enter text followed by new line`

   `>People like to ski. But sometimes it is terrifying.`

   `size: 2`

   `{People like to ski.} But sometimes it is terrifying.`

4. To print nested chunks, look at the *Paragraph detection* recipe that follows.

Paragraph detection

The typical containing structure of a set of sentences is a paragraph. It can be set off explicitly in a markup language such as <p> in HTML or with two or more new lines, which is how paragraphs are usually rendered. We are in the part of NLP where no hard-and-fast rules apply, so we apologize for the hedging. We will handle some common examples in this chapter and leave it to you to generalize.

How to do it...

We have never set up an evaluation harness for paragraph detection, but it can be done in ways similar to sentence detection. This recipe, instead, will illustrate a simple paragraph-detection routine that does something very important—maintain offsets into the original document with embedded sentence detection. This attention to detail will serve you well if you ever need to mark up the document in a way that is sensitive to sentences or other subspans of the document, such as named entities. Consider the following example:

```
Sentence 1. Sentence 2
Sentence 3. Sentence 4.
```

It gets transformed into the following:

```
{[Sentence 1.] [Sentence 2]}

{[Sentence 3.] [Sentence 4.]
}
```

In the preceding snippet, [] designates sentences, and {} designates paragraphs. We will jump right into the code on this recipe from `src/com/lingpipe/cookbook/chapter5/ParagraphSentenceDetection.java`:

1. The example code has little to offer in paragraph-detection techniques. It is an open-ended problem, and you will have to use your wiles to solve it. Our paragraph detector is a pathetic `split("\n\n")` that, in a more sophisticated approach, will take into account context, characters, and other features that are far too idiosyncratic for us to cover. Here is the beginning of the code that reads the entire document as a string and splits it into an array. Note that `paraSeperatorLength` is the number of characters that form the basis of the paragraph split—if the length of the split varies, then that length will have to be associated with the corresponding paragraph:

   ```
   public static void main(String[] args) throws IOException {
     String document = Files.readFromFile(new File(args[0]),
       Strings.UTF8);
     String[] paragraphs = document.split("\n\n");
     int paraSeparatorLength = 2;
   ```

2. The real point of the recipe is to help with the mechanics of maintaining character offsets into the original document and show embedded processing. This will be done by keeping two separate chunkings: one for paragraphs and one for sentences:

```
ChunkingImpl paraChunking = new
   ChunkingImpl(document.toCharArray(),0,document.length());
ChunkingImpl sentChunking = new
   ChunkingImpl(paraChunking.charSequence());
```

3. Next, the sentence detector will be set up in the same way as one in the previous recipe:

```
boolean eosIsSentBoundary = true;
boolean balanceParens = false;
SentenceModel sentenceModel = new
   IndoEuropeanSentenceModel(eosIsSentBoundary, balanceParens);
SentenceChunker sentenceChunker = new
   SentenceChunker(IndoEuropeanTokenizerFactory.INSTANCE,
   sentenceModel);
```

4. The chunking iterates over the array of paragraphs and builds a sentence chunking for each paragraph. The somewhat-complicated part of this approach is that the sentence chunk offsets are with respect to the paragraph string, not the entire document. So, the variables' starts and ends are updated with document offsets in the code. Chunks have no methods to adjust starts and ends, so a new chunk must be created, `adjustedSentChunk`, with appropriate offsets into the paragraph start and must be added to `sentChunking`:

```
int paraStart = 0;
for (String paragraph : paragraphs) {
  for (Chunk sentChunk :
    sentenceChunker.chunk(paragraph).chunkSet()) {
    Chunk adjustedSentChunk =
      ChunkFactory.createChunk(sentChunk.start() +
      paraStart,sentChunk.end() + paraStart, "S");
    sentChunking.add(adjustedSentChunk);
  }
```

5. The rest of the loop adds the paragraph chunk and then updates the start of the paragraph with the length of the paragraph plus the length of the paragraph separator. This will complete the creation of correctly offset sentences and paragraphs into the original document string:

```
paraChunking.add(ChunkFactory.createChunk(paraStart, paraStart +
  paragraph.length(),"P"));
paraStart += paragraph.length() + paraSeparatorLength;
}
```

6. The rest of the program is concerned with printing out the paragraphs and sentences with some markup. First, we will create a chunking that has both sentence and paragraph chunks:

```
String underlyingString =
   paraChunking.charSequence().toString();
ChunkingImpl displayChunking = new
   ChunkingImpl(paraChunking.charSequence());
displayChunking.addAll(sentChunking.chunkSet());
displayChunking.addAll(paraChunking.chunkSet());
```

7. Next, `displayChunking` will be sorted by recovering `chunkSet`, converting it into an array of chunks and the application of the static comparator:

```
Set<Chunk> chunkSet = displayChunking.chunkSet();
Chunk[] chunkArray = chunkSet.toArray(new Chunk[0]);
Arrays.sort(chunkArray,
   Chunk.LONGEST_MATCH_ORDER_COMPARATOR);
```

8. We will use the same trick as we did in the *Marking embedded chunks in a string – sentence chunk example* recipe, which is to insert the markup backwards into the string. We will have to keep an offset counter, because nested sentences will extend the finishing paragraph mark placement. The approach assumes that no chunks overlap and that sentences are contained within paragraphs always:

```
StringBuilder output = new StringBuilder(underlyingString);
int sentBoundOffset = 0;
for (int i = chunkArray.length -1; i >= 0; --i) {
  Chunk chunk = chunkArray[i];
  if (chunk.type().equals("P")) {
    output.insert(chunk.end() + sentBoundOffset,"}");
    output.insert(chunk.start(),"{");
    sentBoundOffset = 0;
  }
  if (chunk.type().equals("S")) {
    output.insert(chunk.end(),"]");
    output.insert(chunk.start(),"[");
    sentBoundOffset += 2;
  }
}
System.out.println(output.toString());
```

9. That's it for the recipe.

Simple noun phrases and verb phrases

This recipe will show you how to find simple **noun phrases** (**NP**) and **verb phrases** (**VP**). By "simple", we mean that there is no complex structure within the phrases. For example, the complex NP "The rain in Spain" will be broken into two simple NP chunks "The rain" and "Spain". These phrases are also called "basal".

This recipe will not go into the details of how the basal NPs/VPs are calculated but rather how to use the class—it can come in handy, and the source can be included if you want to sort out how it works.

How to do it...

Like many of the recipes, we will provide a command-line-interactive interface here:

1. Haul up the command line and type:

   ```
   java -cp lingpipe-cookbook.1.0.jar:lib/lingpipe-4.1.0.jar: com.lingpipe.cookbook.chapter5.PhraseChunker
   ```

   ```
   INPUT> The rain in Spain falls mainly on the plain.
   ```

   ```
   The/at rain/nn in/in Spain/np falls/vbz mainly/rb on/in the/at plain/jj ./.
   ```

   ```
   noun(0,8) The rain
   noun(12,17) Spain
   verb(18,30) falls mainly
   noun(34,43) the plain
   ```

How it works...

The `main()` method starts by deserializing a part-of-speech tagger and then creating `tokenizerFactory`:

```
public static void main(String[] args) throws IOException,
ClassNotFoundException {
  File hmmFile =
new File("models/pos-en-general-brown.HiddenMarkovModel");
  HiddenMarkovModel posHmm =
     (HiddenMarkovModel) AbstractExternalizable.readObject(hmmFile);
  HmmDecoder posTagger  = new HmmDecoder(posHmm);
  TokenizerFactory tokenizerFactory =
     IndoEuropeanTokenizerFactory.INSTANCE;
```

Finding Spans in Text – Chunking

Next, `PhraseChunker` is constructed, which is a heuristic approach to the problem. Look at the source to see how it works—it scans the input left to right for NP/VP starts and attempts to add to the phrase incrementally:

```
PhraseChunker chunker =
  new PhraseChunker(posTagger,tokenizerFactory);
```

Our standard console I/O code is next:

```
BufferedReader bufReader = new BufferedReader(new
InputStreamReader(System.in));
while (true) {
  System.out.print("\n\nINPUT> ");
  String input = bufReader.readLine();
```

Then, the input is tokenized, POS is tagged, and the tokens and tags are printed out:

```
Tokenizer tokenizer =
  tokenizerFactory.tokenizer(input.toCharArray(),
  0,input.length());
String[] tokens = tokenizer.tokenize();
List<String> tokenList = Arrays.asList(tokens);
Tagging<String> tagging = posTagger.tag(tokenList);
for (int j = 0; j < tokenList.size(); ++j) {
  System.out.print(tokens[j] + "/" + tagging.tag(j) + " ");
}
System.out.println();
```

The NP/VP chunkings are then calculated and printed out:

```
Chunking chunking = chunker.chunk(input);
CharSequence cs = chunking.charSequence();
for (Chunk chunk : chunking.chunkSet()) {
  String type = chunk.type();
  int start = chunk.start();
  int end = chunk.end();
  CharSequence text = cs.subSequence(start,end);
  System.out.println("   " + type + "(" + start + ","
    + end + ") " + text);
}
```

There is a more comprehensive tutorial at `http://alias-i.com/lingpipe/demos/tutorial/posTags/read-me.html`.

Regular expression-based chunking for NER

Named Entity Recognition (**NER**) is the process of finding mentions of specific things in text. Consider a simple name; location-named entity recognizer might find `Ford Prefect` and `Guildford` as the name and location mentions, respectively, in the following text:

```
Ford Prefect used to live in Guildford before he needed to move.
```

We will start by building rule-based NER systems and move up to machine-learning methods. Here, we'll take a look at building an NER system that can extract e-mail addresses from text.

How to do it...

1. Enter the following command into the command prompt:

   ```
   java -cp lingpipe-cookbook.1.0.jar:lib/lingpipe-4.1.0.jar com.lingpipe.cookbook.chapter5.RegexNer
   ```

2. Interaction with the program proceeds as follows:

   ```
   Enter text, . to quit:
   >Hello,my name is Foo and my email is foo@bar.com or you can also contact me at foo.bar@gmail.com.
   input=Hello,my name is Foo and my email is foo@bar.com or you can also contact me at foo.bar@gmail.com.
   chunking=Hello,my name is Foo and my email is foo@bar.com or you can also contact me at foo.bar@gmail.com. : [37-48:email@0.0, 79-96:email@0.0]
        chunk=37-48:email@0.0   text=foo@bar.com
        chunk=79-96:email@0.0   text=foo.bar@gmail.com
   ```

3. You can see that both `foo@bar.com` as well as `foo.bar@gmail.com` were returned as valid `e-mail` type chunks. Also, note that the final period in the sentence is not part of the second e-mail.

Finding Spans in Text – Chunking

How it works...

A regular expression chunker finds chunks that match the given regular expression. Essentially, the `java.util.regex.Matcher.find()` method is used to iteratively find matching text segments, and these are then converted into the Chunk objects. The RegExChunker class wraps these steps. The code of `src/com/lingpipe/cookbook/chapter5/RegExNer.java` is described as follows:

```
public static void main(String[] args) throws IOException {
  String emailRegex = "[A-Za-z0-9](([_\\.\\-]?[a-zA-Z0-9]+)*)" +
    + "@([A-Za-z0-9]+)" +
    "((([\\.\\-]?[a-zA-Z0-9]+)*)\\.([A-Za-z]{2,})";
  String chunkType = "email";
  double score = 1.0;
  Chunker chunker = new RegExChunker(emailRegex,chunkType,score);
```

All the interesting work was done in the preceding lines of code. The `emailRegex` is pulled off of the Internet—see the following for the source, and the remaining bits are setting up `chunkType` and `score`.

The rest of the code reads in the input and prints out the chunking:

```
BufferedReader reader = new BufferedReader(new
  InputStreamReader(System.in));
String input = "";
while (true) {
  System.out.println("Enter text, . to quit:");
  input = reader.readLine();
  if(input.equals(".")){
    break;
  }
  Chunking chunking = chunker.chunk(input);
  System.out.println("input=" + input);
  System.out.println("chunking=" + chunking);
  Set<Chunk> chunkSet = chunking.chunkSet();
  Iterator<Chunk> it = chunkSet.iterator();
  while (it.hasNext()) {
    Chunk chunk = it.next();
    int start = chunk.start();
    int end = chunk.end();
    String text = input.substring(start,end);
    System.out.println("     chunk=" + chunk + "
       text=" + text);
  }
 }
}
```

See also

- The regular expression for the e-mail address match is from `regexlib.com` at `http://regexlib.com/DisplayPatterns.aspx?cattabindex=0&categoryId=1`

Dictionary-based chunking for NER

In many websites and blogs and certainly on web forums, you might see keyword highlighting that links pages you can buy a product from. Similarly, news websites also provide topic pages for people, places, and trending events, such as the one at `http://www.nytimes.com/pages/topics/`.

A lot of this is fully automated and is easy to do with a dictionary-based `Chunker`. It is straightforward to compile lists of names for entities and their types. An exact dictionary chunker extracts chunks based on exact matches of tokenized dictionary entries.

The implementation of the dictionary-based chunker in LingPipe is based on the Aho-Corasick algorithm which finds all matches against a dictionary in linear time independent of the number of matches or size of the dictionary. This makes it much more efficient than the naïve approach of doing substring searches or using regular expressions.

How to do it...

1. In the IDE of your choice run the `DictionaryChunker` class in the `chapter5` package or type the following using the command line:

   ```
   java -cp lingpipe-cookbook.1.0.jar:lib/lingpipe-4.1.0.jar com.lingpipe.cookbook.chapter5.DictionaryChunker
   ```

2. Since this particular chunker example is biased (very heavily) towards the Hitchhikers Guide, let's use a sentence that involves some of the characters:

   ```
   Enter text, . to quit:
   Ford and Arthur went up the bridge of the Heart of Gold with Marvin
   CHUNKER overlapping, case sensitive
        phrase=|Ford|   start=0  end=4  type=PERSON    score=1.0
        phrase=|Arthur| start=9  end=15 type=PERSON    score=1.0
        phrase=|Heart|  start=42 end=47 type=ORGAN     score=1.0
      phrase=|Heart of Gold| start=42 end=55 type=SPACECRAFT score=1.0
        phrase=|Marvin| start=61 end=67 type=ROBOT     score=1.0
   ```

3. Note that we have overlapping chunks from `Heart` and `Heart of Gold`. As we will see, this can be configured to behave differently.

Finding Spans in Text – Chunking

How it works...

Dictionary-based NER drives a great deal of automatic linking against unstructured text data. We can build one using the following steps.

The first step of the code will create `MapDictionary<String>` to store the dictionary entries:

```
static final double CHUNK_SCORE = 1.0;

public static void main(String[] args) throws IOException {
  MapDictionary<String> dictionary = new MapDictionary<String>();
  MapDictionary<String> dictionary = new MapDictionary<String>();
```

Next, we will populate the dictionary with `DictionaryEntry<String>`, which includes type information and a score that will be used to create chunks:

```
dictionary.addEntry(new
  DictionaryEntry<String>("Arthur","PERSON",CHUNK_SCORE));
dictionary.addEntry(new
  DictionaryEntry<String>("Ford","PERSON",CHUNK_SCORE));
dictionary.addEntry(new
  DictionaryEntry<String>("Trillian","PERSON",CHUNK_SCORE));
dictionary.addEntry(new
  DictionaryEntry<String>("Zaphod","PERSON",CHUNK_SCORE));
dictionary.addEntry(new
  DictionaryEntry<String>("Marvin","ROBOT",CHUNK_SCORE));
dictionary.addEntry(new DictionaryEntry<String>("Heart of Gold",
  "SPACECRAFT",CHUNK_SCORE));
dictionary.addEntry(new DictionaryEntry<String>("Hitchhikers
  Guide", "PRODUCT",CHUNK_SCORE));
```

In the `DictionaryEntry` constructor, the first argument is the phrase, the second string argument is the type, and the final double argument is the score for the chunk. Dictionary entries are always case sensitive. There is no limit to the number of different entity types in a dictionary. The scores will simply be passed along as chunk scores in the dictionary-based chunker.

Next, we will build `Chunker`:

```
boolean returnAllMatches = true;
boolean caseSensitive = true;
ExactDictionaryChunker dictionaryChunker =
  new ExactDictionaryChunker(dictionary,
  IndoEuropeanTokenizerFactory.INSTANCE,
  returnAllMatches,caseSensitive);
```

An exact dictionary chunker might be configured either to extract all the matching chunks to restrict the results to a consistent set of non-overlapping chunks via the `returnAllMatches` boolean. Look at the Javadoc to understand the exact criteria. There is also a `caseSensitive` boolean. The chunker requires a tokenizer, as it matches tokens as symbols, and whitespaces are ignored in the matching process.

Next is our standard I/O code for console interaction:

```
BufferedReader reader = new BufferedReader(new
  InputStreamReader(System.in));
String text = "";
while (true) {
  System.out.println("Enter text, . to quit:");
  text = reader.readLine();
  if(text.equals(".")){
    break;
  }
}
```

The remaining code creates a chunking, goes through the chunks, and prints them out:

```
System.out.println("\nCHUNKER overlapping, case sensitive");
Chunking chunking = dictionaryChunker.chunk(text);
  for (Chunk chunk : chunking.chunkSet()) {
    int start = chunk.start();
    int end = chunk.end();
    String type = chunk.type();
    double score = chunk.score();
    String phrase = text.substring(start,end);
    System.out.println("     phrase=|" + phrase + "|"
      + " start=" + start + " end=" + end
      + " type=" + type + " score=" + score);
```

Dictionary chunkers are very useful even in machine-learning-based systems. There tends to always be a class of entities that are best identified this way. The *Mixing the NER sources* recipe addresses how to work with multiple sources of named entities.

Translating between word tagging and chunks – BIO codec

In *Chapter 4*, *Tagging Words and Tokens*, we used HMMs and CRFs to apply tags to words/tokens. This recipe addresses the case of creating chunks from taggings that use the **Begin, In, and Out** (**BIO**) tags to encode chunkings that can span multiple words/tokens. This, in turn, is the basis of modern named-entity detection systems.

Finding Spans in Text – Chunking

Getting ready

The standard BIO-tagging scheme has the first token in a chunk of type X tagged B-X (begin), with all the subsequent tokens in the same chunk tagged I-X (in). All the tokens that are not in chunks are tagged O (out). For example, the string with character counts:

```
John Jones Mary and Mr. Jones
012345678901234567890123456 78
0         1         2
```

It can be tagged as:

```
John   B_PERSON
Jones  I_PERSON
Mary   B_PERSON
and    O
Mr     B_PERSON
.      I_PERSON
Jones  I_PERSON
```

The corresponding chunks will be:

```
0-10  "John Jones" PERSON
11-15 "Mary" PERSON
20-29 "Mr. Jones" PERSON
```

How to do it...

The program will show the simplest mapping between taggings and chunkings and the other way around:

1. Run the following:

   ```
   java -cp lingpipe-cookbook.1.0.jar:lib/lingpipe-4.1.0.jar: com.lingpipe.cookbook.chapter5.BioCodec
   ```

2. The program first prints out the string that will be tagged with a tagging:

   Tagging for :The rain in Spain.

   The/B_Weather

   rain/I_Weather

   in/O

   Spain/B_Place

   ./O

3. Next, the chunking is printed:

   ```
   Chunking from StringTagging
   0-8:Weather@-Infinity
   12-17:Place@-Infinity
   ```

4. Then, the tagging is created from the chunking just displayed:

   ```
   StringTagging from Chunking
   The/B_Weather
   rain/I_Weather
   in/O
   Spain/B_Place
   ./O
   ```

How it works...

The code starts by manually constructing `StringTagging`—we will see HMMs and CRFs do the same programmatically, but here it is explicit. It then prints out the created `StringTagging`:

```
public static void main(String[] args) {
  List<String> tokens = new ArrayList<String>();
  tokens.add("The");
  tokens.add("rain");
  tokens.add("in");
  tokens.add("Spain");
  tokens.add(".");
  List<String> tags = new ArrayList<String>();
  tags.add("B_Weather");
  tags.add("I_Weather");
  tags.add("O");
  tags.add("B_Place");
  tags.add("O");
  CharSequence cs = "The rain in Spain.";
  //012345678901234567
  int[] tokenStarts = {0,4,9,12,17};
  int[] tokenEnds = {3,8,11,17,17};
  StringTagging tagging =
    new StringTagging(tokens, tags, cs,
    tokenStarts, tokenEnds);
  System.out.println("Tagging for :" + cs);
  for (int i = 0; i < tagging.size(); ++i) {
    System.out.println(tagging.token(i) + "/"
      + tagging.tag(i));
  }
```

Finding Spans in Text – Chunking

Next, it will construct `BioTagChunkCodec` and convert the tagging just printed out to a chunking followed by printing the chunking:

```
BioTagChunkCodec codec = new BioTagChunkCodec();
Chunking chunking = codec.toChunking(tagging);
System.out.println("Chunking from StringTagging");
for (Chunk chunk : chunking.chunkSet()) {
  System.out.println(chunk);
}
```

The remaining code reverses the process. First, a different `BioTagChunkCodec` is created with `boolean enforceConsistency`, which, if `true`, checks that the tokens created by the supplied tokenizer align exactly with the chunk begins and ends. Without the alignment we end up with a perhaps untenable relationship between chunks and tokens depending on the use case:

```
boolean enforceConsistency = true;
BioTagChunkCodec codec2 =
  new BioTagChunkCodec(IndoEuropeanTokenizerFactory.INSTANCE,
  enforceConsistency);
StringTagging tagging2 = codec2.toStringTagging(chunking);
System.out.println("StringTagging from Chunking");
for (int i = 0; i < tagging2.size(); ++i) {
  System.out.println(tagging2.token(i) + "/" + tagging2.tag(i));
}
```

The last `for` loop simply prints out the tagging returned by the `codec2.toStringTagging()` method.

There's more...

The recipe works through the simplest example of mapping between taggings and chunkings. `BioTagChunkCodec` also takes the `TagLattice<String>` objects to produce n-best output, as will be shown in the HMM and CRF chunkers to follow.

HMM-based NER

`HmmChunker` uses an HMM to perform chunking over tokenized character sequences. Instances contain an HMM decoder for the model and tokenizer factory. The chunker requires the states of the HMM to conform to a token-by-token encoding of a chunking. It uses the tokenizer factory to break the chunks down into sequences of tokens and tags. Refer to the *Hidden Markov Models (HMM) – part of speech* recipe in *Chapter 4, Tagging Words and Tokens*.

We'll look at training `HmmChunker` and using it for the `CoNLL2002` Spanish task. You can and should use your own data, but this recipe assumes that training data will be in the `CoNLL2002` format.

Training is done using an `ObjectHandler` which supplies the training instances.

Getting ready

As we want to train this chunker, we need to either label some data using the **Computational Natural Language Learning** (**CoNLL**) schema or use the one that's publicly available. For speed, we'll choose to get a corpus that is available in the CoNLL 2002 task.

> The ConNLL is an annual meeting that sponsors a bakeoff. In 2002, the bakeoff involved Spanish and Dutch NER.

The data can be downloaded from http://www.cnts.ua.ac.be/conll2002/ner.tgz.

Similar to what we showed in the preceding recipe; let's take a look at what this data looks like:

```
El         O
Abogado    B-PER
General    I-PER
del        I-PER
Estado     I-PER
,          O
Daryl      B-PER
Williams   I-PER
,          O
```

With this encoding scheme, the phrases *El Abogado General del Estado* and *Daryl Williams* are coded as persons, with their beginning and continuing tokens picked out with tags B-PER and I-PER, respectively.

> There are a few formatting errors in the data that must be fixed before our parsers can handle them. After unpacking `ner.tgz` in the `data` directory you will have to go to `data/ner/data`, unzip the following files, and modify as indicated:
> `esp.train, line 221619, change I-LOC to B-LOC`
> `esp.testa, line 30882, change I-LOC to B-LOC`
> `esp.testb, line 9291, change I-LOC to B-LOC`

How to do it...

1. Using the command line, type the following:

   ```
   java -cp lingpipe-cookbook.1.0.jar:lib/lingpipe-4.1.0.jar com.lingpipe.cookbook.chapter5.HmmNeChunker
   ```

Finding Spans in Text – Chunking

2. It will run the training on the CoNLL training data if the model doesn't exist. It might take a while, so be patient. The output of the training will be:

   ```
   Training HMM Chunker on data from: data/ner/data/esp.train
   Output written to : models/Conll2002_ESP.RescoringChunker
   Enter text, . to quit:
   ```

3. Once the prompt to enter the text is presented, type in some Spanish text from the CoNLL test set:

   La empresa también tiene participación en Tele Leste Celular , operadora móvil de los estados de Bahía y Sergipe y que es controlada por la española Iberdrola , y además es socia de Portugal Telecom en Telesp Celular , la operadora móvil de Sao Paulo .

Rank	Conf	Span	Type	Phrase
0	1.0000	(105, 112)	LOC	Sergipe
1	1.0000	(149, 158)	ORG	Iberdrola
2	1.0000	(202, 216)	ORG	Telesp Celular
3	1.0000	(182, 198)	ORG	Portugal Telecom
4	1.0000	(97, 102)	LOC	Bahía
5	1.0000	(241, 250)	LOC	Sao Paulo
6	0.9907	(163, 169)	PER	además
7	0.9736	(11, 18)	ORG	también
8	0.9736	(39, 60)	ORG	en Tele Leste Celular
9	0.0264	(42, 60)	ORG	Tele Leste Celular

4. What we will see is a number of entities, their confidence score, the span in the original sentence, the type of entity, and the phrase that represents this entity.

5. To find out the correct tags, take a look at the annotated `esp.testa` file, which contains the following tags for this sentence:

   ```
   Tele B-ORG
   Leste I-ORG
   Celular I-ORG
   Bahía B-LOC
   Sergipe B-LOC
   Iberdrola B-ORG
   Portugal B-ORG
   Telecom I-ORG
   Telesp B-ORG
   Celular I-ORG
   Sao B-LOC
   Paulo I-LOC
   ```

6. This can be read as follows:

Tele Leste Celular	ORG
Bahía	LOC
Sergipe	LOC
Iberdrola	ORG
Portugal Telecom	ORG
Telesp Celular	ORG
Sao Paulo	LOC

7. So, we got all the ones with 1.000 confidence correct and the rest wrong. This can help us set up a threshold in production.

How it works...

The `CharLmRescoringChunker` provides a long-distance character language model-based chunker that operates by rescoring the output of a contained character language model HMM chunker. The underlying chunker is an instance of `CharLmHmmChunker`, which is configured with the specified tokenizer factory, n-gram length, number of characters, and interpolation ratio provided in the constructor.

Let's start with the `main()` method; here, we will set up the chunker, train it if it doesn't exist, and then allow for some input to get the named entities out:

```
String modelFilename = "models/Conll2002_ESP.RescoringChunker";
String trainFilename = "data/ner/data/esp.train";
```

The training file will be in the correct place if you unpack the CoNLL data (`tar -xvzf ner.tgz`) in the data directory. Remember to correct the annotation on line 221619 of `esp.train`. If you use other data, then modify and recompile the class.

The next bit of code trains the model if it doesn't exist and then loads the serialized version of the chunker. If you have questions about deserialization, see the *Deserializing and running a classifier* recipe in *Chapter 1*, *Simple Classifiers*. Consider the following code snippet:

```
File modelFile = new File(modelFilename);
if(!modelFile.exists()){
  System.out.println("Training HMM Chunker on data
    from: " + trainFilename);
  trainHMMChunker(modelFilename, trainFilename);
  System.out.println("Output written to : "
    + modelFilename);
}

@SuppressWarnings("unchecked")
RescoringChunker<CharLmRescoringChunker> chunker
```

```
    = (RescoringChunker<CharLmRescoringChunker>)
    AbstractExternalizable.readObject(modelFile);
```

The `trainHMMChunker()` method starts with some `File` bookkeeping before setting up configuration parameters for `CharLmRescoringChunker`:

```
static void trainHMMChunker(String modelFilename, String
trainFilename) throws IOException{
    File modelFile = new File(modelFilename);
    File trainFile = new File(trainFilename);

    int numChunkingsRescored = 64;
    int maxNgram = 12;
    int numChars = 256;
    double lmInterpolation = maxNgram;
    TokenizerFactory factory
        = IndoEuropeanTokenizerFactory.INSTANCE;

    CharLmRescoringChunker chunkerEstimator
        = new CharLmRescoringChunker(factory,numChunkingsRescored,
            maxNgram,numChars,
            lmInterpolation);
```

Starting with the first parameter, `numChunkingsRescored` sets the number of chunkings from the embedded `Chunker` that will be rescored in an effort to improve performance. The implementation of this rescoring can vary, but generally, less-localized information is used to improve on the basic HMM output, which is contextually limited. The `maxNgram` sets the maximum character size for the rescoring-bounded character language model per chunk type, and `lmInterpolation` dictates how the models are interpolated. A good value is the character n-gram size. Finally, a tokenizer factory is created. There is a lot going on in this class; consult Javadoc for more information.

Next in the method, we will get a parser to be discussed in the following code snippet, that takes `chunkerEstimator` with the `setHandler()` method, and then, the `parser.parse()` method does the actual training. The last bit of code serializes the model to disk—see the *How to serialize a LingPipe object – classifier example* recipe in *Chapter 1, Simple Classifiers*, to read about what is going on:

```
Conll2002ChunkTagParser parser
    = new Conll2002ChunkTagParser();
parser.setHandler(chunkerEstimator);
parser.parse(trainFile);
AbstractExternalizable.compileTo(chunkerEstimator,modelFile);
```

Now, let's take a look at parsing the CoNLL data. The source for this class is `src/com/lingpipe/cookbook/chapter5/Conll2002ChunkTagParser`:

```
public class Conll2002ChunkTagParser extends StringParser<ObjectHandl
er<Chunking>>
{

  static final String TOKEN_TAG_LINE_REGEX =
    "(\\S+)\\s(\\S+\\s)?(O|[B|I]-\\S+)";
  static final int TOKEN_GROUP = 1;
  static final int TAG_GROUP = 3;
  static final String IGNORE_LINE_REGEX =
    "-DOCSTART(.*)";
  static final String EOS_REGEX =
    "\\A\\Z";
  static final String BEGIN_TAG_PREFIX = "B-";
  static final String IN_TAG_PREFIX = "I-";
  static final String OUT_TAG = "O";
```

The statics set up the configuration of the `com.aliasi.tag.LineTaggingParser` LingPipe class. CoNLL, like many available data sets, uses a token/tag per line format, which is meant to be very easy to parse:

```
private final LineTaggingParser mParser =
  new LineTaggingParser(TOKEN_TAG_LINE_REGEX,
    TOKEN_GROUP, TAG_GROUP, IGNORE_LINE_REGEX, EOS_REGEX);
```

The `LineTaggingParser` constructor requires a regular expression that identifies the token and tag strings via grouping. There is additionally a regular expression for lines to ignore and finally, a regular expression for sentence ends.

Next, we set up `TagChunkCodec`; this will handle the mapping from tagged tokens in the BIO format to proper chunks. See the previous recipe, *Translating between word tagging and chunks – BIO codec*, for more about what is going on here. The remaining parameters customize the tags to match those of the CoNLL training data:

```
private final TagChunkCodec mCodec =
  new BioTagChunkCodec(null, false,
    BEGIN_TAG_PREFIX, IN_TAG_PREFIX, OUT_TAG);
```

The rest of the class provides methods for `parseString()`, which is immediately sent to the `LineTaggingParser` class:

```
public void parseString(char[] cs, int start, int end) {
  mParser.parseString(cs,start,end);
}
```

Finding Spans in Text – Chunking

Next, the `ObjectHandler` parser is properly configured with the codec and supplied handler:

```
public void setHandler(ObjectHandler<Chunking> handler) {

   ObjectHandler<Tagging<String>> taggingHandler
     = TagChunkCodecAdapters.chunkingToTagging(mCodec, handler);
   mParser.setHandler(taggingHandler);
}

public TagChunkCodec getTagChunkCodec(){
   return mCodec;
}
```

It's a lot of odd-looking code, but all this does is set up a parser to read the lines from the input file and extract chunkings out of them.

Finally, let's go back to the `main` method and look at the output loop. We will set up the `MAX_NBEST` chunkings value as 10 and then invoke the `nBestChunkings` method on the chunker. This provides the top 10 chunks and their probabilistic scores. Based on an evaluation, we can choose to cut off at a particular score:

```
char[] cs = text.toCharArray();
Iterator<Chunk> it =
   chunker.nBestChunks(cs,0,cs.length,
   MAX_N_BEST_CHUNKS);
System.out.println(text);
System.out.println("Rank       Conf      Span"  + "    Type    Phrase");
DecimalFormat df = new DecimalFormat("0.0000");

for (int n = 0; it.hasNext(); ++n) {

Chunk chunk = it.next();
double conf = chunk.score();
int start = chunk.start();
int end = chunk.end();
String phrase = text.substring(start,end);
System.out.println(n + " "         + "              "   + df.format(conf)
+ "          (" + start + ", " + end + ")    " + chunk.type()          + "    "
 + phrase);
}
```

There's more...

For more details on running a complete evaluation, refer to the evaluation section of the tutorial at `http://alias-i.com/lingpipe/demos/tutorial/ne/read-me.html`.

See also

For more details on `CharLmRescoringChunker` and `HmmChunker`, refer to:

- `http://alias-i.com/lingpipe/docs/api/com/aliasi/chunk/AbstractCharLmRescoringChunker.html`
- `http://alias-i.com/lingpipe/docs/api/com/aliasi/chunk/HmmChunker.html`

Mixing the NER sources

Now that we've seen how to build a few different types of NERs, we can look at how to combine them. In this recipe, we will take a regular expression chunker, a dictionary-based chunker, and an HMM-based chunker and combine their outputs and look at overlaps.

We will just initialize a few chunkers in the same way we did in the past few recipes and then pass the same text through these chunkers. The easiest possibility is that each chunker returns a unique output. For example, let's consider a sentence such as "President Obama was scheduled to give a speech at the G-8 conference this evening". If we have a person chunker and an organization chunker, we might only get two unique chunks out. However, if we add a `Presidents of USA` chunker, we will get three chunks: PERSON, ORGANIZATION, and PRESIDENT. This very simple recipe will show us one way to handle these cases.

How to do it...

1. Using the command line or equivalent in your IDE, type the following:

   ```
   java -cp lingpipe-cookbook.1.0.jar:lib/lingpipe-4.1.0.jar com.lingpipe.cookbook.chapter5.MultipleNer
   ```

2. The usual interactive prompt follows:

   ```
   Enter text, . to quit:
   President Obama is scheduled to arrive in London this evening. He will address the G-8 summit.
   neChunking: [10-15:PERSON@-Infinity, 42-48:LOCATION@-Infinity, 83-86:ORGANIZATION@-Infinity]
   pChunking: [62-66:MALE_PRONOUN@1.0]
   dChunking: [10-15:PRESIDENT@1.0]
   ----Overlaps Allowed

    Combined Chunks:
   [83-86:ORGANIZATION@-Infinity, 10-15:PERSON@-Infinity, 10-15:PRESIDENT@1.0, 42-48:LOCATION@-Infinity, 62-66:MALE_
   ```

```
PRONOUN@1.0]

----Overlaps Not Allowed

 Unique Chunks:
[83-86:ORGANIZATION@-Infinity, 42-48:LOCATION@-Infinity, 62-
66:MALE_PRONOUN@1.0]

 OverLapped Chunks:
[10-15:PERSON@-Infinity, 10-15:PRESIDENT@1.0]
```

3. We see the output from the three chunkers: `neChunking` is the output of an HMM chunker that is trained to return the MUC-6 entities, `pChunking` is a simple regular expression that recognizes male pronouns, and `dChunking` is a dictionary chunker that recognizes US Presidents.
4. With overlaps allowed, we will see the chunks for `PRESIDENT` as well as `PERSON` in the merged output.
5. With overlaps disallowed, they will be added to the set overlapped chunks and removed from the unique chunks.

How it works...

We initialized three chunkers that should be familiar to you from the previous recipes in this chapter:

```
Chunker pronounChunker =
  new RegExChunker(" He | he | Him | him",
  "MALE_PRONOUN",1.0);
File MODEL_FILE =
  new File("models/ne-en-news.muc6."
  + "AbstractCharLmRescoringChunker");
Chunker neChunker =
  (Chunker) AbstractExternalizable.readObject(MODEL_FILE);

MapDictionary<String> dictionary = new MapDictionary<String>();
dictionary.addEntry(
  new DictionaryEntry<String>("Obama","PRESIDENT",CHUNK_SCORE));
dictionary.addEntry(
  new DictionaryEntry<String>("Bush","PRESIDENT",CHUNK_SCORE));
ExactDictionaryChunker dictionaryChunker =
  new ExactDictionaryChunker(dictionary,
  IndoEuropeanTokenizerFactory.INSTANCE);
```

Now, we will just chunk our input text via all three chunkers, combine the chunks into one set, and pass our `getCombinedChunks` method to it:

```
Set<Chunk> neChunking = neChunker.chunk(text).chunkSet();
Set<Chunk> pChunking = pronounChunker.chunk(text).chunkSet();
Set<Chunk> dChunking = dictionaryChunker.chunk(text).chunkSet();
Set<Chunk> allChunks = new HashSet<Chunk>();
allChunks.addAll(neChunking);
allChunks.addAll(pChunking);
allChunks.addAll(dChunking);
getCombinedChunks(allChunks,true);//allow overlaps
getCombinedChunks(allChunks,false);//no overlaps
```

The meat of this recipe is in the `getCombinedChunks` method. We will just loop through all the chunks and check each pair if they overlap in their starts and ends. If they overlap and overlaps are not allowed, they are added to an overlapped set; otherwise, they are added to a combined set:

```
static void getCombinedChunks(Set<Chunk> chunkSet,
  boolean allowOverlap){
  Set<Chunk> combinedChunks = new HashSet<Chunk>();
  Set<Chunk>overLappedChunks = new HashSet<Chunk>();
  for(Chunk c : chunkSet){
    combinedChunks.add(c);
    for(Chunk x : chunkSet){
      if (c.equals(x)){
        continue;
      }
      if (ChunkingImpl.overlap(c,x)) {
        if (allowOverlap){
          combinedChunks.add(x);
        } else {
          overLappedChunks.add(x);
          combinedChunks.remove(c);
        }
      }
    }
  }
}
```

Here is the place to add more rules for overlapping chunks. For example, you can make it score based, so if the `PRESIDENT` chunk type has a higher score than the HMM-based one, you can choose it instead.

CRFs for chunking

CRFs are best known to provide close to state-of-the-art performance for named-entity tagging. This recipe will tell us how to build one of these systems. The recipe assumes that you have read, understood, and played with the *Conditional random fields – CRF for word/token tagging* recipe in *Chapter 4, Tagging Words and Tokens*, which addresses the underlying technology. Like HMMs, CRFs treat named entity detection as a word-tagging problem, with an interpretation layer that provides chunkings. Unlike HMMs, CRFs use a logistic-regression-based classification approach, which, in turn, allows for random features to be included. Also, there is an excellent tutorial on CRFs that this recipe follows closely (but omits details) at `http://alias-i.com/lingpipe/demos/tutorial/crf/read-me.html`. There is also a lot of information in the Javadoc.

Getting ready

Just as we did earlier, we will use a small hand-coded corpus to serve as training data. The corpus is in `src/com/lingpipe/cookbook/chapter5/TinyEntityCorpus.java`. It starts with:

```
public class TinyEntityCorpus extends Corpus<ObjectHandler<Chunking>>
{

  public void visitTrain(ObjectHandler<Chunking> handler) {
    for (Chunking chunking : CHUNKINGS) handler.handle(chunking);
  }

  public void visitTest(ObjectHandler<Chunking> handler) {
    /* no op */
  }
```

Since we are only using this corpus to train, the `visitTest()` method does nothing. However, the `visitTrain()` method exposes the handler to all the chunkings stored in the `CHUNKINGS` constant. This, in turn, looks like the following:

```
static final Chunking[] CHUNKINGS = new Chunking[] {
  chunking(""), chunking("The"),
  chunking("John ran.", chunk(0,4,"PER")),
  chunking("Mary ran.", chunk(0,4,"PER")),
  chunking("The kid ran."), chunking("John likes Mary.",
  chunk(0,4,"PER"), chunk(11,15,"PER")),
  chunking("Tim lives in Washington", chunk(0,3,"PER"),
  chunk(13,23,"LOC")), chunking("Mary Smith is in New York City",
```

```
    chunk(0,10,"PER"), chunk(17,30,"LOC")),
  chunking("New York City is fun", chunk(0,13,"LOC")),
  chunking("Chicago is not like Washington",
    chunk(0,7,"LOC"), chunk(20,30,"LOC"))
};
```

We are still not done. Given that the creation of `Chunking` is fairly verbose, there are static methods to help dynamically create the requisite objects:

```
static Chunking chunking(String s, Chunk... chunks) {
  ChunkingImpl chunking = new ChunkingImpl(s);
  for (Chunk chunk : chunks) chunking.add(chunk);
  return chunking;
}

static Chunk chunk(int start, int end, String type) {
  return ChunkFactory.createChunk(start,end,type);
}
```

This is all the setup; next, we will train and run a CRF on the preceding data.

How to do it...

1. Type the `TrainAndRunSimplCrf` class in the command line or run the equivalent in your IDE:

   `java -cp lingpipe-cookbook.1.0.jar:lib/lingpipe-4.1.0.jar: com.lingpipe.cookbook.chapter5.TrainAndRunSimpleCrf`

2. This results in loads of screen output that report on the health and progress of the CRF, it is mostly information from the underlying logistic-regression classifier that drives the whole show. The fun bit is that we will get an invitation to play with the new CRF:

   Enter text followed by new line

   >John Smith went to New York.

3. The chunker reports the first best output:

   FIRST BEST

   John Smith went to New York. : [0-10:PER@-Infinity, 19-27:LOC@-Infinity]

4. The preceding output is the first best analysis by the CRF of what sorts of entities are in the sentence. It thinks that `John Smith` is `PER` with the `0-10:PER@-Infinity` output. We know that it applies to the `John Smith` string by taking the substring from 0 to 10 in the input text. Ignore `-Infinity`, which is supplied for chunks that have no score. The first best chunking does not have scores. The other entity that it thinks is in the text is `New York` as an `LOC`.

5. Immediately, the conditional probabilities follow:

```
10 BEST CONDITIONAL
Rank log p(tags|tokens)   Tagging
0    -1.66335590  [0-10:PER@-Infinity, 19-27:LOC@-Infinity]
1    -2.38671498  [0-10:PER@-Infinity, 19-28:LOC@-Infinity]
2    -2.77341747  [0-10:PER@-Infinity]
3    -2.85908677  [0-4:PER@-Infinity, 19-27:LOC@-Infinity]
4    -3.00398856  [0-10:PER@-Infinity, 19-22:LOC@-Infinity]
5    -3.23050827  [0-10:PER@-Infinity, 16-27:LOC@-Infinity]
6    -3.49773765  [0-10:PER@-Infinity, 23-27:PER@-Infinity]
7    -3.58244582  [0-4:PER@-Infinity, 19-28:LOC@-Infinity]
8    -3.72315571  [0-10:PER@-Infinity, 19-22:PER@-Infinity]
9    -3.95386735  [0-10:PER@-Infinity, 16-28:LOC@-Infinity]
```

6. The preceding output provides the 10 best analyses of the whole phrase, along with their conditional (natural log) probabilities. In this case, we will see that the system isn't particularly confident of any of its analyses. For instance, the estimated probability of the first best analysis being correct is `exp(-1.66)=0.19`.

7. Next, in the output, we see probabilities for individual chunks:

```
MARGINAL CHUNK PROBABILITIES
Rank Chunk Phrase
0 0-10:PER@-0.49306887565189683 John Smith
1 19-27:LOC@-1.1957935770408703 New York
2 0-4:PER@-1.3270942262839682 John
3 19-22:LOC@-2.484463373596263 New
4 23-27:PER@-2.6919267821139776 York
5 16-27:LOC@-2.881057607295971 to New York
6 11-15:PER@-3.0868632773744222 went
7 16-18:PER@-3.1583044940140192 to
8 19-22:PER@-3.2036305275847825 New
9 23-27:LOC@-3.536294896211011 York
```

8. As with the previous conditional output, the probabilities are logs, so we can see that the `John Smith` chunk has estimated probability $\exp(-0.49) = 0.61$, which makes sense because in training the CRF saw `John` at the beginning of `PER` and `Smith` at the end of another, but not `John Smith` directly.

9. The preceding kind of probability distributions can really improve systems if there are sufficient resources to consider a broad range of analyses and ways of combining evidence to allow for improbable outcomes to be selected. First best analyses tend to be over committed to conservative outcomes that fit what training data looks like.

How it works...

The code in `src/com/lingpipe/cookbook/chapter5/TrainAndRunSimpleCRF.java` resembles our classifier and HMM recipes with a few differences. These differences are addressed as follows:

```
public static void main(String[] args) throws IOException {
  Corpus<ObjectHandler<Chunking>> corpus =
  new TinyEntityCorpus();

  TokenizerFactory tokenizerFactory =
    IndoEuropeanTokenizerFactory.INSTANCE;
  boolean enforceConsistency = true;
  TagChunkCodec tagChunkCodec =
    new BioTagChunkCodec(tokenizerFactory,
    enforceConsistency);
```

When we previously played with CRFs, the inputs were of the `Tagging<String>` type. Looking back at `TinyEntityCorpus.java`, the types are of the `Chunking` type. The preceding `BioTagChunkCodec` facilitates the translation of `Chunking` into `Tagging` via the efforts of a supplied `TokenizerFactory` and `boolean` that raise an exception if `TokenizerFactory` does not exactly agree with the `Chunk` starts and ends. Look back to the *Translating between word tagging and chunks–BIO codec* recipe better understand the role of this class.

Let's take a look at the following:

```
John Smith went to New York City. : [0-10:PER@-Infinity, 19-32:LOC@-Infinity]
```

This codec will translate into a tagging:

```
Tok     Tag
John    B_PER
Smith   I_PER
went    O
to      O
New     B_LOC
York    I_LOC
City    I_LOC
.       O
```

The codec will do the reverse operation as well. The Javadoc is worth a visit. Once this mapping is established, the rest of the CRF is the same as the word tagging case behind the scenes, as shown by the fact that we use the same feature extractor in the *Conditional random fields – CRF for word/token tagging* recipe, in *Chapter 4, Tagging Words and Tokens*. Consider the following code snippet:

```
ChainCrfFeatureExtractor<String> featureExtractor =
    new SimpleCrfFeatureExtractor();
```

All the mechanics are hidden inside a new `ChainCrfChunker` class, and it is initialized in a manner similar to logistic regression, which is the underlying technology. Refer to the *Logistic regression* recipe of *Chapter 3, Advanced Classifiers*, for more information on the configuration:

```
int minFeatureCount = 1;
boolean cacheFeatures = true;
boolean addIntercept = true;
double priorVariance = 4.0;
boolean uninformativeIntercept = true;
RegressionPrior prior =
    RegressionPrior.gaussian(priorVariance,
    uninformativeIntercept);
int priorBlockSize = 3;
double initialLearningRate = 0.05;
double learningRateDecay = 0.995;
AnnealingSchedule annealingSchedule =
    AnnealingSchedule.exponential(initialLearningRate,
    learningRateDecay);
double minImprovement = 0.00001;
int minEpochs = 10;
int maxEpochs = 5000;
Reporter reporter =
    Reporters.stdOut().setLevel(LogLevel.DEBUG);
System.out.println("\nEstimating");
ChainCrfChunker crfChunker =
```

```
    ChainCrfChunker.estimate(corpus,
    tagChunkCodec, tokenizerFactory,
    featureExtractor, addIntercept,
    minFeatureCount, cacheFeatures,
    prior, priorBlockSize, annealingSchedule,
  minImprovement, minEpochs, maxEpochs, reporter);
```

The only new thing here is the `tagChunkCodec` parameter, which we just described.

Once the training is over, we will access the chunker for first best with the following code:

```
    System.out.println("\nFIRST BEST");
    Chunking chunking = crfChunker.chunk(evalText);
    System.out.println(chunking);
```

Conditional chunkings are delivered by:

```
    int maxNBest = 10;
    System.out.println("\n" + maxNBest + " BEST CONDITIONAL");
    System.out.println("Rank log p(tags|tokens)   Tagging");
    Iterator<ScoredObject<Chunking>> it =
      crfChunker.nBestConditional(evalTextChars,0,
      evalTextChars.length,maxNBest);

    for (int rank = 0; rank < maxNBest && it.hasNext(); ++rank) {
      ScoredObject<Chunking> scoredChunking = it.next();
      System.out.println(rank + "       " +
        scoredChunking.score() + " " +
        scoredChunking.getObject().chunkSet());
    }
```

The individual chunks are accessed with:

```
    System.out.println("\nMARGINAL CHUNK PROBABILITIES");
    System.out.println("Rank Chunk Phrase");
    int maxNBestChunks = 10;
    Iterator<Chunk> nBestIt  = crfChunker.nBestChunks
      (evalTextChars,0, evalTextChars.length,maxNBestChunks);
    for (int n = 0; n < maxNBestChunks && nBestIt.hasNext(); ++n) {
      Chunk chunk = nBestChunkIt.next();
      System.out.println(n + " " + chunk + " " +
        evalText.substring(chunk.start(),chunk.end()));
    }
```

That's it. You have access to one of the world's finest chunking technologies. Next, we will show you how to make it better.

Finding Spans in Text – Chunking

NER using CRFs with better features

In this recipe, we'll show you how to create a realistic, though not quite state-of-the-art, set of features for CRFs. The features will include normalized tokens, part-of-speech tags, word-shape features, position features, and token prefixes and suffixes. Substitute it for the `SimpleCrfFeatureExtractor` in the *CRFs for chunking* recipe to use it.

How to do it...

The source for this recipe is in `src/com/lingpipe/cookbook/chapter5/FancyCrfFeatureExtractor.java`:

1. Open up your IDE or command prompt and type:

   `java -cp lingpipe-cookbook.1.0.jar:lib/lingpipe-4.1.0.jar: com.lingpipe.cookbook.chapter5.FancyCrfFeatureExtractor`

2. Brace yourself for an explosion of features from the console. The data being used for feature extraction is `TinyEntityCorpus` of the previous recipe. Luckily, the first bit of data is just the node features for the "John" in the sentence `John ran.`:

   `Tagging:   John/PN`

   `Node Feats:{PREF_NEXT_ra=1.0, PREF_Jo=1.0, POS_np=1.0, TOK_CAT_LET-CAP=1.0, SUFF_NEXT_an=1.0, PREF_Joh=1.0, PREF_NEXT_r=1.0, SUFF_John=1.0, TOK_John=1.0, PREF_NEXT_ran=1.0, BOS=1.0, TOK_NEXT_ran=1.0, SUFF_NEXT_n=1.0, SUFF_NEXT_ran=1.0, SUFF_ohn=1.0, PREF_J=1.0, POS_NEXT_vbd=1.0, SUFF_hn=1.0, SUFF_n=1.0, TOK_CAT_NEXT_ran=1.0, PREF_John=1.0}`

3. The next word in the sequence adds edge features—we won't bother showing you the node features:

   `Edge Feats:{PREV_TAG_TOKEN_CAT_PN_LET-CAP=1.0, PREV_TAG_PN=1.0}`

How it works...

As with other recipes, we won't bother discussing parts that are very similar to previous recipes—the relevant previous recipe here is the *Modifying CRFs* recipe in *Chapter 4, Tagging Words and Tokens*. This is exactly the same, except for the fact that we will add in a lot more features—perhaps, from unexpected sources.

> The tutorial for CRFs covers how to serialize/deserialize this class. This implementation does not cover it.

Object construction is similar to the `Modifying CRFs` recipe in *Chapter 4, Tagging Words and Tokens*:

```
public FancyCrfFeatureExtractor()
  throws ClassNotFoundException, IOException {
  File posHmmFile = new File("models/pos-en-general"
    + "brown.HiddenMarkovModel");
  @SuppressWarnings("unchecked") HiddenMarkovModel posHmm =
    (HiddenMarkovModel)
  AbstractExternalizable.readObject(posHmmFile);

  FastCache<String,double[]> emissionCache =
    new FastCache<String,double[]>(100000);
  mPosTagger = new HmmDecoder(posHmm,null,emissionCache);
}
```

The constructor sets up a part-of-speech tagger with a cache and shoves it into the `mPosTagger` member variable.

The following method does very little, except supplying an inner `ChunkerFeatures` class:

```
public ChainCrfFeatures<String> extract(List<String> tokens,
List<String> tags) {
  return new ChunkerFeatures(tokens,tags);
}
```

The `ChunkerFeatures` class is where things get more interesting:

```
class ChunkerFeatures extends ChainCrfFeatures<String> {
  private final Tagging<String> mPosTagging;

  public ChunkerFeatures(List<String> tokens,
    List<String> tags) {
    super(tokens,tags);
    mPosTagging = mPosTagger.tag(tokens);
  }
```

The `mPosTagger` function is used to set up `Tagging<String>` for the tokens presented on class creation. This will be aligned with the `tag()` and `token()` superclass methods and be the source of part-of-speech tags as a node feature.

Now, we can get on with the feature extraction. We will start with edge features, as they are the simplest:

```
public Map<String,? extends Number> edgeFeatures(int n, int k) {
  ObjectToDoubleMap<String> feats =
    new ObjectToDoubleMap<String>();
  feats.set("PREV_TAG_" + tag(k),1.0);
  feats.set("PREV_TAG_TOKEN_CAT_" + tag(k)
    + "_" + tokenCat(n-1), 1.0);
  return feats;
}
```

The new feature is prefixed with `PREV_TAG_TOKEN_CAT_`, and the example is `PREV_TAG_TOKEN_CAT_PN_LET-CAP=1.0`. The `tokenCat()` method looks at the word shape feature for the previous token and returns it as a string. Look at the Javadoc for `IndoEuropeanTokenCategorizer` to see what is going on.

Next comes the node features. There are many of these; each will be presented in turn:

```
public Map<String,? extends Number> nodeFeatures(int n) {
  ObjectToDoubleMap<String> feats =
    new ObjectToDoubleMap<String>();
```

The preceding code sets up the method with the appropriate return type. The next two lines set up some state to know where the feature extractor is in the string:

```
boolean bos = n == 0;
boolean eos = (n + 1) >= numTokens();
```

Next, we will compute the token categories, tokens, and part-of-speech tags for the current position, previous position, and the next position of the input:

```
String tokenCat = tokenCat(n);
String prevTokenCat = bos ? null : tokenCat(n-1);
String nextTokenCat = eos ? null : tokenCat(n+1);

String token = normedToken(n);
String prevToken = bos ? null : normedToken(n-1);
String nextToken = eos ? null : normedToken(n+1);

String posTag = mPosTagging.tag(n);
String prevPosTag = bos ? null : mPosTagging.tag(n-1);
String nextPosTag = eos ? null : mPosTagging.tag(n+1);
```

The previous and next methods check if we're at the begin or end of the sentence and return `null` accordingly. The part-of-speech tagging is taken from the saved part-of-speech taggings computed in the constructor.

The token methods provide some normalization of tokens to compress all numbers to the same kind of value. This method is as follows:

```
public String normedToken(int n) {
  return token(n).replaceAll("\\d+","*$0*")
    .replaceAll("\\d","D");
}
```

This just takes every sequence of numbers and replaces it with *D...D*. For instance, 12/3/08 is converted to *DD*/*D*/*DD*.

We will then set feature values for the preceding, current, and following tokens. First, a flag indicates whether it begins or ends a sentence or an internal node:

```
if (bos) {
  feats.set("BOS",1.0);
}
if (eos) {
  feats.set("EOS",1.0);
}
if (!bos && !eos) {
  feats.set("!BOS!EOS",1.0);
}
```

Next, we will include the tokens, token categories, and their parts of speech:

```
feats.set("TOK_" + token, 1.0);
if (!bos) {
  feats.set("TOK_PREV_" + prevToken,1.0);
}
if (!eos) {
  feats.set("TOK_NEXT_" + nextToken,1.0);
}
feats.set("TOK_CAT_" + tokenCat, 1.0);
if (!bos) {
  feats.set("TOK_CAT_PREV_" + prevTokenCat, 1.0);
}
if (!eos) {
  feats.set("TOK_CAT_NEXT_" + nextToken, 1.0);
}
feats.set("POS_" + posTag,1.0);
if (!bos) {
  feats.set("POS_PREV_" + prevPosTag,1.0);
}
if (!eos) {
  feats.set("POS_NEXT_" + nextPosTag,1.0);
}
```

Finding Spans in Text – Chunking

Finally, we will add the prefix and suffix features, which add features for each suffix and prefix (up to a prespecified length):

```
      for (String suffix : suffixes(token)) {
        feats.set("SUFF_" + suffix,1.0);
      }
    }
    if (!bos) {
      for (String suffix : suffixes(prevToken)) {
        feats.set("SUFF_PREV_" + suffix,1.0);
        if (!eos) {
          for (String suffix : suffixes(nextToken)) {
            feats.set("SUFF_NEXT_" + suffix,1.0);
          }
          for (String prefix : prefixes(token)) {
            feats.set("PREF_" + prefix,1.0);
          }
          if (!bos) {
            for (String prefix : prefixes(prevToken)) {
              feats.set("PREF_PREV_" + prefix,1.0);
            }
          }
          if (!eos) {
            for (String prefix : prefixes(nextToken)) {
              feats.set("PREF_NEXT_" + prefix,1.0);
            }
          }
        }
      }
      return feats;
    }
```

After this, we will just return the feature mapping generated.

The `prefix` or `suffix` function is simply implemented with a list:

```
    static int MAX_PREFIX_LENGTH = 4;
      static List<String> prefixes(String s) {
        int numPrefixes = Math.min(MAX_PREFIX_LENGTH,s.length());
        if (numPrefixes == 0) {
          return Collections.emptyList();
        }
        if (numPrefixes == 1) {
          return Collections.singletonList(s);
        }
        List<String> result = new ArrayList<String>(numPrefixes);
        for (int i = 1; i <= Math.min(MAX_PREFIX_LENGTH,s.length()); ++i)
  {
          result.add(s.substring(0,i));
        }
```

```
      return result;
  }

  static int MAX_SUFFIX_LENGTH = 4;
  static List<String> suffixes(String s) {
    int numSuffixes = Math.min(s.length(), MAX_SUFFIX_LENGTH);
    if (numSuffixes <= 0) {
      return Collections.emptyList();
    }
    if (numSuffixes == 1) {
      return Collections.singletonList(s);
    }
    List<String> result = new ArrayList<String>(numSuffixes);
    for (int i = s.length() - numSuffixes; i < s.length(); ++i) {
      result.add(s.substring(i));
    }
    return result;
  }
```

That's a nice feature set for your named-entity detector.

6
String Comparison and Clustering

In this chapter, we will cover the following recipes:

- Distance and proximity – simple edit distance
- Weighted edit distance
- The Jaccard distance
- The Tf-Idf distance
- Using edit distance and language models for spelling correction
- The case restoring corrector
- Automatic phrase completion
- Single-link and complete-link clustering using edit distance
- Latent Dirichlet allocation (LDA) for multitopic clustering

Introduction

This chapter starts off by comparing strings using standard language neutral techniques. Then, we will use these techniques to build some commonly used applications. We will also look at clustering techniques based on distances between strings.

For a string, we use the canonical definition that a string is a sequence of characters. So, clearly, these techniques apply to words, phrases, sentences, paragraphs, and so on, all of which you have learnt to extract in the previous chapters.

String Comparison and Clustering

Distance and proximity – simple edit distance

String comparison refers to techniques used to measure the similarity between two strings. We will use distance and proximity to specify how similar any two strings are. The more similar any two strings are, the lesser the distance between them, so the distance from a string to itself is 0. An inverse measure is proximity, which means that the more similar any two strings are, the greater their proximity.

We will take a look at simple edit distance first. Simple edit distance measures distance in terms of how many edits are required to convert one string to the other. A common distance measure proposed by Levenshtien in 1965 allows deletion, insertion, and substitution as basic operations. Adding in transposition is called Damerau-Levenshtien distance. For example, the distance between `foo` and `boo` is 1, as we're looking at a substitution of `f` with `b`.

> For more on distance metrics, refer to the Wikipedia article on distance at http://en.wikipedia.org/wiki/Distance.

Let's look at some more examples of editable operations:

- **Deletion**: `Bart` and `Bar`
- **Insertion**: `Bar` and `Bart`
- **Substitution**: `Bar` and `Car`
- **Transposition**: `Bart` and `Brat`

How to do it...

Now, we will run a simple example on edit distance:

1. Run the `SimpleEditDistance` class using the command line or your IDE:

   ```
   java -cp lingpipe-cookbook.1.0.jar:lib/lingpipe-4.1.0.jar com.lingpipe.cookbook.chapter6.SimpleEditDistance
   ```

2. In the command prompt, you will be prompted for two strings:

   ```
   Enter the first string:
   ab
   Enter the second string:
   ba
   Allowing Transposition Distance between: ab and ba is 1.0
   No Transposition Distance between: ab and ba is 2.0
   ```

3. You will see the distance between the two strings with transposition allowed and with transposition not allowed.
4. Play with some more examples to get a sense of how it works—try them first by hand and then verify that you got the optimal case.

How it works...

This is a very simple piece of code, and all it does is create two instances of the `EditDistance` class: one that allows transpositions, and the other that does not allow transpositions:

```
public static void main(String[] args) throws IOException {

    EditDistance dmAllowTrans = new EditDistance(true);
    EditDistance dmNoTrans = new EditDistance(false);
```

The remaining code will set up an I/O routing, apply the edit distances, and print them out:

```
BufferedReader reader = new BufferedReader(new
   InputStreamReader(System.in));
while (true) {
  System.out.println("Enter the first string:");
  String text1 = reader.readLine();
  System.out.println("Enter the second string:");
  String text2 = reader.readLine();
  double allowTransDist = dmAllowTrans.distance(text1, text2);
  double noTransDist = dmNoTrans.distance(text1, text2);
  System.out.println("Allowing Transposition Distance "
     +" between: " + text1 + " and " + text2 +
     " is " + allowTransDist);
  System.out.println("No Transposition Distance
     between: " + text1 + " and " + text2 +
     " is " + noTransDist);
 }
}
```

If we wanted the proximity instead of distance, we would just use the `proximity` method instead of the `distance` method.

In simple `EditDistance`, all the editable operations have a fixed cost of 1.0, that is, each editable operation (deletion, substitution, insertion, and, if allowed, transposition) is counted with a cost of 1.0 each. So, in the example where we find the distance between `ab` and `ba`, there is one deletion and one insertion, both of which have a cost of 1.0. Therefore, this makes the distance between `ab` and `ba` 2.0 if transposition is not allowed and 1.0 if it is. Note that typically, there will be more than one way to edit one string into the other.

String Comparison and Clustering

> While `EditDistance` is quite simple to use, it is not simple to implement. This is what the Javadoc has to say about this class:
>
> *Implementation note: This class implements edit distance using dynamic programming in time O(n * m) where n and m are the length of the sequences being compared. Using a sliding window of three lattice slices rather than allocating the entire lattice at once, the space required is that for three arrays of integers as long as the shorter of the two character sequences being compared.*

In the following sections, we will see how to assign varying costs to each edit operation.

See also

- Refer to the LingPipe Javadoc on `EditDistance` at http://alias-i.com/lingpipe/docs/api/com/aliasi/spell/EditDistance.html for more details
- For more details on distance, refer to the Javadoc at http://alias-i.com/lingpipe/docs/api/com/aliasi/util/Distance.html
- For more details on proximity, refer to the Javadoc at http://alias-i.com/lingpipe/docs/api/com/aliasi/util/Proximity.html

Weighted edit distance

Weighted edit distance is essentially a simple edit distance, except that the edits allow different costs to be associated with each kind of edit operation. The edit operations we identified in the previous recipe are substitution, insertion, deletion, and transposition. Additionally, there can be a cost associated with the exact matches to increase the weight for matching – this might be used when edits are required, such as a string-variation generator. Edit weights are generally scaled as log probabilities so that you can assign likelihood to an edit operation. The larger the weight, the more likely that edit operation is. As probabilities are between 0 and 1, log probabilities, or weights, will be between negative infinity and zero. For more on this refer to the Javadoc on the `WeightedEditDistance` class at http://alias-i.com/lingpipe/docs/api/com/aliasi/spell/WeightedEditDistance.html.

On the log scale, weighted edit distance can be generalized to produce exactly the same results as simple edit distance did in the previous recipe by setting the match weight to 0 and substituting, deleting, and inserting weights to -1 and transposition weights to either -1 or negative infinity, if we want to turn transposition off.

We will look at weighted edit distance for spell checking and Chinese word segmentation in other recipes.

In this section, we will use the `FixedWeightEditDistance` instance and create the `CustomWeightEditDistance` class that extends the `WeightedEditDistance` abstract class. The `FixedWeightEditDistance` class is initialized with weights for each edit operation. The `CustomWeightEditDistance` class extends `WeightedEditDistance` and has rules for each edit operation weights. The weight for deleting alphanumeric characters is -1, and for all other characters, that is, punctuation and spaces, it is is 0. We will set insertion weights to be the same as deletion weights.

How to do it...

Let's expand on our previous example and look at a version that runs the simple edit distance as well as our weighted edit distance:

1. In your IDE run the `SimpleWeightedEditDistance class,` or in the command line, type:

   ```
   java -cp lingpipe-cookbook.1.0.jar:lib/lingpipe-4.1.0.jar com.lingpipe.cookbook.chapter6.SimpleWeightedEditDistance
   ```

2. In the command line, you will be prompted for two strings: enter the examples shown here or choose your own:

   ```
   SimpleWeightedEditDistance (Java Application) /Library/Java/JavaVirtualMachines/1.6.0_37-b06-434.jdk
   Enter the first string:
   Bart
   Enter the second string:
   Brat
   Allowing Transposition Distance between: Bart and Brat is 1.0
   No Transposition Distance between: Bart and Brat is 2.0
   Fixed Weight Edit Distance between: Bart and Brat is 4.0
   Custom Weight Edit Distance between: Bart and Brat is 2.0
   Enter the first string:
   abc+
   Enter the second string:
   Abc-
   Allowing Transposition Distance between: abc+ and Abc- is 2.0
   No Transposition Distance between: abc+ and Abc- is 2.0
   Fixed Weight Edit Distance between: abc+ and Abc- is 4.0
   Custom Weight Edit Distance between: abc+ and Abc- is -0.0
   Enter the first string:
   ```

3. As you can see, there are two other distance measures being shown here: a fixed weight edit distance and a custom weight edit distance.

4. Play around with other examples, including punctuation and spaces.

How it works...

We will instantiate a `FixedWeightEditDistance` class with some weights that are, arbitrarily chosen:

```
double matchWeight = 0;
double deleteWeight = -2;
double insertWeight = -2;
double substituteWeight = -2;
double transposeWeight = Double.NEGATIVE_INFINITY;
WeightedEditDistance wed = new FixedWeightEditDistance(matchWeight,del
eteWeight,insertWeight,substituteWeight,transposeWeight);
System.out.println("Fixed Weight Edit Distance: "+ wed.toString());
```

In this example, we set the delete, substitute, and insert weights to be equal. This is very similar to the standard edit distance, except that we modified the weights associated with the edit operations from 1 to 2. Setting the transpose weight to negative infinity effectively turns off transpositions completely. Obviously, it's not necessary that the delete, substitute, and insert weights should be equal.

We will also create a `CustomWeightEditDistance` class, which treats punctuations and whitespaces as matches, that is, zero cost for the insert and delete operations (for letters or digits, the cost remains -1). For substitutions, if the character is different only in case, the cost is zero; for all other cases, the cost is -1. We will also turn off transposition by setting its cost to negative infinity. This will result in `Abc+` matching `abc-`:

```
public static class CustomWeightedEditDistance extends
WeightedEditDistance{

  @Override
  public double deleteWeight(char arg0) {
    return (Character.isDigit(arg0)||Character.isLetter(arg0))
      ? -1 : 0;

}

  @Override
  public double insertWeight(char arg0) {
    return deleteWeight(arg0);
}

  @Override
```

```java
    public double matchWeight(char arg0) {
      return 0;
    }

    @Override
    public double substituteWeight(char cDeleted, char cInserted) {
      return Character.toLowerCase(cDeleted) ==
        Character.toLowerCase(cInserted) ? 0 :-1;

    }

    @Override
    public double transposeWeight(char arg0, char arg1) {
      return Double.NEGATIVE_INFINITY;
    }

}
```

This sort of custom weighted edit distance is particularly useful in comparing strings where minor formatting changes are encountered, such as gene/protein names that vary from `Serpin A3` to `serpina3` but refer to the same thing.

See also

- There is a T&T (Tsuruoka and Tsujii) specification for edit distance to compare protein names, refer to `http://alias-i.com/lingpipe/docs/api/com/aliasi/dict/ApproxDictionaryChunker.html#TT_DISTANCE`
- More details on the `WeightedEditDistance` class can be found on the Javadoc page at `http://alias-i.com/lingpipe/docs/api/com/aliasi/spell/WeightedEditDistance.html`

The Jaccard distance

The Jaccard distance is a very popular and efficient way of comparing strings. The Jaccard distance operates at a token level and compares two strings by first tokenizing them and then dividing the number of common tokens by the total number of tokens. In the *Eliminate near duplicates with the Jaccard distance* recipe in *Chapter 1*, *Simple Classifiers*, we applied the distance to eliminate near-duplicate tweets. This recipe will go into a bit more detail and show you how it is computed.

String Comparison and Clustering

A distance of 0 is a perfect match, that is, the strings share all their terms, and a distance of 1 is a perfect mismatch, that is, the strings have no terms in common. Remember that proximity and distance are additive inverses, so proximity also ranges from 1 to 0. Proximity of 1 is a perfect match, and proximity of 0 is a perfect mismatch:

```
proximity = count(common tokens)/count(total tokens)
distance = 1 - proximity
```

The tokens are generated by `TokenizerFactory`, which is passed in during construction. For example, let's use `IndoEuropeanTokenizerFactory` and take a look at a concrete example. If `string1` is `fruit flies like a banana` and `string2` is `time flies like an arrow`, then the token set for `string1` would be {'fruit', 'flies', 'like', 'a', 'banana'}, and the token set for `string2` would be {'time', 'flies', 'like', 'an', 'arrow'}. The common terms (or the intersection) between these two token sets are {'flies', 'like'}, and the union of these terms is {'fruit',' flies', 'like', 'a', 'banana', 'time', 'an', 'arrow'}. Now, we can calculate the Jaccard proximity by dividing the number of common terms by the total number of terms, that is, 2/8, which equals 0.25. Thus, the distance is 0.75 (1 - 0.25). Obviously, the Jaccard distance is eminently tunable by modifying the tokenizer that the class is initialized with. For example, one could use a case-normalizing tokenizer so that `Abc` and `abc` would be considered equivalent. Similarly, a stemming tokenizer would consider the words `runs` and `run` to be equivalent. We will see a similar ability in the next distance metric, the Tf-Idf distance, as well.

How to do it...

Here's how to run the `JaccardDistance` example:

1. In Eclipse, run the `JaccardDistanceSample` class, or in the command line, type:

   ```
   java -cp lingpipe-cookbook.1.0.jar:lib/lingpipe-4.1.0.jar com.lingpipe.cookbook.chapter6.JaccardDistanceSample
   ```

2. As in the previous recipes, you will be prompted for two strings. The first string that we will use is `Mimsey Were the Borogroves`, which is an excellent sci-fi short-story title, and the second string `All mimsy were the borogoves,` is the actual line from *Jabberwocky* that inspired it:

   ```
   Enter the first string:
   Mimsey Were the Borogroves
   Enter the second string:
   All mimsy were the borogoves,


   IndoEuropean Tokenizer
   Text1 Tokens: {'Mimsey''Were''the'}
   ```

```
Text2 Tokens: {'All''mimsy''were''the''borogoves'}
IndoEuropean Jaccard Distance is 0.8888888888888888


Character Tokenizer
Text1 Tokens: {'M''i''m''s''e''y''W''e''r''e''t''h''e''B''o''r''o'
'g''r''o''v''e'}
Text2 Tokens: {'A''l''l''m''i''m''s''y''w''e''r''e''t''h''e''b''o'
'r''o''g''o''v''e''s'}
Character Jaccard Distance between is 0.42105263157894735


EnglishStopWord Tokenizer
Text1 Tokens: {'Mimsey''Were'}
Text2 Tokens: {'All''mimsy''borogoves'}
English Stopword Jaccard Distance between is 1.0
```

3. The output contains the tokens and the distances using three different tokenizers. The `IndoEuropean` and `EnglishStopWord` tokenizers are pretty close and show that these two lines are far apart. Remember that the closer two strings are, the lesser is the distance between them. The character tokenizer, however, shows that these lines are closer to each other with characters as the basis of comparison. Tokenizers can make a big difference in calculating the distance between strings.

How it works...

The code is straightforward, and we will just cover the creation of the `JaccardDistance` objects. We will start with three tokenizer factories:

```
TokenizerFactory indoEuropeanTf =
    IndoEuropeanTokenizerFactory.INSTANCE;

TokenizerFactory characterTf =
    CharacterTokenizerFactory.INSTANCE;

TokenizerFactory englishStopWordTf =
    new EnglishStopTokenizerFactory(indoEuropeanTf);
```

Note that `englishStopWordTf` uses a base tokenizer factory to construct itself. Refer to *Chapter 2, Finding and Working with Words*, if there are questions on what is going on here.

String Comparison and Clustering

Next, the Jaccard distance classes are constructed, given a tokenizer factory as an argument:

```
JaccardDistance jaccardIndoEuropean =
  new JaccardDistance(indoEuropeanTf);
JaccardDistance jaccardCharacter =
  new JaccardDistance(characterTf);

JaccardDistance jaccardEnglishStopWord =
  new JaccardDistance(englishStopWordTf);
```

The rest of the code is just our standard I/O loop and some print statements. That's it! On to more sophisticated measures of string distance.

The Tf-Idf distance

A very useful distance metric between strings is provided by the `TfIdfDistance` class. It is, in fact, closely related to the distance metric from the popular open source search engine, Lucene/SOLR/Elastic Search, where the strings being compared are the query against documents in the index. Tf-Idf stands for the core formula that is **term frequency** (**TF**) times **inverse document frequency** (**IDF**) for terms shared by the query and the document. A very cool thing about this approach is that common terms (for example, `the`) that are very frequent in documents are downweighted, while rare terms are upweighted in the distance comparison. This can help focus the distance on terms that are actually discriminating in the document collection.

Not only does `TfIdfDistance` come in handy for search-engine-like applications, it can be very useful for clustering and for any problem that calls for document similarity without supervised training data. It has a desirable property; scores are normalized to a score between 0 and 1, and for a fixed document d1 and varying length documents d2, do not overwhelm the assigned score. In our experience, the scores for different pairs of documents are fairly robust if you were trying to rank the quality of match for a pair of documents.

> Note that there are a range of different distances called Tf-Idf distances. The one in this class is defined to be symmetric, unlike typical Tf-Idf distances that are defined for information-retrieval purposes.

There is a lot of information in the Javadoc that is well worth a good look. However, for the purposes of these recipes, all you need to know is that the Tf-Idf distance is useful for finding similar documents on a word-by-word basis.

How to do it...

In the quest to keep things a little interesting, we will use our `TfIdfDistance` class to build a really simple search engine over tweets. We will perform the following steps:

1. If you have not done it already, run the `TwitterSearch` class from *Chapter 1, Simple Classifiers*, and get some tweets to play with, or go with our provided data. We will use the tweets found by running the `Disney World` query, and they are already in the `data` directory.

2. Type the following in the command line—this uses our defaults:

    ```
    java -cp lingpipe-cookbook.1.0.jar:lib/lingpipe-4.1.0.jar:lib/opencsv-2.4.jar com.lingpipe.cookbook.chapter6.TfIdfSearch
    Reading search index from data/disney.csv
    Getting IDF data from data/connecticut_yankee_king_arthur.txt
    enter a query:
    ```

3. Enter a query that has some likely word matches:

    ```
    I want to go to disney world
    0.86 : I want to go to Disneyworld
    0.86 : I want to go to disneyworld
    0.75 : I just want to go to DisneyWorld...
    0.75 : I just want to go to Disneyworld ???
    0.65 : Cause I wanna go to Disneyworld.
    0.56 : I wanna go to disneyworld with Demi
    0.50 : I wanna go back to disneyworld
    0.50 : I so want to go to Disneyland I've never been. I've been to Disneyworld in Florida.
    0.47 : I want to go to #DisneyWorld again... It's so magical!!
    0.45 : I want to go to DisneyWorld.. Never been there :( #jadedchildhood
    ```

4. That's it. Try different queries and play around with the scores. Then, have a look at the source.

String Comparison and Clustering

How it works...

This code is a very simple way to build a search engine rather than a good way to build one. However, it is a decent way to explore how the concept of string distance works in the search context. Later in the book, we will perform clustering based on the same distance metric. Start with the `main()` class in `src/com/lingpipe/cookbook/chapter6/TfIdfSearch.java`:

```
public static void main(String[] args) throws IOException {
  String searchableDocs = args.length > 0
    ? args[0] : "data/disneyWorld.csv";
  System.out.println("Reading search index
    from " + searchableDocs);

  String idfFile = args.length > 1
  ? args[1] : "data/connecticut_yankee_king_arthur.txt";
  System.out.println("Getting IDF data from " + idfFile);
```

This program can take command-line-supplied files for the searched data in the `.csv` format and a text file for use as the source of training data. Next, we will set up a tokenizer factory and `TfIdfDistance`. If you are not familiar with tokenizer factories, then refer to the *Modifying tokenizer factories* recipe in *Chapter 2, Modifying Tokenizer Factories*, for an explanation:

```
TokenizerFactory tokFact = IndoEuropeanTokenizerFactory.INSTANCE;
TfIdfDistance tfIdfDist = new TfIdfDistance(tokFact);
```

Then, we will get the data that will be the IDF component by splitting the training text on ".", which approximates sentence detection—we could have done a proper sentence detection like we did in the *Sentence detection* recipe in *Chapter 5, Finding Spans in Text – Chunking*, but we chose to keep the example as simple as possible:

```
String training =
  Files.readFromFile(new File(idfFile), Strings.UTF8);
for (String line: training.split("\\.")) {
  tfIdfDist.handle(line);
}
```

Inside the `for` loop, there is `handle()`, which trains the class with knowledge of the token distributions in the corpus, with sentences being the document. It often happens that the concept of document is either smaller (sentence, paragraph, and word) or larger than what is typically termed `document`. In this case, the document frequency will be the number of sentences the token is in.

Next, the documents that we are searching are loaded:

```
List<String[]> docsToSearch =
  Util.readCsvRemoveHeader(new File(searchableDocs));
```

The console is set up to read in the query:

```
BufferedReader reader =
  new BufferedReader(new InputStreamReader(System.in));
while (true) {
  System.out.println("enter a query: ");
  String query = reader.readLine();
```

Next, each document is scored against the query with `TfIdfDistance` and put into `ObjectToDoubleMap`, which keeps track of the proximity:

```
ObjectToDoubleMap<String> scoredMatches =
  new ObjectToDoubleMap<String>();
for (String [] line : docsToSearch) {
  scoredMatches.put(line[Util.TEXT_OFFSET],
    tfIdfDist.proximity(line[Util.TEXT_OFFSET],
    query));
}
```

Finally, `scoredMatches` is retrieved in the proximity order, and the first 10 examples are printed out:

```
List<String> rankedDocs = scoredMatches.keysOrderedByValueList();
for (int i = 0; i < 10; ++i) {
  System.out.printf("%.2f : ",
    scoredMatches.get(rankedDocs.get(i)));
  System.out.println(rankedDocs.get(i));
}
}
```

While this approach is very inefficient, in that, each query iterates over all the training data, does an explicit `TfIdfDistance` comparison, and stores it, it is not a bad way to play around with small datasets and comparison metrics.

There's more...

There are some subtleties worth highlighting about `TfIdfDistance`.

Difference between supervised and unsupervised trainings

When we train `TfIdfDistance`, there are some important differences in the use of training from the ones used in the rest of the book. The training done here is unsupervised, which means that no human or other external source has marked up the data for the expected outcome. Most of the recipes in this book that train use human annotated, or supervised, data.

Training on test data is OK

As this is unsupervised data, there is no requirement that the training data should be be distinct from the evaluation or production data.

Using edit distance and language models for spelling correction

Spelling correction takes a user input text and provides a corrected form. Most of us are familiar with automatic spelling correction via our smart phones or editors such as Microsoft Word. There are obviously quite a few amusing examples of these on the Web where the spelling correction fails. In this example, we'll build our own spelling-correction engine and look at how to tune it.

LingPipe's spelling correction is based on a noisy-channel model which models user mistakes and expected user input (based on the data). Expected user input is modeled by a character-language model, and mistakes (or noise) is modeled by weighted edit distance. The spelling correction is done using the `CompiledSpellChecker` class. This class implements the noisy-channel model and provides an estimate of the most likely message, given that the message actually received. We can express this through a formula in the following manner:

```
didYouMean(received) = ArgMaxintended P(intended | received)
        = ArgMaxintended P(intended, received) / P(received)
        = ArgMaxintended P(intended, received)
        = ArgMaxintended P(intended) * P(received | intended)
```

In other words, we will first create a model of the intended message by creating an n-gram character-language model. The language model stores the statistics of seen phrases, that is, essentially, it stores counts of how many times the n-grams occurred. This gives us `P(intended)`. For example, `P(intended)` is how likely is the character sequence `the`. Next, we will create the channel model, which is a weighted edit distance and gives us the probability that the error was typed for that intended text. Again, for example, how likely is the error `teh` when the user intended to type `the`. In our case, we will model the likeliness using weighted edit distance where the weights are scaled as log probabilities. Refer to the *Weighted edit distance* recipe earlier in the chapter.

The usual way of creating a compiled spell checker is through an instance of `TrainSpellChecker`. The result of compiling the spell-checker-training class and reading it back in is a compiled spell checker. `TrainSpellChecker` creates the basic models, weighted edit distance, and token set through the compilation process. We will then need to set various parameters on the `CompiledSpellChecker` object.

A tokenizer factory can be optionally specified to train token-sensitive spell checkers. With tokenization, input is further normalized to insert a single whitespace between all the tokens that are not already separated by a space in the input. The tokens are then output during compilation and read back into the compiled spell checker. The output of set of tokens may be pruned to remove any below a given count threshold. The thresholding doesn't make sense in the absence of tokens because we only have characters to count in the absence of tokens. Additionally, the set of known tokens can be used to constrain the set of alternative spellings suggested during spelling correction to include only tokens in the observed token set.

This approach to spell check has several advantages over a pure dictionary-based solution:

- The context is usefully modeled. `Frod` can be corrected to `Ford` if the next word is `dealership` and to `Frodo` if the next word is `Baggins`—a character from *The Lord of the Rings* trilogy.

- Spell checking can be sensitive to domains. Another big advantage of this approach over dictionary-based spell checking is that the corrections are motivated by data in the training corpus. So, `trt` will be corrected to `tort` in a legal domain, `tart` in a cooking domain, and `TRt` in a bioinformatics domain.

How to do it...

Let's look at the steps involved in running spell checking:

1. In your IDE, run the `SpellCheck` class, or in the command line, type the following—note that we are allocating 1 gigabyte of heap space with the `-Xmx1g` flag:

   ```
   java -Xmx1g -cp lingpipe-cookbook.1.0.jar:lib/lingpipe-
   4.1.0.jar:lib/opencsv-2.4.jar com.lingpipe.cookbook.chapter6.
   SpellCheck
   ```

2. Be patient; the spell checker takes a minute or two to train.

3. Now, let's enter some misspelled words such as `beleive`:

   ```
   Enter word, . to quit:
   >beleive
   Query Text: beleive
   Best Alternative: believe
   Nbest: 0: believe Score:-13.97322991490364
   Nbest: 1: believed Score:-17.326215342327487
   Nbest: 2: believes Score:-20.8595682233572
   Nbest: 3: because Score:-21.468056442099623
   ```

4. As you can see, we got the best alternative to the input text as well as some other alternatives. They are sorted by the likelihood of being the best alternative.

String Comparison and Clustering

5. Now, we can play around with different input and see how well this spell checker does. Try multiple words in the input and see how it performs:

    ```
    The rain in Spani falls mainly on the plain.
    Query Text: The rain in Spani falls mainly on the plain.
    Best Alternative: the rain in spain falls mainly on the plain .
    Nbest: 0: the rain in spain falls mainly on the plain .
    Score:-96.30435947472415
    Nbest: 1: the rain in spain falls mainly on the plan .
    Score:-100.55447634639404
    Nbest: 2: the rain in spain falls mainly on the place .
    Score:-101.32592701496742
    Nbest: 3: the rain in spain falls mainly on the plain ,
    Score:-101.81294112237359
    ```

6. Also, try inputting some proper names to see how they get evaluated.

How it works...

Now, let's look at what makes all this tick. We will start off by setting up `TrainSpellChecker`, which requires a `NGramProcessLM` instance, `TokenizerFactory`, and an `EditDistance` object that sets up weights for edit operations such as deletion, insertion, substitution, and so on:

```
public static void main(String[] args) throws IOException,
  ClassNotFoundException {
  double matchWeight = -0.0;
  double deleteWeight = -4.0;
  double insertWeight = -2.5;
  double substituteWeight = -2.5;
  double transposeWeight = -1.0;

  FixedWeightEditDistance fixedEdit =
    new FixedWeightEditDistance(matchWeight,
      deleteWeight,
      insertWeight,
      substituteWeight,
      transposeWeight);
  int NGRAM_LENGTH = 6;
  NGramProcessLM lm = new NGramProcessLM(NGRAM_LENGTH);

  TokenizerFactory tokenizerFactory =
    IndoEuropeanTokenizerFactory.INSTANCE;
  tokenizerFactory =
    new com.aliasi.tokenizer.LowerCaseTokenizerFactory(tokenizerFactory);
```

`NGramProcessLM` needs to know the number of characters to sample in its modeling of the data. Reasonable values have been supplied in this example for the weighted edit distance, but they can be played with to help with variations due to particular datasets:

```
TrainSpellChecker sc =
   new TrainSpellChecker(lm,fixedEdit,tokenizerFactory);
```

`TrainSpellChecker` can now be constructed, and next, we will load 150,000 lines of books from Project Gutenberg. In a search-engine context, this data will be the data in your index:

```
File inFile = new File("data/project_gutenberg_books.txt");
String bigEnglish =
   Files.readFromFile(inFile,Strings.UTF8);
sc.handle(bigEnglish);
```

Next, we will add entries from a dictionary to help with rare words:

```
File dict = new File("data/websters_words.txt");
String webster =
   Files.readFromFile(dict, Strings.UTF8);
sc.handle(webster);
```

Next, we will compile `TrainSpellChecker` so that we can instantiate `CompiledSpellChecker`. Typically, the output of the `compileTo()` operation is written to disk, and `CompiledSpellChecker` is read and instantiated from the disk, but the in-memory option is being used here:

```
CompiledSpellChecker csc =
   (CompiledSpellChecker) AbstractExternalizable.compile(sc);
```

Note that there is also a way to deserialize to `TrainSpellChecker` in cases where more data might be added later. `CompiledSpellChecker` will not accept further training instances.

`CompiledSpellChecker` admits many fine-tuning methods that are not relevant during training but are relevant in use. For example, it can take a set of strings that are not to be edited; in this case, the single value is `lingpipe`:

```
Set<String> dontEdit = new HashSet<String>();
dontEdit.add("lingpipe");
csc.setDoNotEditTokens(dontEdit);
```

If these tokens are seen in the input, they will not be considered for edits. This can have a huge impact on the run time. The larger this set is, the faster the decoder will run. Configure the set of do-not-edit tokens to be as large as possible if execution speed is important. Usually, this is done by taking the object to counter-map from the compiled spell checker and saving tokens with high counts.

String Comparison and Clustering

During training, the tokenizer factory was used to normalize data into tokens separated by a single whitespace. It is not serialized in the compile step, so if token sensitivity is needed in do-not-edit tokens, then it must be supplied:

```
csc.setTokenizerFactory(tokenizerFactory);
int nBest = 3;
csc.setNBest(64);
```

The nBest parameter is set for the number of hypotheses that will be considered in modifying inputs. Even though the `nBest` size in the output is set to 3, it is advisable to allow for a larger hypothesis space in the left-to-right exploration of best performing edits. Also, the class has methods to control what edits are allowed and how they are scored. See the tutorial and Javadoc for more about them.

Finally, we will do a console I/O loop to generate spelling variations:

```
BufferedReader reader =
  new BufferedReader(new InputStreamReader(System.in));
String query = "";
while (true) {
  System.out.println("Enter word, . to quit:");
  query = reader.readLine();
  if (query.equals(".")){
    break;
  }
  String bestAlternative = csc.didYouMean(query);
  System.out.println("Best Alternative: "
    + bestAlternative);
  int i = 0;
  Iterator<ScoredObject<String>> iterator =
    csc.didYouMeanNBest(query);
  while (i < nBest) {
    ScoredObject<String> so = iterator.next();
    System.out.println("Nbest: " + i + ": "
      + so.getObject() + " Score:" + so.score());
    i++;
  }
}
```

> We have included a dictionary in this model, and we will just feed the dictionary entries into the trainer like any other data.
>
> It might be worthwhile to boost the dictionary by training each word in the dictionary more than once. Depending on the count of the dictionary, it might dominate or be dominated by the source training data.

See also

- The spelling-correction tutorial is more complete and covers evaluation at `http://alias-i.com/lingpipe/demos/tutorial/querySpellChecker/read-me.html`
- The Javadoc for `CompiledSpellChecker` can be found at `http://alias-i.com/lingpipe/docs/api/com/aliasi/spell/CompiledSpellChecker.html`
- More information on how spell checkers work is given in the textbook, *Speech and Language Processing*, *Jurafsky, Dan*, and *James H. Martin, 2000, Prentice-Hall*

The case restoring corrector

A case-restoring spell corrector, also called a truecasing corrector, only restores the case and does not change anything else, that is, it does not correct spelling errors. This is very useful when dealing with low-quality text from transcriptions, automatic speech-recognition output, chat logs, and so on, which contain a variety of case challenges. We typically want to enhance this text to build better rule-based or machine-learning systems. For example, news and video transcriptions (such as closed captions) typically have errors, and this makes it harder to use this data to train NER. Case restoration can be used as a normalization tool across different data sources to ensure that all the data is consistent.

How to do it...

1. In your IDE, run the `CaseRestore` class, or in the command line, type the following:

   ```
   java -cp lingpipe-cookbook.1.0.jar:lib/lingpipe-4.1.0.jar com.lingpipe.cookbook.chapter6.CaseRestore
   ```

2. Now, let's type in some mangled-case or single-case input:

   ```
   Enter input, . to quit:
   george washington was the first president of the u.s.a
   Best Alternative: George Washington was the first President of the U.S.A
   Enter input, . to quit:
   ITS RUDE TO SHOUT ON THE WEB
   Best Alternative: its rude to shout on the Web
   ```

3. As you can see, the mangled case gets corrected. If we use more modern text, such as current newspaper data or something similar, this would be directly applicable to case-normalizing broadcast news transcripts or closed captions.

String Comparison and Clustering

How it works...

The class works in a manner similar to the spelling correction in which we have a model specified by the language model and a channel model specified by the edit distance metric. The distance metric, however, only allows case changes, that is, case variants are zero cost, and all other edit costs are set to `Double.NEGATIVE_INFINITY`:

We will focus on what is different from the previous recipe rather than going over all the source. We will train the spell checker with some English text from Project Gutenberg and use the `CASE_RESTORING` edit distance from the `CompiledSpellChecker` class:

```
int NGRAM_LENGTH = 5;
NGramProcessLM lm = new NGramProcessLM(NGRAM_LENGTH);
TrainSpellChecker sc = new
  TrainSpellChecker(lm,CompiledSpellChecker.CASE_RESTORING);
```

Once again, by invoking the `bestAlternative` method, we will get the best estimate of case-restored text:

```
String bestAlternative = csc.didYouMean(query);
```

That's it. Case restoration is made easy.

See also

- The paper by Lucian Vlad Lita et al., 2003, at `http://acl.ldc.upenn.edu/P/P03/P03-1020.pdf` is a good reference on truecasing

Automatic phrase completion

Automatic phrase completion is different from spelling correction, in that, it finds the most likely completion among a set of fixed phrases for the text entered so far by a user.

Obviously, automatic phrase completion is ubiquitous on the Web, for instance, on `https://google.com`. For example, if I type `anaz` as a query, Google pops up the following suggestions:

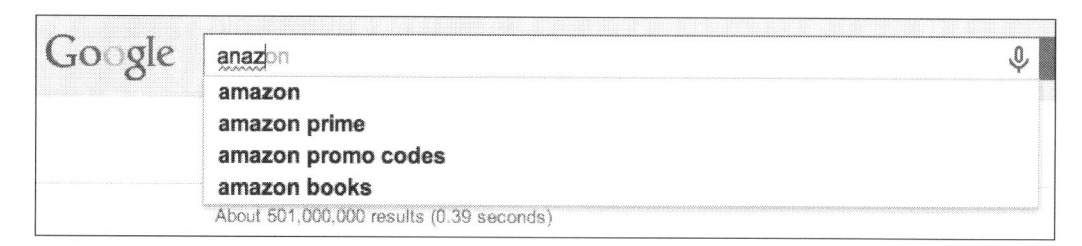

Note that the application is performing spelling checking at the same time as completion. For instance, the top suggestion is **amazon**, even though the query so far is **anaz**. This is not surprising, given that the number of results reported for the phrases that start with **anaz** is probably very small.

Next, note that it's not doing word suggestion but phrase suggestion. Some of the results, such as **amazon prime** are two words.

One important difference between autocompletion and spell checking is that autocompletion typically operates over a fixed set of phrases that must match the beginning to be completed. What this means is that if I type a query `I want to find anaz`, there are no suggested completions. The source of phrases for a web search is typically high-frequency queries from the query logs.

In LingPipe, we use the `AutoCompleter` class, which maintains a dictionary of phrases with counts and provides suggested completions based on prefix matching by weighted edit distance and phrase likelihood.

The autocompleter finds the best scoring phrases for a given prefix. The score of a phrase versus a prefix is the sum of the score of the phrase and the maximum score of the prefix against any prefix of the phrase. The score for a phrase is just its maximum likelihood probability estimate, that is, the log of its count divided by the sum of all counts.

Google and other search engines most likely use their query counts as the data for the best scoring phrases. As we don't have query logs here, we'll use US census data about cities in the US with populations greater than 100,000. The phrases are the city names, and their counts are their populations.

How to do it...

1. In your IDE, run the `AutoComplete` class, or in the command line, type the following command:
   ```
   java -cp lingpipe-cookbook.1.0.jar:lib/lingpipe-4.1.0.jar com.lingpipe.cookbook.chapter6.AutoComplete
   ```

2. Enter some US city names and look at the output. For example, typing `new` will result in the following output:
   ```
   Enter word, . to quit:
   new
   |new|
   -13.39 New York,New York
   -17.89 New Orleans,Louisiana
   -18.30 Newark,New Jersey
   -18.92 Newport News,Virginia
   ```

String Comparison and Clustering

```
-19.39 New Haven,Connecticut
If we misspell 'new' and type 'mew' instead,
Enter word, . to quit:
mew

|mew |
-13.39 New York,New York
-17.89 New Orleans,Louisiana
-19.39 New Haven,Connecticut
```

3. Typing city names that don't exist in our initial list will not return any output:

    ```
    Enter word, . to quit:
    Alta,Wyoming
    |Alta,Wyoming|
    ```

How it works...

Configuring an autocompleter is very similar to configuring spelling, except that instead of training a language model, we will supply it with a fixed list of phrases and counts, an edit distance metric, and some configuration parameters. The initial portion of this code just reads a file and sets up a map of phrases to counts:

```
File wordsFile = new File("data/city_populations_2012.csv");
String[] lines =
  FileLineReader.readLineArray(wordsFile,"ISO-8859-1");
ObjectToCounterMap<String> cityPopMap = new
ObjectToCounterMap<String>();
int lineCount = 0;
for (String line : lines) {
if(lineCount++ <1) continue;
  int i = line.lastIndexOf(',');
  if (i < 0) continue;
  String phrase = line.substring(0,i);
  String countString = line.substring(i+1);
  Integer count = Integer.valueOf(countString);

  cityPopMap.set(phrase,count);
}
```

The next step is to configure the edit distance. This will measure how close a prefix of a target phrase is to the query prefix. This class uses a fixed weight edit distance, but any edit distance might be used in general:

```
double matchWeight = 0.0;
double insertWeight = -10.0;
double substituteWeight = -10.0;
double deleteWeight = -10.0;
double transposeWeight = Double.NEGATIVE_INFINITY;
FixedWeightEditDistance editDistance =
  new FixedWeightEditDistance(matchWeight,
    deleteWeight,
    insertWeight,
    substituteWeight,
    transposeWeight);
```

There are a few parameters to tune autocompletion: the edit distance and search parameters. The edit distance is tuned in exactly the same way as it is for spelling. The maximum number of results to return is more of an application's decision than a tuning's decision. Having said this, smaller result sets are faster to compute. The maximum queue size indicates how big the set of hypotheses can get inside the autocompleter before being pruned. Set `maxQueueSize` as low as possible while still performing adequately to increase speed:

```
int maxResults = 5;
int maxQueueSize = 10000;
double minScore = -25.0;
AutoCompleter completer =
  new AutoCompleter(cityPopMap, editDistance,
    maxResults, maxQueueSize, minScore);
```

See also

- Review the Javadoc for the `AutoCompleter` class at http://alias-i.com/lingpipe/docs/api/com/aliasi/spell/AutoCompleter.html

Single-link and complete-link clustering using edit distance

Clustering is the process of grouping a collection of objects by their similarities, that is, using some sort of distance measure. The idea behind clustering is that objects within a cluster are located close to each other, but objects in different clusters are farther away from each other. We can divide clustering techniques very broadly into hierarchical (or agglomerative) and divisional techniques. Hierarchical techniques start by assuming that every object is its own cluster and merge clusters together until a stopping criterion has been met.

For example, a stopping criterion can be a fixed distance between every cluster. Divisional techniques go the other way and start by grouping all the objects into one cluster and split it until a stopping criterion has been met, such as the number of clusters.

We will review hierarchical techniques in the next few recipes. The two clustering implementations we will provide in LingPipe are single-link clustering and complete-link clustering; the resulting clusters form what is known as a partition of the input set. A set of sets is a partition of another set if each element of the set is a member of exactly one set of the partition. In mathematical terms, the sets that make up a partition are pair-wise disjoint, and the union is the original set.

A clusterer takes a set of objects as input and returns a set of sets of objects as output, that is, in code, `Clusterer<String>` has a `cluster` method, which operates on `Set<String>` and returns `Set<Set<String>>`.

A hierarchical clusterer extends the `Clusterer` interface and also operates on a set of objects, but it returns `Dendrogram` instead of a set of sets of objects. A dendrogram is a binary tree over the elements being clustered, with distances attached to each branch, which indicates the distance between the two sub-branches. For the aa, aaa, aaaaa, bbb, bbbb strings, the single-link based dendrogram with `EditDistance` as the metric looks like this:

```
3.0
    2.0
        1.0
            aaa
            aa
        aaaaa
    1.0
        bbbb
        bbb
```

The preceding dendrogram is based on single-link clustering, which takes the minimum distance between any two elements as the measure of similarity. So, when `{ 'aa', 'aaa' }` is merged with `{ 'aaaa' }`, the score is 2.0 by adding two a to aaa. Complete-link clustering takes the maximum distance between any two elements, which would be 3.0, with an addition of three a to aa. Single-link clustering tends to create highly separated clusters, whereas complete-link clustering tends to create more tightly centered clusters.

There are two ways to extract clusterings from dendrograms. The simplest way is to set a distance bound and maintain every cluster formed at less than or equal to this bound. The other way to construct a clustering is to continue cutting the highest distance cluster until a specified number of clusters is obtained.

In this example, we will look at single-link and complete-link clustering with edit distance as the distance metric. We will try to cluster city names by `EditDistance`, where the maximum distance is 4.

How to do it...

1. In your IDE, run the `HierarchicalClustering` class, or in the command line, type the following:

   `java -cp lingpipe-cookbook.1.0.jar:lib/lingpipe-4.1.0.jar com.lingpipe.cookbook.chapter6.HierarchicalClustering`

2. The output is various clustering approaches to the same underlying set of `Strings`. In this recipe, we will intersperse the source and output. First, we will create our set of strings:

   ```
   public static void main(String[] args) throws
   UnsupportedEncodingException, IOException {
   
     Set<String> inputSet = new HashSet<String>();
     String [] input =
       { "aa", "aaa", "aaaaa", "bbb", "bbbb" };
     inputSet.addAll(Arrays.asList(input));
   ```

3. Next, we will set up a single-link instance with `EditDistance` and create the dendrogram for the preceding set and print it out:

   ```
   boolean allowTranspositions = false;
   Distance<CharSequence> editDistance =
     new EditDistance(allowTranspositions);
   
   AbstractHierarchicalClusterer<String> slClusterer =
     new SingleLinkClusterer<String>(editDistance);
   
   Dendrogram<String> slDendrogram =
     slClusterer.hierarchicalCluster(inputSet);
   
   System.out.println("\nSingle Link Dendrogram");
   System.out.println(slDendrogram.prettyPrint());
   ```

4. The output will be as follows:

   ```
   Single Link Dendrogram
   
   3.0
       2.0
           1.0
               aaa
               aa
           aaaaa
       1.0
           bbbb
           bbb
   ```

String Comparison and Clustering

5. Next up, we will create and print out the complete-link treatment of the same set:

   ```
   AbstractHierarchicalClusterer<String> clClusterer =
     new CompleteLinkClusterer<String>(editDistance);

   Dendrogram<String> clDendrogram =
     clClusterer.hierarchicalCluster(inputSet);

   System.out.println("\nComplete Link Dendrogram");
   System.out.println(clDendrogram.prettyPrint());
   ```

6. This will produce the same dendrogram, but with different scores:

   Complete Link Dendrogram

   ```
   5.0
       3.0
           1.0
               aaa
               aa
           aaaaa
       1.0
           bbbb
           bbb
   ```

7. Next, we will produce the clusters where the number of clusters is being controlled for the single-link case:

   ```
   System.out.println("\nSingle Link Clusterings with k Clusters");
   for (int k = 1; k < 6; ++k ) {
     Set<Set<String>> slKClustering =
       slDendrogram.partitionK(k);
     System.out.println(k + "   " + slKClustering);
   }
   ```

8. This will produce the following—it will be the same for the complete link, given the input set:

   Single Link Clusterings with k Clusters
   ```
   1   [[bbbb, aaa, aa, aaaaa, bbb]]
   2   [[aaa, aa, aaaaa], [bbbb, bbb]]
   3   [[aaaaa], [bbbb, bbb], [aaa, aa]]
   4   [[bbbb, bbb], [aa], [aaa], [aaaaa]]
   5   [[bbbb], [aa], [aaa], [aaaaa], [bbb]]
   ```

9. The following code snippet is the complete-link clustering without a max distance:

    ```
    Set<Set<String>> slClustering = slClusterer.cluster(inputSet);
    System.out.println("\nComplete Link Clustering No "
      + "Max Distance");
    System.out.println(slClustering + "\n");
    ```

10. The output will be:

    Complete Link Clustering No Max Distance

    [[bbbb, aaa, aa, aaaaa, bbb]]

11. Next, we will control the max distance:

    ```
    for(int k = 1; k < 6; ++k ){
      clClusterer.setMaxDistance(k);
      System.out.println("Complete Link Clustering at " +
        "Max Distance= " + k);

      Set<Set<String>> slClusteringMd =
        clClusterer.cluster(inputSet);
      System.out.println(slClusteringMd);
    }
    ```

12. The following is the effects of clustering limited by maximum distance for the complete-link case. Note that the single-link input here will have all elements in the same cluster at 3:

    Complete Link Clustering at Max Distance= 1
    [[bbbb, bbb], [aaa, aa], [aaaaa]]
    Complete Link Clustering at Max Distance= 2
    [[bbbb, bbb], [aaa, aa], [aaaaa]]
    Complete Link Clustering at Max Distance= 3
    [[bbbb, bbb], [aaa, aa, aaaaa]]
    Complete Link Clustering at Max Distance= 4
    [[bbbb, bbb], [aaa, aa, aaaaa]]
    Complete Link Clustering at Max Distance= 5
    [[bbbb, aaa, aa, aaaaa, bbb]]

13. That's it! We have exercised a good portion of LingPipe's clustering API.

There's more...

Clustering is very sensitive to `Distance` that is used for the comparison of clusters. Consult the Javadoc for the 10 implementing classes for possible variations. `TfIdfDistance` can come in very handy to cluster language data.

K-means (++) clustering is a feature-extractor-based clustering. This is what Javadoc says about it:

> K-means clustering may be viewed as an iterative approach to the minimization of the average square distance between items and their cluster centers...

See also...

- For a detailed tutorial including details on evaluations, go over to http://alias-i.com/lingpipe/demos/tutorial/cluster/read-me.html

Latent Dirichlet allocation (LDA) for multitopic clustering

Latent Dirichlet allocation (**LDA**) is a statistical technique to document clustering based on the tokens or words that are present in the document. Clustering such as classification generally assumes that categories are mutually exclusive. The neat thing about LDA is that it allows for documents to be in multiple topics at the same time, instead of just one category. This better reflects the fact that a tweet can be about *Disney* and *Wally World*, among other topics.

The other neat thing about LDA, like many clustering techniques, is that it is unsupervised, which means that no supervised training data is required! The closest thing to training data is that the number of topics must be specified before hand.

LDA can be a great way to explore a dataset where you don't know what you don't know. It can also be difficult to tune, but generally, it does something interesting. Let's get a system working.

For each document, LDA assigns a probability of belonging to a topic based on the words in that document. We will start with documents that are converted to sequences of tokens. LDA uses the count of the tokens and does not care about the context or order in which those words appear. The model that LDA operates on for each document is called "a bag of words" to denote that the order is not important.

Chapter 6

The LDA model consists of a fixed number of topics, each of which is modeled as a distribution over words. A document under LDA is modeled as a distribution over topics. There is a Dirichlet prior on both the topic distributions over words and the document distributions over topics. Check out the Javadoc, referenced tutorial, and research literature if you want to know more about what is going on behind the scenes.

Getting ready

We will continue to work with the .csv data from tweets. Refer to *Chapter 1*, *Simple Classifiers*, to know how to get tweets, or use the example data from the book. The recipe uses data/gravity_tweets.csv.

This recipe closely follows the tutorial at http://alias-i.com/lingpipe/demos/tutorial/cluster/read-me.html, which goes into much more detail than we do in the recipe. The LDA portion is at the end of the tutorial.

How to do it...

This section will be a source code review for src/com/lingpipe/cookbook/chapter6/Lda.java with some references to the src/com/lingpipe/cookbook/chapter6/LdaReportingHandler.java helping class that will get discussed as we use parts of it:

1. The top of the main() method gets data from a standard csv reader:

    ```
    File corpusFile = new File(args[0]);
     List<String[]> tweets = Util.readCsvRemoveHeader(corpusFile);
    ```

2. Next up is a pile of configuration that we will address line by line. The minTokenCount filters all tokens that are seen less than five times in the algorithm. As datasets get bigger, this number can get larger. For 1100 tweets, we are assuming that at least five mentions will help reduce the overall noisiness of Twitter data:

    ```
    int minTokenCount = 5;
    ```

3. The numTopics parameter is probably the most critical configuration value, because it informs the algorithm about how many topics to find. Changes to this number can produce very different topics. You can experiment with it. By choosing 10, we are saying that the 1100 tweets talk about 10 things overall. This is clearly wrong; maybe, 100 is closer to the mark. It is possible that the 1100 tweets had more than 1100 topics, since a tweet can be in more than one topic. Play around with it:

    ```
    short numTopics = 10;
    ```

4. According to the Javadoc, a rule of thumb for `documentTopicPrior` is to set it to 5 divided by the number of topics (or less if there are very few topics; 0.1 is typically the maximum value used):

   ```
   double documentTopicPrior = 0.1;
   ```

5. A generally useful value for the `topicWordPrior` is as follows:

   ```
   double topicWordPrior = 0.01;
   ```

6. The `burninEpochs` parameter sets how many epochs to run before sampling. Setting this to greater than 0 has desirable properties, in that, it avoids correlation in the samples. The `sampleLag` controls how often the sample is taken after burning is complete, and `numSamples` controls how many samples to take. Currently, 2000 samples will be taken. If `burninEpochs` were 1000, then 3000 samples would be taken with a sample lag of 1 (every time). If `sampleLag` was 2, then there would be 5000 iterations (1000 burnin, 2000 samples taken every 2 epochs for a total of 4000 epochs). Consult the Javadoc and tutorial for more about what is going on here:

   ```
   int burninEpochs = 0;
   int sampleLag = 1;
   int numSamples = 2000;
   ```

7. Finally, `randomSeed` initializes the random process in `GibbsSampler`:

   ```
   long randomSeed = 6474835;
   ```

8. `SymbolTable` is constructed; this will store the mapping from strings to integers for efficient processing:

   ```
   SymbolTable symbolTable = new MapSymbolTable();
   ```

9. A tokenizer is next with our standard one:

   ```
   TokenzierFactory tokFactory = IndoEuropeanTokenizerFactory.INSTANCE;
   ```

10. Next, the configuration of LDA is printed out:

    ```
    System.out.println("Input file=" + corpusFile);
    System.out.println("Minimum token count=" + minTokenCount);
    System.out.println("Number of topics=" + numTopics);
    System.out.println("Topic prior in docs=" + documenttopicPrior);
    System.out.println("Word prior in topics=" + wordPrior);
    System.out.println("Burnin epochs=" + burninEpochs);
    System.out.println("Sample lag=" + sampleLag);
    System.out.println("Number of samples=" + numSamples);
    ```

11. Then, we will create a matrix of documents and tokens that will be input to LDA and a report on how many tokens are present:

    ```
    int[][] docTokens = LatentDirichletAllocation.tokenizeDocuments(Id
    aTexts,tokFactory,symbolTable, minTokenCount);
    System.out.println("Number of unique words above count"
      + " threshold=" + symbolTable.numSymbols());
    ```

12. A sanity check will follow by reporting a total token count:

    ```
    int numTokens = 0;
    for (int[] tokens : docTokens){
      numTokens += tokens.length;
    }
    System.out.println("Tokenized.   #Tokens After Pruning=" +
    numTokens);
    ```

13. In order to get progress reports on the epochs/samples, a handler is created to deliver the desired news. It takes `symbolTable` as an argument to be able to recreate the tokens in reporting:

    ```
    LdaReportingHandler handler = new LdaReportingHandler(symbolTab
    le);
    ```

14. The method that the search accesses in `LdaReportingHandler` follows:

    ```
    public void handle(LatentDirichletAllocation.GibbsSample sample) {
      System.out.printf("Epoch=%3d    elapsed time=%s\n",
        sample.epoch(),
        Strings.msToString(System.currentTimeMillis()
        - mStartTime));

      if ((sample.epoch() % 10) == 0) {
        double corpusLog2Prob = sample.corpusLog2Probability();
        System.out.println("      log2 p(corpus|phi,theta)="
          + corpusLog2Prob + "   token cross" +
          entropy rate=" +
          (-corpusLog2Prob/sample.numTokens()));
      }
    }
    ```

15. After all this setup, we will get to run LDA:

    ```
    LatentDirichletAllocation.GibbsSample sample =
      LatentDirichletAllocation.gibbsSampler(docTokens,
      numTopics,
      documentTopicPrior,
      wordPrior,
      burninEpochs,
      sampleLag,
      numSamples,
      new Random(randomSeed),
      handler);
    ```

String Comparison and Clustering

16. Wait, there's more! However, we are almost done. We just need a final report:

    ```
    int maxWordsPerTopic = 20;
    int maxTopicsPerDoc = 10;
    boolean reportTokens = true;
    handler.reportTopics(sample,maxWordsPerTopic,
      maxTopicsPerDoc,reportTokens);
    ```

17. Finally, we will get to run this code. Type the following command:

    ```
    java -cp lingpipe-cookbook.1.0.jar:lib/lingpipe-4.1.0.jar:lib/
    opencsv-2.4.jar com.lingpipe.cookbook.chapter6.LDA
    ```

18. Have a look at a sample of the resulting output that confirms the configuration and the early reports from the search epochs:

    ```
    Input file=data/gravity_tweets.csv
    Minimum token count=1
    Number of topics=10
    Topic prior in docs=0.1
    Word prior in topics=0.01
    Burnin epochs=0
    Sample lag=1
    Number of samples=2000
    Number of unique words above count threshold=1652
    Tokenized.   #Tokens After Pruning=10101
    Epoch=  0    elapsed time=:00
         log2 p(corpus|phi,theta)=-76895.71967475882
      token cross-entropy rate=7.612683860484983
    Epoch=  1    elapsed time=:00
    ```

19. After the epochs are done, we will get a report on the topics found. The first topic starts with a listing of words ordered by count. Note that the topic does not have a title. The topic `meaning` can be gleaned by scanning the words that have high counts and a high Z score. In this case, there is a word `movie` with a Z score of 4.0, a gets 6.0, and looking down the list, we see `good` with a score of 5.6. The Z score reflects how nonindependent the word is from the topic with a higher score; this means that the word is more tightly associated with the topic. Look at the source for `LdaReportingHandler` to get the exact definition:

    ```
    TOPIC 0  (total count=1033)
             WORD    COUNT         Z
    --------------------------------------------
            movie      109       4.0
          Gravity       73       1.9
    ```

```
            a      72        6.0
           is      57        4.9
            !      52        3.2
          was      45        6.0
            .      42       -0.4
            ?      41        5.8
         good     39        5.6
```

20. The preceding output is pretty awful, and the other topics don't look any better. The next topic shows no more potential, but some obvious problems are arising because of tokenization:

```
TOPIC 1    (total count=1334)
           WORD     COUNT        Z
--------------------------------------------
             /       144         2.2
             .       117         2.5
             #        91         3.5
             @        73         4.2
             :        72         1.0
             !        50         2.7
            co        49         1.3
             t        47         0.8
          http        47         1.2
```

21. Donning our system tuner's hats, we will adjust the tokenizer to be the new `RegExTokenizerFactory("[^\\s]+")` tokenizer, which really cleans up the clusters, increases clusters to 25, and applies `Util.filterJaccard(tweets, tokFactory, .5)` to remove duplicates (1100 to 301). These steps were not performed one at a time, but this is a recipe, so we present the results of some experimentation. There was no evaluation harness, so this was a process that was made up of making a change, seeing if the output looks better and so on. Clusters are notoriously difficult to evaluate and tune on such an open-ended problem. The output looks a bit better.

22. On scanning the topics, we get to know that there are still lots of low-value words that crap up the topics, but Topic 18 looks somewhat promising, with a high Z score for best and ever:

```
OPIC 18    (total count=115)
           WORD     COUNT        Z
--------------------------------------------
         movie        24         1.0
           the        24         1.3
```

of	15	1.7
best	10	3.0
ever	9	2.8
one	9	2.8
I've	8	2.7
seen	7	1.8
most	4	1.4
it's	3	0.9
had	1	0.2
can	1	0.2

23. Looking further into the output, we will see some documents that score high for `Topic 18`:

```
DOC 34
TOPIC     COUNT     PROB
----------------------
   18        3      0.270
    4        2      0.183
    3        1      0.096
    6        1      0.096
    8        1      0.096
   19        1      0.096
```

Gravity(4) is(6) the(8) best(18) movie(19) I've(18) seen(18) in(3) a(4)

```
DOC 50
TOPIC     COUNT     PROB
----------------------
   18        6      0.394
   17        4      0.265
    5        2      0.135
    7        1      0.071
```

The(17) movie(18) Gravity(7) has(17) to(17) be(5) one(18) of(18) the(18) best(18) of(18) all(17) time(5)

24. Both seem reasonable for a `best movie ever` topic. However, be warned that the other topics/document assignments are fairly bad.

We can't really claim victory over this dataset in all honesty, but we have laid out the mechanics of how LDA works and its configuration. LDA has not been a huge commercial success, but it has produced interesting concept-level implementations for National Institutes of Health and other customers. LDA is a tuner's paradise with many ways to play with the resulting clustering. Check out the tutorial and Javadoc, and send us your success stories.

7
Finding Coreference Between Concepts/People

In this chapter, we will cover the following recipes:

- Named entity coreference with a document
- Adding pronouns to coreference
- Cross-document coreference
- The John Smith problem

Introduction

Coreference is a basic mechanism in human language that allows two sentences to be about the same thing. It's a big deal for human communication—it functions much in the same way as variable names do in programming languages, with the additional subtly that scope is defined by very different rules than blocks. Coreference is less important commercially—maybe this chapter will help change that. Here is an example:

    Alice walked into the garden. She was surprised.

Coreference exists between `Alice` and `She`; the phrases talk about the same thing. It all gets very interesting when we start asking whether Alice in one document is the same as Alice in another.

Finding Coreference Between Concepts/People

Coreference, like word-sense disambiguation, is a next-generation industrial capacity. The challenges of coreference contribute to the insistence of the IRS to have a social security number that unambiguously identifies persons independent of their names. Many of the techniques discussed were developed to help track persons and organizations in text data with varying degrees of success.

Named entity coreference with a document

As seen in *Chapter 5*, *Finding Spans in Text – Chunking*, LingPipe can use a variety of techniques to recognize proper nouns that correspond to persons, places, things, genes, and so on. However, chunking doesn't quite finish the job, because it doesn't help with finding an entity when two named entities are the same. Being able to say that John Smith is the same entity as Mr. Smith, John or even an exact repeat, John Smith, can be very useful—so useful that the idea was the basis of our company when we were a baby-defense contractor. Our novel contribution was the generation of sentences indexed by what entities they mentioned, which turned out to be an excellent way to summarize what was being said about that entity, particularly if the mapping spanned languages—we call it **entity-based summarization**.

> The idea for entity-based summarization came about as a result of a talk Baldwin gave at the University of Pennsylvania at a graduate student seminar. Mitch Marcus, the then department chair, thought that showing all sentences that mentioned an entity—including pronouns—will be an excellent summary of that entity. In some sense, this comment is why LingPipe exists. It led to Baldwin leading a UPenn DARPA project and then the creation of Alias-i. Lesson learned—talk to everybody about your ideas and research.

This recipe will take you through the basics of computing coreferences.

Getting ready

Lay your hands on some narrative text; we will use a simple example that we know works—coreference systems usually need a lot of tuning to the domain. Feel free to pick something else, but it will need to be in English.

How to do it...

As usual, we will take you through running code from the command line and then dive into what the code actually does. Off we go.

1. We will start with a simple text to illustrate coreference. The file is in `data/simpleCoref.txt`, and it contains:

   ```
   John Smith went to Washington. Mr. Smith is a business man.
   ```

2. Get thee to a command line and a Java interpreter and reproduce the following:

   ```
   java -cp lingpipe-cookbook.1.0.jar:lib/lingpipe-4.1.0.jar: com.
   lingpipe.cookbook.chapter7.NamedEntityCoreference
   ```

3. This results in:

   ```
   Reading in file :data/simpleCoref.txt
   Sentence Text=John Smith went to Washington.
        mention text=John Smith type=PERSON id=0
        mention text=Washington type=LOCATION id=1
   Sentence Text=Mr. Smith is a business man.
        mention text=Mr. Smith type=PERSON id=0
   ```

4. There are three named entities found. Note that there is an `ID` field in the output. The `John Smith` and `Mr. Smith` entities have the same ID, `id=0`. This means that the phrases are considered to be coreferent. The remaining entity `Washington` has a different ID, `id=1`, and is not coreferent with John Smith / Mr. Smith.

5. Create your own text file, supply it as an argument on the command line, and see what gets computed.

How it works...

The coreference code in LingPipe is a heuristic system built on top of sentence detection and named-entity recognition. The overall flow is as follows:

1. Tokenize the text.
2. Detect sentences in the document, for each sentence, detect named entities in the sentence in the left-to-right order, and for each named entity, perform the following tasks:
   1. Create a mention. A mention is a single instance of a named entity.
   2. Mentions can be added to the existing mention chains, or they can start their own mention chains.
   3. Try to resolve the mention to a mention chain that is already created. If a unique match is found, then add the mention to the mention chain; otherwise, create a new mention chain.

The code is in `src/com/lingpipe/cookbook/chapter7/NamedEntityCoreference.java`. The `main()` method starts by setting up the parts of this recipe, starting with a tokenizer factory, sentence chunker, and finally, a named-entity chunker:

```
public static void main(String[] args)
    throws ClassNotFoundException, IOException {
  String inputDoc = args.length > 0 ? args[0]
        : "data/simpleCoref.txt";
  System.out.println("Reading in file :"
```

```
      + inputDoc);
TokenizerFactory mTokenizerFactory
   = IndoEuropeanTokenizerFactory.INSTANCE;
SentenceModel sentenceModel
   = new IndoEuropeanSentenceModel();
Chunker sentenceChunker
   = new SentenceChunker(mTokenizerFactory,sentenceModel);
 File modelFile
   = new File("models/ne-en-news-"
     + "muc6.AbstractCharLmRescoringChunker");
Chunker namedEntChunker
   = (Chunker) AbstractExternalizable.readObject(modelFile);
```

Now, we have set up the basic infrastructure for the recipe. Next is a coreference-specific class:

```
MentionFactory mf = new EnglishMentionFactory();
```

The `MentionFactory` class creates mentions from phrases and types—the current source is named `entities`. Next, the coreference class is created with `MentionFactory` as a parameter:

```
WithinDocCoref coref = new WithinDocCoref(mf);
```

The `WithinDocCoref` class wraps all the mechanics of computing coreference. From *Chapter 5*, *Finding Spans in Text - Chunking*, you should be familiar with the code to get the document text, detect sentences, and iterate over the sentences that apply a named-entity chunker to each sentence:

```
File doc = new File(inputDoc);
String text = Files.readFromFile(doc,Strings.UTF8);
Chunking sentenceChunking
   = sentenceChunker.chunk(text);
Iterator sentenceIt
   = sentenceChunking.chunkSet().iterator();

for (int sentenceNum = 0; sentenceIt.hasNext(); ++sentenceNum) {
  Chunk sentenceChunk = (Chunk) sentenceIt.next();
  String sentenceText
     = text.substring(sentenceChunk.start(),
         sentenceChunk.end());
  System.out.println("Sentence Text=" + sentenceText);

  Chunking neChunking = namedEntChunker.chunk(sentenceText);
```

In the context of the current sentence, the named entities from the sentence are iterated over in the left-to-right order as they would be read. We know this because the `ChunkingImpl` class returns chunks in the order that they were added, and our `HMMChunker` adds them in the left-to-right order:

```
Chunking neChunking = namedEntChunker.chunk(sentenceText);
for (Chunk neChunk : neChunking.chunkSet()) {
```

The following code takes the information from the chunk—type and phrase, but *not* the offset information, and creates a mention:

```
String mentionText
    = sentenceText.substring(neChunk.start(),
        neChunk.end());
String mentionType = neChunk.type();
Mention mention = mf.create(mentionText,mentionType);
```

The next line runs coreference with the mention and what sentence it is in and returns its ID:

```
int mentionId = coref.resolveMention(mention,sentenceNum);

System.out.println("    mention text=" + mentionText
        + " type=" + mentionType
        + " id=" + mentionId);
```

If the mention was resolved to an existing entity, it will have that ID, as we saw with Mr. Smith. Otherwise, it will get a distinct ID and itself be available as an antecedent for subsequent mentions.

This covers the mechanics of running within a document coreference. The upcoming recipes will cover the modification of this class. The next recipe will add pronouns and provide references.

Adding pronouns to coreference

The preceding recipe handled coreference between named entities. This recipe will add pronouns to the mix.

Finding Coreference Between Concepts/People

How to do it...

This recipe will use an interactive version to help you explore the properties of the coreference algorithm. The system is very dependent on the quality of the named-entity detection, so use examples that the HMM is likely to get right. This was trained on *Wall Street Journal* articles from the '90s.

1. Saddle up your console and type the following command:

    ```
    java -cp lingpipe-cookbook.1.0.jar:lib/lingpipe-4.1.0.jar: com.
    lingpipe.cookbook.chapter7.Coreference
    ```

2. In the resulting command prompt, type this:

    ```
    Enter text followed by new line
    >John Smith went to Washington. He was a senator.
    Sentence Text=John Smith went to Washington.
    mention text=John Smith type=PERSON id=0
    mention text=Washington type=LOCATION id=1
    Sentence Text= He was a senator.
    mention text=He type=MALE_PRONOUN id=0
    ```

3. The shared ID between `He` and `John Smith` indicates the coreference between the two. More examples will follow, with comments. Note that each input is considered a distinct document with separate ID spaces.

4. If pronouns are not resolved to a named entity, they get the index -1 as shown here:

    ```
    >He went to Washington.
    Sentence Text= He went to Washington.
    mention text=He type=MALE_PRONOUN id=-1
    mention text=Washington type=LOCATION id=0
    ```

5. The following case also results in a -1 value for `id`, because there is not one unique person in the prior context but two. This is called a failed uniqueness presupposition:

    ```
    >Jay Smith and Jim Jones went to Washington. He was a senator.
    Sentence Text=Jay Smith and Jim Jones went to Washington.
    mention text=Jay Smith type=PERSON id=0
    mention text=Jim Jones type=PERSON id=1
    mention text=Washington type=LOCATION id=2
    Sentence Text= He was a senator.
    mention text=He type=MALE_PRONOUN id=-1
    ```

6. The following code shows that `John Smith` can be resolved to a female pronoun as well. This is because there is no data about what names indicate which genders. It can be added, but generally, the context will disambiguate. `John` could be a female name. The key here is that the pronoun will disambiguate the gender, and a following male pronoun will fail to match:

    ```
    Frank Smith went to Washington. She was a senator.
    Sentence Text=Frank Smith went to Washington.
        mention text=Frank Smith type=PERSON id=0
    ```

```
        mention text=Washington type=LOCATION id=1
Sentence Text=She was a senator.
        mention text=She type=FEMALE_PRONOUN id=0
```

7. The gender assignment will block reference by an incorrect gender. The `He` pronoun in the following code is resolved to ID -1, because the only person is resolved to a female pronoun:

```
John Smith went to Washington. She was a senator. He is now a
lobbyist.
Sentence Text=John Smith went to Washington.
        mention text=John Smith type=PERSON id=0
        mention text=Washington type=LOCATION id=1
Sentence Text=She was a senator.
        mention text=She type=FEMALE_PRONOUN id=0
Sentence Text=He is now a lobbyist.
        mention text=He type=MALE_PRONOUN id=-1
```

8. Coreference can happen inside a sentence as well:

```
>Jane Smith knows her future.
Sentence Text=Jane Smith knows her future.
        mention text=Jane Smith type=PERSON id=0
        mention text=her type=FEMALE_PRONOUN id=0
```

9. The order of the mentions (ordered by the most recent mention) matters when resolving mentions. In the following code, `He` is resolved to `James`, not `John`:

```
John is in this sentence. Another sentence about nothing. James is
in this sentence. He is here.
Sentence Text=John is in this sentence.
        mention text=John type=PERSON id=0
Sentence Text=Another sentence about nothing.
Sentence Text=James is in this sentence.
        mention text=James type=PERSON id=1
Sentence Text=He is here.
        mention text=He type=MALE_PRONOUN id=1
```

10. The same effect takes place with named-entity mentions. The `Mr. Smith` entity resolves to the last mention:

```
John Smith is in this sentence. Random sentence. James Smith is in
this sentence. Mr. Smith is mention again here.
Sentence Text=John Smith is in this sentence.
        mention text=John Smith type=PERSON id=0
Sentence Text=Random sentence.
        mention text=Random type=ORGANIZATION id=1
Sentence Text=James Smith is in this sentence.
        mention text=James Smith type=PERSON id=2
Sentence Text=Mr. Smith is mention again here.
        mention text=Mr. Smith type=PERSON id=2
```

11. The distinction between `John` and `James` goes away if there are too many intervening sentences:

    ```
    John Smith is in this sentence. Random sentence. James Smith is
    in this sentence. Random sentence. Random sentence. Mr. Smith is
    here.
    Sentence Text=John Smith is in this sentence.
          mention text=John Smith type=PERSON id=0
    Sentence Text=Random sentence.
          mention text=Random type=ORGANIZATION id=1
    Sentence Text=James Smith is in this sentence.
          mention text=James Smith type=PERSON id=2
    Sentence Text=Random sentence.
          mention text=Random type=ORGANIZATION id=1
    Sentence Text=Random sentence.
          mention text=Random type=ORGANIZATION id=1
    Sentence Text=Mr. Smith is here.
          mention text=Mr. Smith type=PERSON id=3
    ```

The preceding examples are meant to demonstrate the properties of the within-document coreference system.

How it works...

The code changes to add pronouns are straightforward. The code for this recipe is in `src/com/lingpipe/cookbook/chapter7/Coreference.java`. The recipe assumes that you understood the previous recipe, so it just covers the addition of pronoun mentions:

```
Chunking mentionChunking
   = neChunker.chunk(sentenceText);
Set<Chunk> chunkSet = new TreeSet<Chunk> (Chunk.TEXT_ORDER_
COMPARATOR);
chunkSet.addAll(mentionChunking.chunkSet());
```

We added the `Mention` objects from multiple sources, so there are no order guarantees on the order of elements anymore. Correspondingly, we created `TreeSet` and the appropriate comparator and added all the chunkings from the `neChunker`.

Next, we will add the male and female pronouns:

```
addRegexMatchingChunks(MALE_EN_PRONOUNS,"MALE_PRONOUN",
      sentenceText,chunkSet);
addRegexMatchingChunks(FEMALE_EN_PRONOUNS,"FEMALE_PRONOUN",
      sentenceText,chunkSet);
```

The `MALE_EN_PRONOUNS` constant is a regular expression, `Pattern`:

```
static Pattern MALE_EN_PRONOUNS =    Pattern.compile("\\
b(He|he|Him|him)\\b");
```

The following lines of code show the `addRegExMatchingChunks` subroutine. It adds chunks based on regular expression matches and removes the overlapping, existing HMM-derived chunks:

```
static void addRegexMatchingChunks(Pattern pattern, String type,
String text, Set<Chunk> chunkSet) {

  java.util.regex.Matcher matcher = pattern.matcher(text);

  while (matcher.find()) {
    Chunk regexChunk
      = ChunkFactory.createChunk(matcher.start(),
            matcher.end(),
            type);
    for (Chunk chunk : chunkSet) {
    if (ChunkingImpl.overlap(chunk,regexChunk)) {
      chunkSet.remove(chunk);
    }
    }
  chunkSet.add(regexChunk);
  }
}
```

The one complex bit is that the type for the `MALE_PRONOUN` and `FEMALE_PRONOUN` pronouns will be used to match against `PERSON` entities, with the consequence that the resolution sets the gender of the resolved-to entity.

Other than that, the code should look very familiar with our standard I/O loop running the interaction in the command prompt.

See also

The algorithm behind the system is based on the PhD. thesis of Baldwin. The system was called CogNIAC, and the work is from the mid '90s and is not a current state-of-the-art coreference system. A more modern approach would most likely use a machine-learning framework to take the features generated by Baldwin's approach and many other features and use it to develop a better performing system. A paper on the system is at `http://www.aclweb.org/anthology/W/W97/W97-1306.pdf`.

Cross-document coreference

Cross-document coreference (XDoc) takes the `id` space of an individual document and makes it global to a larger universe. This universe typically includes other processed documents and databases of known entities. While the annotation is trivial, all that one needs to do is swap the document-scope IDs for the universe-scope IDs. The calculation of XDoc can be quite difficult.

This recipe will tell us how to use a lightweight implementation of XDoc developed over the course of deploying such systems over the years. We will provide a code overview for those who might want to extend/modify the code—but there is a lot going on, and the recipe is quite dense.

The input is in the XML format where each file can contain multiple documents:

```
<doc id="1">
<title/>
<content>
Breck Baldwin and Krishna Dayanidhi wrote a book about LingPipe.
</content>
</doc>

<doc id="2">
<title/>
<content>
Krishna Dayanidhi is a developer. Breck Baldwin is too.
</content>
</doc>

<doc id="3">
<title/>
<content>
K-dog likes to cook as does Breckles.
</content>
</doc>
```

The goal is to produce annotations where the mentions of Breck Baldwin share the same ID across documents as for Krishna. Note that both are mentioned by their nicknames in the last document.

A very common elaboration of XDoc is linking a **database** (**DB**) of known entities to text mentions of these entities. This bridges the divide between structured DB and unstructured data (text), which many consider to be the next big thing in business intelligence / voice of the customer / enterprise-knowledge management. We have built systems that linked DBs of genes/proteins to MEDLINE abstracts and persons-of-interest lists to free text, and so on. DBs also provide a natural way for human editors to control how XDoc behaves.

Chapter 7

How to do it...

All the code for this recipe is in the `com.lingpipe.cookbook.chapter7.tracker` package.

1. Gain access to your IDE and run `RunTracker` or type the following command in the command line:

   ```
   java -cp lingpipe-cookbook.1.0.jar:lib/lingpipe-4.1.0.jar: com.lingpipe.cookbook.chapter7.tracker.RunTracker
   ```

2. The screen will scroll by with the analysis of documents, but we will go to the designated output file and examine it. Open `cookbook/data/xDoc/output/docs1.xml` in your favorite text editor. You will see a poorly formatted version of the example output, unless your editor automatically formats XML usefully—the Firefox web browser does a decent job of rendering XML. The output should look like this:

   ```xml
   <docs>
   <doc id="1">
   <title/>
   <content>
   <s index="0">
   <entity id="1000000001" type="OTHER">Breck Baldwin</entity> and <entity id="1000000002" type="OTHER">Krishna Dayanidhi</entity> wrote a book about <entity id="1000000003" type="OTHER">LingPipe.</entity>
   </s>
   </content>
   </doc>
   <doc id="2">
   <title/>
   <content><s index="0">
   <entity id="1000000002" type="OTHER">Krishna Dayanidhi</entity> is a developer.
   </s>
   <s index="1"><entity id="1000000001" type="OTHER">Breck Baldwin</entity> is too.
   </s>
   </content>
   </doc>
   <doc id="3"><title/><content><s index="0">K-dog likes to cook as does <entity id="1000000004" start="28" type="OTHER">Breckles</entity>.</s></content></doc>
   </docs>
   ```

Finding Coreference Between Concepts/People

3. `Krishna` is recognized in the first two documents with the shared ID, `1000000002`, but the nickname, `K-dog`, is not recognized at all. `Breck` is recognized in all three documents, but since the ID on the third mention, `Breckles`, is different from the one in the first two mentions, the system does not consider them to be the same entity.

4. Next, we will use a DB in the form of a dictionary to improve the recognition of the authors when they are mentioned via nicknames. There is a dictionary at `data/xDoc/author-dictionary.xml`; it looks like this:

```
<dictionary>
<entity canonical="Breck Baldwin" id="1" speculativeAliases="0" type="MALE">
   <alias xdc="1">Breck Baldwin</alias>
   <alias xdc="1">Breckles</alias>
   <alias xdc="0">Breck</alias>
</entity>

<entity canonical="Krishna Dayanidhi" id="2" speculativeAliases="0" type="MALE">
   <alias xdc="1">Krishna Dayanidhi</alias>
   <alias xdc="1">K-Dog</alias>
   <alias xdc="0">Krishna</alias>
</entity>
```

5. The aforementioned dictionary contains nicknames for both authors, in addition to their first names. Aliases that have the `xdc=1` value will be used to link entities across documents. The `xdc=0` value will only apply within a document. All aliases will be used to identify named entities via a dictionary lookup.

6. Run the following command, which specifies the entity dictionary or IDE equivalent:

```
java -cp lingpipe-cookbook.1.0.jar:lib/lingpipe-4.1.0.jar: com.lingpipe.cookbook.chapter7.tracker.RunTracker data/xDoc/author-dictionary.xml
```

7. The output in `xDoc/output/docs1.xml` is very different from that of the previous run. First, note that the IDs for us are now the same as specified in the dictionary file: `1` for `Breck` and `2` for `Krishna`. This is a link between the structured DB, such as the nature of the dictionary and unstructured text. Second, notice that both our nicknames have been correctly identified and assigned to the correct IDs. Third, note that the types are now `MALE` instead of `OTHER`:

```
<docs>
<doc id="1">
<title/>
<content>
<s index="0">
<entity id="1" type="MALE">Breck Baldwin</entity> and <entity id="2" type="MALE">Krishna Dayanidhi</entity> wrote a book about
```

```
              <entity id="1000000001" type="OTHER">LingPipe.</entity>
            </s>
          </content>
        </doc>
        <doc id="2">
          <title/>
          <content>
            <s index="0">
              <entity id="2" start="0" type="MALE">K-dog</entity> likes to cook
              as does <entity id="1" start="28" type="MALE">Breckles</entity>.
            </s>
          </content>
        </doc>
      </docs>
```

This was a very quick introduction to how to run XDoc. In the next section, we will see how it works.

How it works...

Up until this recipe, we have attempted to keep code simple, straightforward, and understandable without a deep dive into piles of source. This recipe is more complicated. The code that backs this recipe is not going to fit into the allocated space for complete explanation. The exposition assumes that you will explore entire classes on your own and that you will refer to other recipes in this book for explanation. We offer this recipe because XDoc coreference is a very interesting problem, and our existing infrastructure might help others explore the phenomenon. Welcome to the deep end of the pool.

The batch process life cycle

The entire process is controlled by the `RunTracker.java` class. The overall flow of the `main()` method is as follows:

1. Read the DB of known entities that will be a source of named-entity recognition via `Dictionary` and a known mapping from aliases to dictionary entries. Aliases come with instructions regarding whether they should be used for matching entities across documents via the `xdc=1` or `xdc=0` flag.

2. Set up `EnitityUniverse`, which is the global data structure of IDs for what is found in the texts and from the mentioned dictionary of known entities.

3. Set up what is needed for within-document coreference—things such as a tokenizer, sentence detector, and named-entity detector. It gets a bit fancy with a POS tagger and some word counts.

4. There is a Boolean that controls whether speculative entities will be added. If this Boolean is `true`, it means that we will update our universe of cross-document entities with the ones that we have never seen before. It is a much tougher task to reliably compute with this set to `true`.
5. All the mentioned configuration goes into creating a `Tracker` object.
6. Then, the `main()` method reads in documents to process, hands them off to the `Tracker` object for processing, and writes them to disk. The major steps of the `Tracker.processDocuments()` method are as follows:

    1. Take a set of documents in the XML format and get the individual documents.
    2. For each document, apply the `processDocument()` method, which runs within-document coreference using the dictionary to help find entities as well as the named-entity detector and returns `MentionChain[]`. Then, resolve the individual mentions' chains against the entity universe to update document-level IDs to entity universe IDs. The last step is to write the document to disk with the entity universe IDs.

That is all that we will say about `RunTracker`; there is nothing in there that you should not be able to handle in the context of this book. In the following sections, we will address the individual components that `RunTracker` uses.

Setting up the entity universe

The entity universe `EntityUniverse.java`, is an in-memory representation of the global entities mentioned in a document/database collection. The entity universe also contains various indexes into these entities, which support computing XDoc on individual documents.

The dictionary seeds the `EntityUniverse` file with known entities, and the documents processed subsequently are sensitive to these entities. The XDoc algorithm tries to merge with existing entities before creating new ones, so the dictionary entities are strong attractors for mentions of these entities.

Each entity consists of a unique long ID, a set of aliases partitioned into four separate lists and a type (person, location, and so on). Whether the entity is in the user-defined dictionary and whether speculative mentions are allowed to be added to the entity are also mentioned. The `toString()` method lists an entity as:

```
id=556 type=ORGANIZATION userDefined=true allowSpec=false user
  XDC=[Nokia Corp., Nokia] user non-XDC=[] spec XDC=[] spec non-XDC
=[]
```

The global data structures are as follows:

```
private long mLastId = FIRST_SYSTEM_ID;
```

Entities need unique IDs, and we have a convention that the `FIRST_SYSTEM_ID` value is a large integer, such as `1,000,000`. This provides a space (IDs < 1,000,000) for users to add new entities without collisions with entities found by the system.

We will instantiate a tokenizer for use across the tracker:

```
private final TokenizerFactory mTokenizerFactory;
```

There is a global mapping from unique entity IDs to the entities:

```
private final Map<Long,Entity> mIdToEntity
    = new HashMap<Long,Entity>();
```

Another important data structure is a mapping from aliases (phrases) to entities that have the alias—`mXdcPhraseToEntitySet`. Only phrases that are candidates for finding likely matches for cross-document coreference get added here. From the dictionary, the aliases that are `xdc=1` are added:

```
private final ObjectToSet<String,Entity> mXdcPhraseToEntitySet
    = new ObjectToSet<String,Entity>();
```

For speculatively found aliases, if the alias has at least two tokens and is not already on another entity, it is added to this set. This reflects a heuristic that tries hard to not split the entities apart. The logic of this is quite twisted and beyond the scope of this tutorial. You can refer to `EntityUniverse.createEntitySpeculative` and `EntityUniverse.addPhraseToEntity` for the code.

Why are some aliases not used in finding candidate entities? Consider that `George` has very little descriptive content to discriminate entities in `EntityUniverse`, but `George H.W. Bush` has much more information to work with.

ProcessDocuments() and ProcessDocument()

The interesting bits start to happen in the `Tracker.processDocuments()` method, which calls the XML parsing of each document and then incrementally calls the `processDocument()` method. The code is straightforward for the former, so we will move on to where the more task-specific work happens with the `processDocument()` method called:

```
public synchronized OutputDocument processDocument(
        InputDocument document) {

    WithinDocCoref coref
        = new WithinDocCoref(mMentionFactory);

    String title = document.title();
```

```
            String content = document.content();

            List<String> sentenceTextList = new ArrayList<String>();
            List<Mention[]> sentenceMentionList
                = new ArrayList<Mention[]>();

            List<int[]> mentionStartList = new ArrayList<int[]>();
            List<int[]> mentionEndList = new ArrayList<int[]>();

            int firstContentSentenceIndex
                = processBlock(title,0,
                               sentenceTextList,
                               sentenceMentionList,
                               mentionStartList,mentionEndList,
                               coref);

            processBlock(content,firstContentSentenceIndex,
                         sentenceTextList,
                         sentenceMentionList,
                         mentionStartList,mentionEndList,
                         coref);

            MentionChain[] chains = coref.mentionChains();
```

We used a document format that supports distinguishing the title from the body of the document. This is a good idea if title case is distinct from body case, as is usual with newswire. The `chains` variable will have chains from the title and body of the text, with possible coreference between them. The `mentionStartList` and `mentionEndList` arrays will make it possible to realign the document scoped IDs with the entity universe scoped IDs later in the method:

```
    Entity[] entities   = mXDocCoref.xdocCoref(chains);
```

Computing XDoc

The XDoc code is the result of many hours of hand-tuning the algorithm to work well on news-style data. It has been run on datasets in the 20,000 document range and is designed to support dictionary entries very aggressively. The code also attempts to prevent **short circuits**, which occur when obviously different entities have been merged together. If you mistakenly make Barbara Bush and George Bush coreferent in your global database, then you will have embarrassingly bad results that users will see.

The other sort of error is having two entities in the global store when one will do. This is a sort of *Superman/Clark Kent problem* that can also apply to multiple mentions of the same name.

We will begin with the top-level code:

```
public Entity[] xdocCoref(MentionChain[] chains) { Entity[]
    entities = new Entity[chains.length];

    Map<MentionChain,Entity> chainToEntity
        = new HashMap<MentionChain,Entity>();
    ObjectToSet<Entity,MentionChain> entityToChainSet
        = new ObjectToSet<Entity,MentionChain>();


    for (MentionChain chain : chains)
        resolveMentionChain((TTMentionChain) chain,
                        chainToEntity, entityToChainSet);

    for (int i = 0; i < chains.length; ++i) {
        TTMentionChain chain = (TTMentionChain) chains[i];
        Entity entity = chainToEntity.get(chain);

        if (entity != null) {
            if (Tracker.DEBUG) {
                System.out.println("XDOC: resolved to" + entity);
        Set chainSetForEntity = entityToChainSet.get(entity);
                if (chainSetForEntity.size() > 1)
                    System.out.println("XDOC: multiple chains
  resolved to same entity " + entity.id());
            }
            entities[i] = entity;
            if (entity.addSpeculativeAliases())
                addMentionChainToEntity(chain,entity);
        } else {
            Entity newEntity = promote(chain);
            entities[i] = newEntity;
        }
    }
    return entities;
}
```

A document has a list of mention chains, and each mention chain will be either added to an existing entity, or the mention chain will be promoted to being a new entity. Mention chains must contain a mention that is not pronominal, which is handled at the within-document coreference level.

Finding Coreference Between Concepts/People

Three data structures are updated as each mention chain is processed:

- The `Entity[]` entities are returned by the `xdocCoref` method to support the inline annotation of the documents.
- `Map<MentionChain,Entity> chainToEntity` maps from mention chains to entities.
- `ObjectToSet<Entity,MentionChain> entityToChainSet` is the converse of `chainToEntity`. It is possible that multiple chains in the same document get mapped to the same entity, so this data structure is sensitive to this possibility. This version of the code allows this to happen—in effect, XDoc is setting up a within-doc resolution as a side effect.

Simple enough, if an entity is found, then the `addMentionChainToEntity()` method adds any new information from the mention chain to the entity. New information can include new aliases and type changes (that is, a person is moved to being male or female in virtue of a disambiguating pronoun reference). If no entity is found, then the mention chain goes to `promote()`, which creates a new entity in the entity universe. We will start with `promote()`.

The promote() method

The entity universe is a minimalist data structure that just keeps track of phrases, types, and IDs. The `TTMentionChain` class is a more complex representation of the mentions of a particular document:

```
private Entity promote(TTMentionChain chain) {
    Entity entity
        = mEntityUniverse.createEntitySpeculative(
          chain.normalPhrases(),
                        chain.entityType());
    if (Tracker.DEBUG)
        System.out.println("XDOC: promoted " + entity);
    return entity;
}
```

The call to `mEntityUniverse.createEntitySpeculative` only requires the phrases for the chain (in this case, normalized phrases that have been lowercased and in which all sequences of whitespaces converted into a single space) and the type of the entity. No record is kept of the document from which the mention chain came, counts, or other potentially useful information. This is to keep the memory representation as small as possible. If there is a need to find all the sentences or documents that an entity is mentioned in (a common task), then that mapping from entity IDs has to be stored elsewhere. The XML representation produced for the document after XDoc is run is a natural place to start addressing these needs.

The createEntitySpeculative() method

Creation of a speculatively found new entity only requires determining which of its aliases are the good candidates to link mention chains. Those that are good for cross-document coreference go into the `xdcPhrases` set, and the others go into the `nonXdc` phrases:

```java
public Entity createEntitySpeculative(Set<String> phrases,
                                      String entityType) {
    Set<String> nonXdcPhrases = new HashSet<String>();
    Set<String> xdcPhrases = new HashSet<String>();
    for (String phrase : phrases) {
        if (isXdcPhrase(phrase,hasMultiWordPhrases))
            xdcPhrases.add(phrase);
        else
            nonXdcPhrases.add(phrase);
    }
    while (mIdToEntity.containsKey(++mLastId)) ; // move up to next untaken ID
    Entity entity = new Entity(mLastId,entityType,
                               null,null,xdcPhrases,nonXdcPhrases);
    add(entity);
    return entity;
}
```

The `boolean` method, `XdcPhrase()`, plays a critical role in the XDoc process. The current approach supports a very conservative notion of what a good XDoc phrase is. Intuitively, in the domain of newswire, phrases such as `he`, `Bob`, and `John Smith` are poor indicators of a unique individual being talked about. Good phrases might be `Breckenridge Baldwin`, because that is likely a unique name. There are lots of fancy theories for what is going on here, see rigid designators (http://en.wikipedia.org/wiki/Rigid_designator). The next few lines of code run roughshod over 2,000 years of philosophical thought:

```java
public boolean isXdcPhrase(String phrase,
        boolean hasMultiWordPhrase) {

    if (mXdcPhraseToEntitySet.containsKey(phrase)) {
        return false;
    }
    if (phrase.indexOf(' ') == -1 && hasMultiWordPhrase) {
        return false;
    }
    if (PronounChunker.isPronominal(phrase)) {
        return false;
    }
    return true;
}
```

Finding Coreference Between Concepts/People

This approach attempts to identify the bad phrases for XDoc rather than the good ones. The reasoning is as follows:

- **There is already an entity associated with the phrase**: This enforces an assumption that there is only one John Smith in the world. This worked very well for intelligence-gathering applications, where the analysts had little trouble teasing apart the `John Smith` cases. You can refer to the *The John Smith problem* recipe at the end of this chapter for more about this.
- **The phrase is only one word, and there are multiword phrases associated with the mention chain or entity**: This assumes that longer words are better for XDoc. Note that different orders of entity creation can result in one-word phrases having `xdc` to be `true` on entities with multiword aliases.
- **The phrase is a pronoun**: This is a fairly safe assumption, unless we are in religious texts where `He` or `Him` capitalized in the middle of a sentence indicate reference to God.

Once the sets of `xdc` and `nonXdc` phrases are known, then the entity is created. Refer to the source code for `Entity.java` to understand how entities are created.

Then, the entity is created, and an `add` method updates a mapping in the `EntityUniverse` file of `xdc` phrases to entity IDs:

```
public void add(Entity e) {
    if (e.id() > mLastId)
        mLastId = e.id();
    mIdToEntity.put(new Long(e.id()),e);
    for (String phrase : e.xdcPhrases()) {
        mXdcPhraseToEntitySet.addMember(phrase,e);
    }
}
```

The `EntityUniverse` file's global `mXdcPhraseToEntitySet` variable is the key to finding candidate entities for XDoc as used in `xdcEntitiesToPhrase()`.

The XDocCoref.addMentionChainToEntity() entity

Returning to the `XDocCoref.xdocCoref()` method, we have covered how to create a new entity via `XDocCoref.promote()`. The next option to cover is what happens when a mention chain is resolved to an existing entity, namely `XDocCoref.addMentionChainToEntity()`. For the speculative mentions to be added, the entity must allow speculatively found mentions as provided by the `Entity.allowSpeculativeAliases()` method. This is a feature of the user-defined dictionary entities discussed in user-defined entities. If speculative entities are allowed, then the mention chains are added to the entity with a sensitivity to whether they are `xdc` phrases or not:

```
private void addMentionChainToEntity(TTMentionChain chain,
        Entity entity) {
```

```
        for (String phrase : chain.normalPhrases()) {
                mEntityUniverse.addPhraseToEntity(normalPhrase,
                    entity);
        }
    }
```

The only change that adding a mention chain can add to an entity is the addition of a new phrase. The additional phrases are classified for whether they are xdc or not in the same way as was done in the promotion of a mention chain.

At this point, we have gone over the basics of how mention chains from documents are either promoted to speculative entities or are merged with existing entities in EntityUniverse. Next, we will take a look at how resolution occurs in XDocCoref.resolveMentionChain().

The XDocCoref.resolveMentionChain() entity

The XDocCoref.resolveMentionChain() method assembles a covering set of entities that can possibly match the mention chain being resolved and then attempt to find a unique entity via a call to XDocCoref.resolveCandates():

```
    private void resolveMentionChain(TTMentionChain chain,
                            Map<MentionChain,Entity> chainToEntity,
    ObjectToSet<Entity,MentionChain> entityToChainSet) {
        if (Tracker.DEBUG)
            System.out.println("XDOC: resolving mention chain "
              + chain);
        int maxLengthAliasOnMentionChain = 0;
        int maxLengthAliasResolvedToEntityFromMentionChain = -1;
        Set<String> tokens = new HashSet<String>();
        Set<Entity> candidateEntities = new HashSet<Entity>();
        for (String phrase : chain.normalPhrases()) {
        String[] phraseTokens = mEntityUniverse.normalTokens(phrase);
          String normalPhrase
      = mEntityUniverse.concatenateNormalTokens(phraseTokens);
          for (int i = 0; i < phraseTokens.length; ++i) {
                 tokens.add(phraseTokens[i]);
            }
    }
        int length = phraseTokens.length;
        if (length > maxLengthAliasOnMentionChain) {
            maxLengthAliasOnMentionChain = length;
        }
          Set<Entity> matchingEntities
            = mEntityUniverse.xdcEntitiesWithPhrase(phrase);
          for (Entity entity : matchingEntities) {
            if (null != TTMatchers.unifyEntityTypes(
              chain.entityType(),
```

```
                    entity.type())) {
                        if (maxLengthAliasResolvedToEntityFromMentionChain
< length)
                                    maxLengthAliasResolvedToEntityFromMentionChain
= length;
           candidateEntities.add(entity);
        }
    }
}
resolveCandidates(chain,
                  tokens,
                  candidateEntities,

maxLengthAliasResolvedToEntityFromMentionChain ==
maxLengthAliasOnMentionChain,
                        chainToEntity,
                        entityToChainSet);}
```

The code assembles a set of entities by doing a lookup into the entity universe with `EntityUniverse.xdcEntitiesWithPhrase()`. All aliases for the mention chain are tried without consideration of whether they are good XDoc aliases. Before the entities are added to `candidateEntities`, the type returned must be consistent with the type of the mention chain as determined by `TTMatchers.unifyEntityTypes`. This way, `Washington`, a location is not resolved to `Washington`, a person. A bit of record keeping is done to determine whether the longest alias on the mention chain has matched an entity.

The resolveCandidates() method

The `resolveCandidates()` method captures a key assumption that holds both for within-document and XDoc coreferences—this unambiguous reference is the only basis of resolution. In the within-document case, an example where humans have this problem is the sentence, `Bob and Joe were working together. He fell into the threshing machine.` Who is `he` referring to? The linguistic expectation that a singular referring term have a unique antecedent is called a uniqueness presupposition. An example XDoc case is as follows:

- **Doc1**: John Smith is a character from Pocohontas
- **Doc2**: John Smith is the chairman or GM
- **Doc3**: John Smith is admired

Which `John Smith` does the `John Smith` from Doc3 go with? Perhaps, neither. The algorithm in this software requires that there should be a single possible entity that survives the matching criteria. If there is more than one or zero, then a new entity is created. The implementation is as follows:

```
            private void resolveCandidates(TTMentionChain chain,
                              Set<String> tokens,
                              Set<Entity> candidateEntities,
```

```java
                              boolean resolvedAtMaxLength,
                              Map<MentionChain,Entity> chainToEntity,
                              ObjectToSet<Entity,MentionChain>
    entityToChainSet) {
            filterCandidates(chain,tokens,candidateEntities,resolvedAtMax
    Length);
            if (candidateEntities.size() == 0)
                return;
            if (candidateEntities.size() == 1) {
                Entity entity = Collections.<Entity>getFirst(candidateEnt
    ities);
                chainToEntity.put(chain,entity);
                entityToChainSet.addMember(entity,chain);
                return;
            }
            // BLOWN Uniqueness Presupposition; candidateEntities.size() >
    1
            if (Tracker.DEBUG)
                System.out.println("Blown UP; candidateEntities.size()=" +
    candidateEntities.size());
        }
```

The `filterCandidates` method eliminates all the candidate entities that fail for various semantic reasons. Coreference with an entity in the entity universe only happens if there is a single possible solution. There is not a distinction between too many candidate entities (more than one) or too few (zero). In a more advanced system, one could try and further disambiguate if there are too many entities via `context`.

This is the heart of the XDoc code. The rest of the code marks up the document with entity-universe-relevant indices as returned by the `xdocCoref` method, which we just covered:

```java
    Entity[] entities  = mXDocCoref.xdocCoref(chains);
```

The following `for` loop iterates over the mention chains, which are aligned with `Entities[]` returned by `xdocCoref`. For each mention chain, the mention is mapped to its cross-document entity:

```java
    Map<Mention,Entity> mentionToEntityMap
        = new HashMap<Mention,Entity>();
    for (int i = 0; i < chains.length; ++i){
      for (Mention mention : chains[i].mentions()) {
            mentionToEntityMap.put(mention,entities[i]);
        }
    }
```

Finding Coreference Between Concepts/People

Next, the code will set up a bunch of mappings to create chunks that reflect the entity universe IDs:

```
String[] sentenceTexts
        = sentenceTextList
            .<String>toArray(new String[sentenceTextList.size()])
Mention[][] sentenceMentions
        = sentenceMentionList
            .<Mention[]>toArray(new Mention[sentenceMentionList.size()][]);
int[][] mentionStarts
        = mentionStartList
            .<int[]>toArray(new int[mentionStartList.size()][]);

int[][] mentionEnds
        = mentionEndList
            .<int[]>toArray(new int[mentionEndList.size()][]);
```

The actual creation of the chunks happens next:

```
Chunking[] chunkings = new Chunking[sentenceTexts.length];
  for (int i = 0; i < chunkings.length; ++i) {
   ChunkingImpl chunking = new ChunkingImpl(sentenceTexts[i]);
   chunkings[i] = chunking;
   for (int j = 0; j < sentenceMentions[i].length; ++j) {
    Mention mention = sentenceMentions[i][j];
    Entity entity = mentionToEntityMap.get(mention);
    if (entity == null) {
     Chunk chunk = ChunkFactory.createChunk(mentionStarts[i][j],
        mentionEnds[i][j],
        mention.entityType()
        + ":-1");
       //chunking.add(chunk); //uncomment to get unresolved ents as -1
   indexed.
    } else {
     Chunk chunk = ChunkFactory.createChunk(mentionStarts[i][j],
        mentionEnds[i][j],
        entity.type()
        + ":" + entity.id());
     chunking.add(chunk);
    }
   }
  }
```

The chunkings are then used to create the relevant portions of the document, and `OutputDocument` is returned:

```
        // needless allocation here and last, but simple
        Chunking[] titleChunkings = new Chunking[firstContentSentence
Index];
        for (int i = 0; i < titleChunkings.length; ++i)
            titleChunkings[i] = chunkings[i];

        Chunking[] bodyChunkings = new Chunking[chunkings.length -
firstContentSentenceIndex];
        for (int i = 0; i < bodyChunkings.length; ++i)
            bodyChunkings[i] = chunkings[firstContentSentenceIndex+i];

        String id = document.id();

        OutputDocument result = new OutputDocument(id,titleChunkings,
bodyChunkings);
        return result;
    }
```

So, this is what we have to offer as a starting place for XDoc coreference. Hopefully, we have explained the intentions behind the more opaque methods. Good luck!

The John Smith problem

Different people, locations, and concepts can have the same orthographic representation but be distinct. There are multiple instances of "John Smith", "Paris", and "bank" in the world, and a proper cross-document coreference system should be able to handle it. For the case of concepts such as "bank" (a river bank versus a financial bank), the term of art is word-sense disambiguation. This recipe will demonstrate one approach to the problem that Baldwin developed back in the day with Amit Bagga for person disambiguation.

Getting ready

The code for this recipe closely follows the clustering tutorial at `http://alias-i.com/lingpipe/demos/tutorial/cluster/read-me.html` but changes it to more closely fit the original Bagga-Baldwin work. There is a fair amount of code but nothing very complicated. The source is in `src/com/lingpipe/cookbook/chapter7/JohnSmith.java`.

Finding Coreference Between Concepts/People

The class starts with the standard panoply of NLP tools for tokenization, sentence detection, and named-entity detection. Refer to the previous recipes if this stack is unfamiliar:

```
public static void main(String[] args)
    throws ClassNotFoundException, IOException {
  TokenizerFactory tokenizerFactory = IndoEuropeanTokenizerFactory.
INSTANCE;
  SentenceModel sentenceModel
    = new IndoEuropeanSentenceModel();
  SENTENCE_CHUNKER
    = new SentenceChunker(tokenizerFactory,sentenceModel);
  File modelFile
    = new File("models/ne-en-news-muc6.
AbstractCharLmRescoringChunker");
  NAMED_ENTITY_CHUNKER
    = (Chunker) AbstractExternalizable.readObject(modelFile);
```

Next up, we will revisit `TfIdfDistance`. However, the task requires that we wrap the class to operate over `Documents` rather than `CharSequences`, because we would like to retain the filename and be able to manipulate what text is used for the calculations to come:

```
TfIdfDocumentDistance tfIdfDist = new TfIdfDocumentDistance(tokenizer
Factory);
```

Dropping to the referenced class, we have the following code:

```
public class TfIdfDocumentDistance implements Distance<Document> {
  TfIdfDistance mTfIdfDistance;
  public TfIdfDocumentDistance (TokenizerFactory tokenizerFactory) {
  mTfIdfDistance = new TfIdfDistance(tokenizerFactory);
  }

   public void train(CharSequence text) {
      mTfIdfDistance.handle(text);
   }

  @Override
  public double distance(Document doc1, Document doc2) {
    return mTfIdfDistance.distance(doc1.mCoreferentText,
         doc2.mCoreferentText);
  }

}
```

The `train` method interfaces with the `TfIdfDistance.handle()` method and provides an implementation of a `distance(Document doc1, Document doc2)` method that will drive the clustering code discussed below. All that the `train` method does is pull out the relevant text and hand it off to the `TfIdfDistance` class for the relevant value.

The reference class, `Document`, is an inner class in `JohnSmith`, and it is quite simple. It gets sentences that have entities which match the `.*John Smith.*` pattern and puts them in the `mCoreferentText` variable:

```
static class Document {
        final File mFile;
        final CharSequence mText;
        final CharSequence mCoreferentText;
        Document(File file) throws IOException {
            mFile = file; // includes name
            mText = Files.readFromFile(file,Strings.UTF8);
            Set<String> coreferentSents
      = getCoreferentSents(".*John "                              +
"Smith.*",mText.toString());
            StringBuilder sb = new StringBuilder();
            for (String sentence : coreferentSents) {
               sb.append(sentence);
            }
            mCoreferentText = sb.toString();
        }

        public String toString() {
            return mFile.getParentFile().getName() + "/"
            + mFile.getName();
        }
    }
```

Going deeper into the code, we will now visit the `getCoreferentSents()` method:

```
static final Set<String> getCoreferentSents(String targetPhrase,
String text) {
     Chunking sentenceChunking
      = SENTENCE_CHUNKER.chunk(text);
   Iterator<Chunk> sentenceIt
      = sentenceChunking.chunkSet().iterator();
   int targetId = -2;
   MentionFactory mentionFactory = new EnglishMentionFactory();
   WithinDocCoref coref = new WithinDocCoref(mentionFactory);
   Set<String> matchingSentenceAccumulator
      = new HashSet<String>();
   for (int sentenceNum = 0; sentenceIt.hasNext(); ++sentenceNum) {
```

```java
      Chunk sentenceChunk = sentenceIt.next();
      String sentenceText
        = text.substring(sentenceChunk.start(),
              sentenceChunk.end());
      Chunking neChunking
        = NAMED_ENTITY_CHUNKER.chunk(sentenceText);
      Set<Chunk> chunkSet
        = new TreeSet<Chunk>(Chunk.TEXT_ORDER_COMPARATOR);
      chunkSet.addAll(neChunking.chunkSet());      Coreference.
addRegexMatchingChunks(
        Pattern.compile("\\bJohn Smith\\b"),
              "PERSON",sentenceText,chunkSet);
      Iterator<Chunk> neChunkIt = chunkSet.iterator();
      while (neChunkIt.hasNext()) {
        Chunk neChunk = neChunkIt.next();
        String mentionText
            = sentenceText.substring(neChunk.start(),
              neChunk.end());
        String mentionType = neChunk.type();
        Mention mention
        = mentionFactory.create(mentionText,mentionType);
        int mentionId
        = coref.resolveMention(mention,sentenceNum);
        if (targetId == -2 && mentionText.matches(targetPhrase)) {
        targetId = mentionId;
        }
        if (mentionId == targetId) {
    matchingSentenceAccumulator.add(sentenceText);
          System.out.println("Adding " + sentenceText);
          System.out.println("    mention text=" + mentionText
              + " type=" + mentionType
              + " id=" + mentionId);
        }
      }
    }
    if (targetId == -2) {
      System.out.println("!!!Missed target doc " + text);
    }
    return matchingSentenceAccumulator;
    }
```

Look at the *Cross-document coreference* recipe for most of the moving parts of the preceding method. We will call out a few notable bits. We are cheating in some sense by using a regular expression chunker to find any string that has as a `John Smith` substring and adding it in as a `PERSON` entity. Like most kinds of cheating, this is quite useful if your sole purpose in life is tracking `John Smith`. The cheating we did in reality was to use dictionary matching to find all variations of high-value intelligence targets such as `Osama bin Laden`. In the end, we had over 40 versions of his name scouring openly available news sources as a part of the MiTAP project.

Further, as each sentence is processed, we will check all the mentions for a matching pattern for `John Smith`, and if so, we will collect any sentence that has a mention of this ID. This means that a sentence that refers back to `John Smith` with a pronoun will be included, as will the `Mr. Smith` cases if coreference is doing its job. Note that we need to see a match for `John Smith` before we start collecting contextual information, so we will miss the first sentence of `He awoke. John Smith was a giant cockroach`. Also note that if a second `John Smith` shows up with a different ID, it will be ignored—this can happen.

Finally, note that there is some error checking, in that if `John Smith` is not found, then an error is reported to `System.out`.

If we pop back to mundane I/O slinging in our `main()` method after setting up `TfIdfDocumentDistance`, we would have:

```
File dir = new File(args[0]);
      Set<Set<Document>> referencePartition
            = new HashSet<Set<Document>>();
      for (File catDir : dir.listFiles()) {
          System.out.println("Category from file=" + catDir);
          Set<Document> docsForCat = new HashSet<Document>();
          referencePartition.add(docsForCat);
          for (File file : catDir.listFiles()) {
              Document doc = new Document(file);
              tfIdfDist.train(doc.mText);
              docsForCat.add(doc);
          }
      }
```

We have not discussed this, but the truth annotation of which document references which `Mr. Smith` is encoded in the directory structure of the data. Each subdirectory in the top `johnSmith` directory is treated as the truth cluster. So, `referencePartition` contains the truth. We could have wrapped this as a classification problem with each subdirectory, the correct classification. We will leave it as an exercise to you to stuff this into a cross-validating corpus with a logistic regression solution.

Finding Coreference Between Concepts/People

Moving on, we will construct the test set by flattening our previous categories into a single set of `Document`s. We could have done this in the previous step, but mixing tasks tends to produce bugs, and the extra `for` loop does very little damage to the execution speed:

```
Set<Document> docSet = new HashSet<Document>();
for (Set<Document> cluster : referencePartition) {
    docSet.addAll(cluster);
}
```

Next, we will tee up the clustering algorithms. We will do both `CompleteLink` and `SingleLink` driven by `TfIdfDocumentDistance` that runs the show:

```
HierarchicalClusterer<Document> clClusterer
    = new CompleteLinkClusterer<Document>(tfIdfDist);
Dendrogram<Document> completeLinkDendrogram
    = clClusterer.hierarchicalCluster(docSet);

HierarchicalClusterer<Document> slClusterer
    = new SingleLinkClusterer<Document>(tfIdfDist);
Dendrogram<Document> singleLinkDendrogram
    = slClusterer.hierarchicalCluster(docSet);
```

The details of the clustering algorithms are covered in *Chapter 5, Finding Spans in Texts – Chunking*. Now, we will report performance based on the number of clusters varied from `1` to the number of inputs. The one fancy bit is that the `Cross` category uses `SingleLinkClusterer` as the reference and `CompleteLinkClusterer` as the response:

```
System.out.println();
System.out.println(" ----------------------------------------"
    + "-------------");
System.out.println("|   K   |    Complete      |    Single       | "
    + " Cross       |");
System.out.println("|       |   P   R   F      |   P   R   F     | P"
    + "   R   F     |");
System.out.println(" ----------------------------------------"
    +"-------------");
for (int k = 1; k <= docSet.size(); ++k) {
    Set<Set<Document>> clResponsePartition
        = completeLinkDendrogram.partitionK(k);
    Set<Set<Document>> slResponsePartition
        = singleLinkDendrogram.partitionK(k);

    ClusterScore<Document> scoreCL
        = new ClusterScore<Document>(referencePartition,
                                     clResponsePartition)
    PrecisionRecallEvaluation clPrEval
```

```
          = scoreCL.equivalenceEvaluation();
    ClusterScore<Document> scoreSL
        = new ClusterScore<Document>(referencePartition,
                                     slResponsePartition);
    PrecisionRecallEvaluation slPrEval
      = scoreSL.equivalenceEvaluation();

    ClusterScore<Document> scoreX
        = new ClusterScore<Document>(clResponsePartition
                                     slResponsePartition);
    PrecisionRecallEvaluation xPrEval
      = scoreX.equivalenceEvaluation();

    System.out.printf("| %3d | %3.2f %3.2f %3.2f | %3.2f %3.2f %3.2f"
        + " | %3.2f %3.2f %3.2f |\n",
                    k,
                    clPrEval.precision(),
                    clPrEval.recall(),
                    clPrEval.fMeasure(),
                    slPrEval.precision(),
                    slPrEval.recall(),
                    slPrEval.fMeasure(),
                    xPrEval.precision(),
                    xPrEval.recall(),
                    xPrEval.fMeasure());
  }
  System.out.println(" -----------------------------------------"
        + "------------");
}
```

That's all that we need to do to get ready for this recipe. This is a rare phenomenon to be computed, and this is a toy implementation, but the key concepts should be evident.

How to do it...

We will just run this code and then mess with it a bit:

1. Get yourself to a terminal and type:

   `java -cp lingpipe-cookbook.1.0.jar:lib/lingpipe-4.1.0.jar: com.lingpipe.cookbook.chapter7.JohnSmith`

2. The result will be piles of information that indicate what sentences are being extracted for use in the clustering—remember that the truth annotation is determined by the directory that the files are in. The first cluster is 0:

   `Category from file=data/johnSmith/0`

Finding Coreference Between Concepts/People

3. The code reports sentences that contain references to `John Smith`:

   ```
   Adding I thought John Smith marries Pocahontas.''
       mention text=John Smith type=PERSON id=5
   Adding He's bullets , she's arrows.''
       mention text=He type=MALE_PRONOUN id=5
   ```

4. The pronominal reference to `John Smith` is the basis of inclusion of the second sentence.

5. The system output goes on, and finally, we will get the results for a single-link clustering against the truth and a complete link against the truth. The `K` column indicates how many clusters the algorithm was allowed with precision, recall, and F-measure reported. The first row is in this case that there is only one cluster that will allow for 100 percent recall and 23 percent precision for both complete and single links. Looking down at the scores, we can see that the complete link reports the best F-measure with 11 clusters at `0.60`—in truth, there are 35 clusters. The single-link approach maxes out F-measure at 68 clusters with `0.78` and shows much greater robustness on varying numbers of clusters. The cross case shows that single link and complete link are quite different in direct comparison as well. Note that some `K` values have been eliminated for readability:

```
| K  | Complete         | Single           |
|    | P    R    F      | P    R    F      |
-------------------------------------------------
|  1 | 0.23 1.00 0.38   | 0.23 1.00 0.38
|  2 | 0.28 0.64 0.39   | 0.24 1.00 0.38
|  3 | 0.29 0.64 0.40   | 0.24 1.00 0.39
|  4 | 0.30 0.64 0.41   | 0.24 1.00 0.39
|  5 | 0.44 0.63 0.52   | 0.24 0.99 0.39
|  6 | 0.45 0.63 0.52   | 0.25 0.99 0.39
|  7 | 0.45 0.63 0.52   | 0.25 0.99 0.40
|  8 | 0.49 0.62 0.55   | 0.25 0.99 0.40
|  9 | 0.55 0.61 0.58   | 0.25 0.99 0.40
| 10 | 0.55 0.61 0.58   | 0.25 0.99 0.41
| 11 | 0.59 0.61 0.60   | 0.27 0.99 0.42
| 12 | 0.59 0.61 0.60   | 0.27 0.98 0.42
| 13 | 0.56 0.41 0.48   | 0.27 0.98 0.43
| 14 | 0.71 0.41 0.52   | 0.27 0.98 0.43
| 15 | 0.71 0.41 0.52   | 0.28 0.98 0.43
| 16 | 0.68 0.34 0.46   | 0.28 0.98 0.44
| 17 | 0.68 0.34 0.46   | 0.28 0.98 0.44
| 18 | 0.69 0.34 0.46   | 0.29 0.98 0.44
| 19 | 0.67 0.32 0.43   | 0.29 0.98 0.45
| 20 | 0.69 0.29 0.41   | 0.29 0.98 0.45
| 30 | 0.84 0.22 0.35   | 0.33 0.96 0.49
```

```
|  40 | 0.88 0.18 0.30 | 0.61 0.88 0.72
|  50 | 0.89 0.16 0.28 | 0.64 0.86 0.73
|  60 | 0.91 0.14 0.24 | 0.66 0.77 0.71
|  61 | 0.91 0.14 0.24 | 0.66 0.75 0.70
|  62 | 0.93 0.14 0.24 | 0.87 0.75 0.81
|  63 | 0.94 0.13 0.23 | 0.87 0.69 0.77
|  64 | 0.94 0.13 0.23 | 0.87 0.69 0.77
|  65 | 0.94 0.13 0.23 | 0.87 0.68 0.77
|  66 | 0.94 0.13 0.23 | 0.87 0.66 0.75
|  67 | 0.95 0.13 0.23 | 0.87 0.66 0.75
|  68 | 0.95 0.13 0.22 | 0.95 0.66 0.78
|  69 | 0.94 0.11 0.20 | 0.95 0.66 0.78
|  70 | 0.94 0.11 0.20 | 0.95 0.65 0.77
|  80 | 0.98 0.11 0.19 | 0.97 0.43 0.59
|  90 | 0.99 0.10 0.17 | 0.97 0.30 0.46
| 100 | 0.99 0.08 0.16 | 0.96 0.20 0.34
| 110 | 0.99 0.07 0.14 | 1.00 0.11 0.19
| 120 | 1.00 0.07 0.12 | 1.00 0.08 0.14
| 130 | 1.00 0.06 0.11 | 1.00 0.06 0.12
| 140 | 1.00 0.05 0.09 | 1.00 0.05 0.10
| 150 | 1.00 0.04 0.08 | 1.00 0.04 0.08
| 160 | 1.00 0.04 0.07 | 1.00 0.04 0.07
| 170 | 1.00 0.03 0.07 | 1.00 0.03 0.07
| 180 | 1.00 0.03 0.06 | 1.00 0.03 0.06
| 190 | 1.00 0.02 0.05 | 1.00 0.02 0.05
| 197 | 1.00 0.02 0.04 | 1.00 0.02 0.04
```

6. The following output constrains clustering not by cluster size but by the max distance threshold. The output is for the single-link cluster with .05 increases the distance and the evaluation is the B-cubed metric. The output is the distance, precision, recall, and the size of the resulting cluster. The performance at .80 and .9 is quite good, but beware of setting production thresholds in this after the fact fashion. In a production environment, we will want to see much more data before setting the threshold:

```
B-cubed eval
Dist: 0.00 P: 1.00 R: 0.77 size:189
Dist: 0.05 P: 1.00 R: 0.80 size:171
Dist: 0.10 P: 1.00 R: 0.80 size:164
Dist: 0.15 P: 1.00 R: 0.81 size:157
Dist: 0.20 P: 1.00 R: 0.81 size:153
Dist: 0.25 P: 1.00 R: 0.82 size:148
Dist: 0.30 P: 1.00 R: 0.82 size:144
Dist: 0.35 P: 1.00 R: 0.83 size:142
```

```
Dist: 0.40 P: 1.00 R: 0.83 size:141
Dist: 0.45 P: 1.00 R: 0.83 size:141
Dist: 0.50 P: 1.00 R: 0.83 size:138
Dist: 0.55 P: 1.00 R: 0.83 size:136
Dist: 0.60 P: 1.00 R: 0.84 size:128
Dist: 0.65 P: 1.00 R: 0.84 size:119
Dist: 0.70 P: 1.00 R: 0.86 size:108
Dist: 0.75 P: 0.99 R: 0.88 size: 90
Dist: 0.80 P: 0.99 R: 0.94 size: 60
Dist: 0.85 P: 0.95 R: 0.97 size: 26
Dist: 0.90 P: 0.91 R: 0.99 size:  8
Dist: 0.95 P: 0.23 R: 1.00 size:  1
Dist: 1.00 P: 0.23 R: 1.00 size:  1
```

7. The B-cubed (Bagga, Bierman, and Baldwin) evaluation was created to heavily penalize pushing large clusters together. It assumes that it is more of a problem to push lots of documents about George W. Bush together with George H. W. Bush, both large clusters, than to mistake George Bush, the mechanic who got mentioned once in the dataset. Other scoring metrics will count both the mistakes as equally bad. It is the standard scoring metric used in the literature for this phenomenon.

See also

There is a fair amount of work in the research literature on this exact problem. We were not the first ones to think about this, but we came up with the dominant evaluation metric, and we released a corpus for other groups to compare themselves with us and each other. Our contribution is *Entity-based cross-document coreferencing using the Vector Space Model* by Bagga and Baldwin in *ACL '98 Proceedings of the 36th Annual Meeting of the Association for Computational Linguistics and 17th International Conference on Computational Linguistics*. There has been much progress since—there are more than 400 citations to this model on Google Scholar; they are worth a look if this problem is of importance to you.

Index

Symbol

.csv file
  classifier, applying to 22-24

A

active learning
  about 126-133
  working 133-136
addInterceptFeature Boolean 90
AGPL
  URL 8
AnnealingSchedule 91
annotated data
  parsing 179-182
annotation
  about 136-138
  working 138
AutoCompleter class
  URL 243
automatic phrase completion
  about 240
  working 241-243

B

background model
  running, on tweets 146-148
BaseClassifier<E> classifier interface 14
baseline
  with cross metrics, establishing 108, 109
  with cross validation, establishing 108, 109
batch process life cycle
  about 269
  createEntitySpeculative() method 275, 276
  entity universe file, setting up 270, 271
  processDocument() method 271, 272
  processDocuments() method 271, 272
  promote() method 274
  resolveCandidates() method 278-281
  XDoc, computing 272, 273
  XDocCoref.addMentionChainToEntity()
    entity 276
  XDocCoref.resolveMentionChain()
    entity 277, 278
Begin, In, and Out (BIO) tags 195
books on similar topics
  about 146
  background model 146
  foreground model 146
  interesting phrases 146
Brown Corpus
  URL 150

C

case-restoring spell corrector
  about 239
  working 240
ChainCrfFeatureExtractor interface 166
character stream
  words, finding in 52-55
CharacterTokenizerFactory 56
CharLmRescoringChunker
  URL 205
checkTokensAndWhiteSpaces() method 67
checkTokens() method 67
Chinese word segmentation tutorial
  URL 73
classifier
  about 76
  applying, to .csv file 22-24

confidence estimates,
    obtaining from 15-19
deserializing 11-14
evaluating 24-28
evaluating, with cross validation 32-36
running 11-14
thresholding 119-126
training, with cross validation 32-36
working 76-78
classifier.bestCategory() method 119
classifier-building life cycle
    about 106, 107
    baseline with cross validation,
        establishing 108, 109
    baseline with metrics, establishing 108, 109
    evaluation metric, implementing 111-113
    single metric, selecting 110
    training data, testing on 108
ClearTK 9
cluster
    URL 249
clustering
    about 243
    URL, for tutorial 281
CogNIAC 265
competitors, LingPipe
    ClearTK 9
    DkPro 9
    GATE 9
    JavaNLP 9
    Learning Based Java (LBJ) 9
    Mallet 9
    NLTK 9
    OpenNLP 9
    SVM 9
    Vowpal Wabbit 9
CompiledSpellChecker 73
complete-link clustering
    with edit distance 244-247
**Computational Natural Language
    Learning (CoNLL) 199**
Conditional random fields. *See* **CRFs**
confidence-based tagging 153, 154
confidence estimates
    obtaining, from classifier 15-19
confusion matrix 26, 109

coreference
    about 257
    pronouns, adding to 261-265
CRFs
    about 163
    candidate-edge features 171
    modifying 167-170
    node features 171
    URL 163, 208
    used, for named entity recognition 214-219
    used, for word/token tagging 163, 164
CRFs, for chunking 208-213
cross-document coreference (XDoc)
    overview 266-269
cross validation
    about 32
    classifier, evaluating with 32-36
    classifier, training with 32-36

D

Damerau-Levenstein distance 222
data
    obtaining, from Twitter API 19-22
database (DB) 266
dictionary-based chunking, NER 193-195
distance
    URL 224
distance metrics
    URL 222
DkPro 9

E

early stopping 103
editable operations
    Deletion 222
    Insertion 222
    Substitution 222
    Transposition 222
edit distance
    used, for complete-link clustering 244-247
    used, for single-link clustering 244-247
    using, for spelling correction 234-238
EditDistance class 71, 224
embedded chunks
    marking, in string 184, 185
entity-based summarization 258

error categories
  viewing 37-39
evaluation metric
  implementing 111-113
evaluations
  URL, for tutorial 248
eXtensible Business Reporting Language (XBRL) 48
Externalizable 13

F

feature extraction
  customizing 103, 104
  tuning 100, 101
feature extractors
  about 85-87
  combining 105, 106
filtered tokenizers, Javadoc page
  URL 60
foreground model
  about 145
  running, on tweets 146-148

G

GATE 9
gold standard data 25
Google
  URL 240

H

handle() method 31, 77
hidden Marcov models (HMM) 41, 149-151
hierarchical clusterer 244
HMM-based NER
  overview 198-204
HmmChunker
  about 198
  URL 205

I

incrementToken() method 65
IndoEuropeanTokenizerFactory 52, 55, 56
Infrequently Asked Questions (IAQs) 48
installation, LingPipe 8

interesting phrases
  detecting, from small dataset 142-145
interfaces
  BaseClassifier<E> 15
  ConditionalClassifier<E> extends
      RankedClassifier<E> 15
  JointClassifier<E> extends
      ConditionalClassifier<E> 15
  RankedClassifier<E> extends
      BaseClassifer<E> 15
  ScoredClassifier<E> extends
      RankedClassifier<E> 15
inverse document frequency (IDF) 230
issues, as classification problem
  about 48
  degree of sentiment 49
  non-exclusive category classification 49
  person/company/location detection 49
  question answering 48
  topic detection 48

J

Jaccard distance
  about 227
  near duplicates, eliminating with 42-45
JaccardDistance example
  running 228, 229
Japanese classifier
  URL 12
Javadoc, for CompiledSpellChecker
  URL 239
JavaNLP 9
John Smith problem
  overview 281-290

K

K-means (++) clustering 248

L

language model classifier
  training 29-31
  with tokens 78, 79
language model (LM)
  properties 16, 17
  URL 19

using, for spelling correction 234-238
Latent Dirichlet allocation (LDA)
  about 248
  for multitopic clustering 248-255
LingPipe
  about 8, 86
  advantages 9
  book code, downloading 10
  data, downloading 10
  downloading 11
  installing 8
  Lucene tokenizers, using with 62-65
  Solr tokenizers, using with 62-65
  URL, for downloading 11
LingPipe 1.0 8
LingPipe Javadoc, EditDistance
  URL 224
LingPipe object
  serializing 40, 41
linguistic pipeline. *See* **LingPipe**
linguistic tuning 114-119
LMClassifier 17
logistic regression
  about 87-93
  annealing schedule and epochs 103
  feature extraction, tuning 100
  parameters, tuning in 97, 98
  priors 101, 102
  URL 87
  working 87-99
lowercase tokenizer 56-58
LowerCaseTokenizerFactory 60
Lucene
  URL 60
Lucene tokenizers
  using 60-62
  using, with LingPipe 62-65

M

MAchine Learning for LanguagE Toolkit (Mallet) 9
MarginalTaggerEvaluator 162
maximum entropy 87
MedlineSentenceModel 177
Message Understanding Conference. *See* **MUC-6**

minImprovement parameter 91
MUC-6 52
multithreaded cross validation
  about 93
  working 94-97
MultivariateDistribution 16

N

Naïve Bayes
  about 79-84
  expectation maximization tutorial, URL 85
  features 80
  URL 85
named entity coreference, document 258-261
Named Entity Recognition. *See* **NER**
natural language processing. *See* **NLP**
NBestTaggerEvaluator 162
N-best word tagging 151, 152
near duplicates
  eliminating, with Jaccard distance 42-45
NER
  about 191
  dictionary-based chunking 193-195
  regular expression-based chunking 191, 192
  with CRFs 214-219
NER sources
  mixing 205-208
nested sentences 177
nextToken() method 65
nextWhitespace() method 65
NLP 8
NLTK 9
noun phrases (NP)
  about 189
  finding 189, 190

O

OpenNLP 9

P

paragraph detection
  overview 186-188
parameters
  tuning, in logistic regression 97, 98

part-of-speech (POS) 149
precision
  about 39
  scenarios 40
priors 101, 102
Project Gutenberg
  URL 70
pronouns
  adding, to coreference 261-265
proximity
  URL 224

R

recall
  about 39
  scenarios 40
regular expression-based chunking, NER 191, 192
regular expression, e-mail address match
  URL 193

S

sentence chunk
  example 184, 185
sentence detection
  evaluating 178, 179
  overview 174-177
  tuning 182-184
sentence detector 175
sentiment
  classifying 45-48
Serializable 13
short circuits 272
SimpleCrfFeatureExtractor 165, 166
simple edit distance
  about 222
  example 222, 223
single-link clustering
  with edit distance 244-247
single metric
  selecting 110
smoothing 81
Solr tokenizers
  using 60-62
  using, with LingPipe 62-65

SortedSet<ScoredObject<String[]>> collocation 145
spell checking
  running 235-238
spelling correction
  about 234
  edit distance, using for 234-238
  language models, using for 234-238
spelling-correction tutorial
  URL 239
statistically improbable phrases (SIP)
  about 145
  URL 145
StopTokenizerFactory filter 59
stop word tokenizers 58-60
string
  embedded chunks, marking in 184, 185
string comparison 222
supervised trainings
  versus unsupervised trainings 233
Support Vector Machine (SVM) 9

T

tag clouds
  URL 142
tagging evaluation
  URL 160
term frequency (TF) 230
Tf-Idf distance
  about 230
  working 232, 233
time-separated Twitter data
  about 146
  background model 146
  foreground model 146
  interesting phrases 146
token-based language model
  issues 148, 149
tokenization 55
tokenized language model
  about 144
  URL 145
tokenize() method 52
tokenizer factories
  about 52
  modifying 68, 69

TokenizerFactory instance 52
TokenizerFactory interface 52
tokenizer() method 64
tokenizer.nextToken() method 55
Tokenizer object 52
tokenizers
  combining 56-59
  evaluating, with unit tests 66, 67
tokens
  impossible penultimates 183
  impossible starts 183
  language model classifier with 78, 79
  possible stops 183
topic pages
  URL 193
topic-separated Twitter data
  background model 146
  foreground model 146
  interesting phrases 146
toString() method 29
train() method 31
truecasing
  reference link 240
T&T specification, edit distance
  URL 227
tuning 145
tuning feature extraction 101
Twitter
  URL 19
twitter4j
  URL, for documentation 22
Twitter API
  data, obtaining from 19-22
  URL, for documentation 22

U

unit tests
  tokenizers, evaluating with 66, 67
unsupervised trainings
  versus supervised trainings 233

V

verb phrases (VP)
  about 189
  finding 189, 190
Vowpal Wabbit 9

W

weighted edit distance
  about 224
  working 225-227
WeightedEditDistance class
  about 73
  URL 224, 227
words
  finding, in character stream 52-55
words, for languages
  finding, without white spaces 70-73
word tagging
  training 154-160
word tagging, and chunks
  translating between 195-198
word-tagging evaluation 160-162

Thank you for buying
Natural Language Processing with Java and LingPipe Cookbook

About Packt Publishing

Packt, pronounced 'packed', published its first book "*Mastering phpMyAdmin for Effective MySQL Management*" in April 2004 and subsequently continued to specialize in publishing highly focused books on specific technologies and solutions.

Our books and publications share the experiences of your fellow IT professionals in adapting and customizing today's systems, applications, and frameworks. Our solution based books give you the knowledge and power to customize the software and technologies you're using to get the job done. Packt books are more specific and less general than the IT books you have seen in the past. Our unique business model allows us to bring you more focused information, giving you more of what you need to know, and less of what you don't.

Packt is a modern, yet unique publishing company, which focuses on producing quality, cutting-edge books for communities of developers, administrators, and newbies alike. For more information, please visit our website: www.packtpub.com.

About Packt Open Source

In 2010, Packt launched two new brands, Packt Open Source and Packt Enterprise, in order to continue its focus on specialization. This book is part of the Packt Open Source brand, home to books published on software built around Open Source licenses, and offering information to anybody from advanced developers to budding web designers. The Open Source brand also runs Packt's Open Source Royalty Scheme, by which Packt gives a royalty to each Open Source project about whose software a book is sold.

Writing for Packt

We welcome all inquiries from people who are interested in authoring. Book proposals should be sent to author@packtpub.com. If your book idea is still at an early stage and you would like to discuss it first before writing a formal book proposal, contact us; one of our commissioning editors will get in touch with you.

We're not just looking for published authors; if you have strong technical skills but no writing experience, our experienced editors can help you develop a writing career, or simply get some additional reward for your expertise.

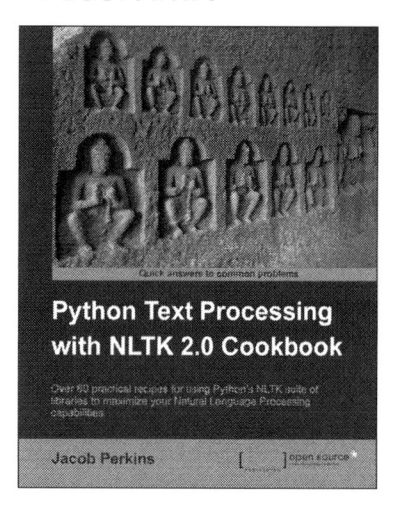

[PACKT] open source
community experience distilled
PUBLISHING

Python Text Processing with NLTK 2.0 Cookbook

ISBN: 978-1-84951-360-9　　　　Paperback: 272 pages

Over 80 practical recipes for using Python's NLTK suite of libraries to maximize your Natural Language Processing capabilities

1. Quickly get to grips with Natural Language Processing—with Text Analysis, Text Mining, and beyond.
2. Learn how machines and crawlers interpret and process natural languages.
3. Easily work with huge amounts of data and learn how to handle distributed processing.
4. Part of Packt Publishing's cookbook series: each recipe is a carefully organized sequence of instructions to complete the task as efficiently as possible.

Python 2.6 Text Processing: Beginner's Guide

ISBN: 978-1-84951-212-1　　　　Paperback: 380 pages

The easiest way to learn how to manipulate text with Python

1. The easiest way to learn text processing with Python.
2. Deals with the most important textual data formats you will encounter.
3. Learn to use the most popular text processing libraries available for Python.
4. Packed with examples to guide you through.

Please check www.PacktPub.com for information on our titles

Mastering Python Regular Expressions

ISBN: 978-1-78328-315-6   Paperback: 110 pages

Leverage regular expressions in Python even for the most complex features

1. Explore the workings of regular expressions in Python.

2. Learn all about optimizing regular expressions using RegexBuddy.

3. Full of practical and step-by-step examples, tips for performance, and solutions for performance-related problems faced by users all over the world.

Storm Blueprints: Patterns for Distributed Real-time Computation

ISBN: 978-1-78216-829-4   Paperback: 336 pages

Use Storm design patterns to perform distributed, real-time big data processing, and analytics for real-world use cases

1. Process high-volume logfiles in real time while learning the fundamentals of Storm topologies and system deployment.

2. Deploy Storm on Hadoop (YARN) and understand how the systems complement each other for online advertising and trade processing.

Please check www.PacktPub.com for information on our titles

Made in the USA
Middletown, DE
29 December 2016